LITERATURE AND

LITERATURE AND THE CREATIVE ECONOMY

Sarah Brouillette

STANFORD UNIVERSITY PRESS

STANFORD, CALIFORNIA

Stanford University Press
Stanford, California

Printed in the United States of America on acid-free, archival-quality paper

Library of Congress Cataloging-in-Publication Data

Brouillette, Sarah, 1977– author.
    Literature and the creative economy / Sarah Brouillette.
        pages   cm
    Includes bibliographical references and index.
    ISBN 978-0-8047-8948-6 (cloth : alk. paper)
    ISBN 978-1-5036-0280-9 (pbk. : alk. paper)
    1. English literature—21st century—History and criticism. 2. Creation
(Literary, artistic, etc.)—Economic aspects. 3. Authorship—Economic aspects.
4. Cultural industries. 5. Cultural policy. I. Title.
PR481.B76 2014
820.9'0092—dc23

                                                                    2013028369

ISBN 978-0-8047-9243-1 (electronic)

Contents

Acknowledgments

I first wish to thank Lina Shoumarova, the amazing graduate assistant I have been working with for the past few years. Having helped me to remake and improve this book on several occasions, she may well know it better than I do.

I started thinking concretely about this research while I held a Rockefeller Humanities Fellowship at the Smithsonian Centre for Folklife and Cultural Heritage. I was generously mentored there by James Early and lucked out in having Bill Anthes as my cubicle mate. I completed much of the manuscript as a Leverhulme Visiting Fellow at Queen Margaret University in Edinburgh, a position I held thanks to David Finkelstein. It was there that I met Jeremy Valentine, who shared many of my interests and welcomed me to ramble on about them, and Mark Banks, whose scholarship has thoroughly informed my own stance on creative work. All the while a Standard Research Grant from the Social Sciences and Humanities Council of Canada supported semi-frequent research trips to London and made it possible for me to fund my invaluable research assistants—Lina, Steve McLeod, and Mike Labreque.

At MIT, Shankar Raman and Jim Buzard were inspiring examples and gracious readers of my work, and Joshua Green was a constant source of comfort and provocation. Since moving to the Department of English at Carleton University, I have benefited greatly from having Paul Keen as my chair and from working with remarkably convivial, supportive, engaging colleagues. Brian Greenspan and Franny Nudelman in the Department of English, and Miranda Brady, Chris Russill, and Melissa Aronczyk in the School of Journalism and Communication, have been particularly necessary friends and interlocutors, as has Tai Zimmer, a member of Carleton's wider community.

When the manuscript for this book first started to cohere, discussions with Matthew Hart and Michael Szalay determined how I ended up conceiving my project. I cannot thank them enough. Since beginning to work with Stanford University Press, I have appreciated the guidance and support of Emily-Jane Cohen, and my work has benefited greatly from Cynthia Lindlof's editorial precision and insight. The two readers who reported on the manuscript managed to be both incisive and kind.

Thank you as well to the network of scholars who in various ways kept me reading and writing, outraged and informed, thinking and laughing. These include Daniel Allington, Sara Amon, Jasper Bernes, Sarah Blacker, Nicholas Brown, Piers Brown, Sam Cohen, Sharae Deckard, David Farrier, Alan Finlayson, Elaine Freedgood, Jenny Godfrey, James Graham, Dave Gunning, Max Haiven, Stefan Helgesson, Doug Henwood, Andrew Hoberek, Graham Huggan, Joseph Jeon, Aaron Kilner, Lee Konstantinou, Sara Malton, John Marx, Sophie Mayer, John McLeod, Ana Mendes, Padmini Ray Murray, Pashmina Murthy, Mathias Nilges, Andrew Pendakis, Rashmi Sadana, Kulpreet Sasan, Emilio Sauri, Min Hyoung Song, Claire Squires, Neelam Srivastava, Imre Szeman, Rebecca Tierney-Hynes, Trysh Travis, Andrew van der Vlies, Eva Hemmungs Wirtén, and Daniel Worden.

The thought and writing behind this book often happened because I had occasion to give talks and contribute chapters to books and journals. Material from Chapter 2 appeared in short form in *Mediations* 24.2 (2009); it was expanded for inclusion in *Literary Materialisms*, ed. Mathias Nilges and Emilio Sauri (London: Palgrave, 2013), and is reproduced with permission of *Mediations* and Palgrave Macmillan. Material from Chapter 3 appeared in short form in *Mediations* 26.1–2 (2012–13); it was expanded and modified for *Theorizing Cultural Work*, ed. Mark Banks et al. (London: Routledge, 2013), and is reproduced with permission of *Mediations* and Routledge. Part of Chapter 4 was published in a longer and different form in *Modern Fiction Studies* 58.3 (2012), copyright © 2012 The Johns Hopkins University Press.

I would be remiss if I did not mention my appreciation for the staff at Bridgehead Coffee in Old Ottawa South and Coffee Angel in Edinburgh, where I regularly worked or eavesdropped on nearby conversations when work was not happening.

This book has two dedicatees: Travis DeCook, who is a model of careful and heartfelt scholarship and a presence in everything I write; and our son Ben—my favorite dance partner and cherished playmate.

dialectic of art + work

Introduction

Britain's New Labour government, in power from 1997 to 2010, attempted an unprecedented incorporation of culture into governance. At the heart of this effort was circulation of the idea that the UK was becoming increasingly dependent on the profitability of its creative economy. Faith in this idea has spread with remarkable speed. United Nations agencies have, for example, embraced the idea of the creative economy and attempted to devise ways to measure its impact. UNESCO's Creative Cities Network, and designation of official Cities of Literature, Cities of Film, Cities of Music, and so on, reflects its desire to "help unlock the creative, social and economic potential of cultural industries."[1] This yoking together of cultural, social, and economic goals is at the heart of the creative-economy frameworks adopted by local and national governments in the UK and elsewhere. What subtends the ready adoption of these frameworks?

I argue in this book that we find some answers to this question in literary studies. I consider, first, how long-standing ideas about literature and literary writers have informed creative-economy policymaking and the discourses that have arisen with it and complement it. I then examine how writers have articulated complicity with and distance from various facets of the placement of art in instrumental service to the economy—a placement that was of heightened concern for many cultural workers during the New Labour years but is of course by no means exclusive to it. Among the phenomena that have served to heighten concern are the presentation of artists as models of contentedly flexible and self-managed workers, the treatment of training in and exposure to art as a pathway to social inclusion, use of the presence of culture and cultural institutions to increase property values, and support for cultural diversity as a means of growing cultural markets and fostering an inclusive society of active cultural consumers. The literature I discuss engages these phenomena, and I read it in relation to a broader wariness about how the linking up of culture, economy, and governance—a linking up that might have had welcome repercussions—has in fact tended to unfold. For just as creative-industries frameworks have found legitimacy within government institutions in the UK and around the world, many policymakers, analysts, writers, and artists, including those on the left who had seen a progressive potential in the expanding recognition of the importance of culture, have experienced what Justin O'Connor calls "affective disinvestment from the creative industries imaginary."[2]

Reference to the creative economy, as to the attendant creative industries and creative class, first emerged in relation to claims about the empirically measurable economic might of the practices, institutions, and individuals ostensibly served by the intellectual property regime. However, it would be unwise to perpetuate the binary positioning of positivist approaches that take the existence of the creative economy for granted versus the more suspicious treatment of the creative economy as a script designed to serve political interests.[3] Attempts to account for the creative economy, even those sponsored by government, are rarely free of contradiction and ambivalence, and we risk overlooking observable economic and cultural change if we treat the creative economy as little more than a fantastic projection of political will. Instead, I stress the dialectical interplay between the discourse of the creative economy and the real world of cultural economics that it is meant to encompass and quantify; my goal is not to debunk the notion that there is such a thing as the creative economy but rather to focus attention on how and why faith in its existence has become consequential.

One of my core claims, supported by several scholars, is that creative-economy discourse dovetails importantly with neoliberalism, conceived as a set of shifting practices whose net effect is to erode public welfare, valorize private property and free markets, position government as a facilitator and "pre-eminent narrator" of the shift to neoliberal policy, and orchestrate or justify a corresponding notion that capitalism's continued and insuperable expansion is at once inevitable and welcome.[4] Britain's first neoliberal government, under Conservative prime minister Margaret Thatcher (1979–90), established many of the expedient forms of state relation to the arts common under New Labour. Support for the kind of grassroots community-based work that flourished in the 1970s was significantly abrogated. Arts organizations and practitioners found that funding for culture was increasingly indexed to a centralized Conservative agenda: to preservation of the national heritage, which meant money for established British institutions; to the regeneration of deindustrialized cities that might thrive in a world of increasingly fluid capital and labor markets, which meant the linking of cultural events and institutions to urban renewal schemes; and to the running of the public sector based on private-sector models of efficiency and return, which meant that arts organizations would need to prove they could operate like viable businesses and even find private-sector collaborators if they hoped to be favored by government.[5] If all of these developments—the imagining of the arts as an offshoot of a branded heritage and tourist product, the appeal to cultural infrastructure as a gentrifying force, and emphasis on artists as collaborators with private-sector development—continued under New Labour, there was a difference.

New Labour politicians campaigned against the Conservatives' blinkered focus on free-market economics and against the traditional Labour Party's opposition to the deregulation of markets. New Labour insisted that social welfare and economic deregulation were intertwined. The party developed the idea of the Third Way to brand its mediation between market-based Thatcherite policymaking and Labour's traditional focus on social needs and capacities. While New Labour policy would remain predominantly economistic—the party's premier intellectual urged it to consider "its orientation . . . in a world where there are no alternatives to capitalism"[6]—it would position economic reform as a way to reach more intangible goals such as social integration and personal well-being. New welfare, health, and education policies were justified as the means to economic ends.[7] Culture would be central to negotiating the symbiosis between economic and social goals. The research director of the premier

New Labour think tank had written that it was only through culture that a "viable capitalist social order" would manage to "organise and sustain itself."[8] New Labour embraced this maxim to stress the usefulness of culture and the arts to securing individual and collective interests. It put forward a comprehensive creative-economy program to monitor and foster the economic value of culture and the arts. Its public and cultural diplomacy policies at times blurred into one another, as it trumpeted the use of culture, including literature, in nation-branding strategies that would encourage investment in the UK and sell British foreign policy decisions. Policymakers imagined that arts organizations could forward a social inclusion agenda by bringing minorities into a nation of happily multicultural communities. Urban regeneration policy positioned the presence of cultural institutions and of those who do cultural work as the key to increasing property values and to renewing troubled neighborhoods.

Meanwhile, in several social science and policy fields the cultural worker was constructed as a model flexible self-manager, committed to introspection, self-expression, and self-direction.[9] Creative work tends to be figured contradictorily by creative-economy rhetoric, as at once newly valuable to capitalism and romantically honorable and free. A recent study by The Work Foundation, commissioned by the Department of Culture, Media and Sport, reports that

the creative industries are peopled by creative talents who themselves get pleasure and utility from what they do. They are "called to their art." One upside from the business perspective (although it attracts complaints of exploitation) is that their "reservation" wages—the lowest they are prepared to work for—are lower than the marginal value of what they produce, making labour particularly cheap. A downside is that the "talent" care deeply about how the creative work is organized, which may discourage concessions or compromises to management.[10]

My study troubles this model. It questions the images of creative workers' enterprising individualism present in policy documents, management and planning literature focused on cultural-sector businesses, and in much social science research on the creative economy. Its two parts reflect my two-pronged approach to forwarding more socially responsive conceptions of the creative self: we need to challenge the model of the asocial or antisocial flexible individualist by stressing that, though it is disseminated as a natural given, it is in fact historically produced, highly contested, and contingent; and we need to identify and articulate alternative visions of a self not sufficient to itself, a self whose anti-egoism and need for sympathetic community are no less essential or natural than the predilections of the flexibly creative individual.

**

Though neoliberal Britain is my particular case, I stress the transnational political currents—especially the US-based social science and management thought—at work in British creative-economy discourse and position the literature I discuss as part of a global conversation about the evolving relationship between cultural commerce and artistic autonomy. The first part of this study provides a partial genealogy of the mainstream model of the creative personality. I emphasize in particular how creative-economy frameworks, informed by management theory, have drawn upon mainly US-based social scientific observation of writers' working lives and have come to incorporate concepts bearing a literary provenance. These include the idea that the best work expresses the interiority of talented individuals, the idea that the creative realm is a space of pure introspection unbounded by necessity and expedience, and the related notion that though creative people may work within markets, serious ones will be motivated by internal directives to which profit is irrelevant. Placed in this light, mainstream creative-industries and creative-economy discourse evidently emboldens an established management conception—a conception that is in a sense originally American but now globally resonant—of the reflexive individual's enterprising and expressive labor, a vocabulary that itself leans on depictions of artists' expressive creativity.

Chapter 1 provides a closer look at the key features of the new vocabulary of creativity. I begin by considering the influence of *The Rise of the Creative Class* by Richard Florida, the American management guru now installed at the Rotman School of Management at the University of Toronto. *The Rise of the Creative Class* has become a handbook for government officials and done more than any other work to crystallize and disseminate globally the ostensible virtues of the conception of culture that New Labour campaigned on and then fostered as it governed. In it Florida argues that the work of the creative class is to render ideas amendable to market circulation. It is precisely this rendering that is the mark of *links to language poetry — era of neoliberalism*

originality or creative genius. Florida thus imagines that true creativity is indivisible from marketability. This conception accords with and shapes how the creative economy has been posited, defined, and discussed in the UK and globally. The particular vocabulary of creativity he helps foster, highlighting the economic impact of culture and the importance to urban growth of the presence of creative workers, informed the New Labour government's emphasis on creativity as the particular form of expertise that would secure a postindustrial UK's viability within the global economy. This emphasis became in turn a key branding strategy for the party itself. New Labour claimed it would be able to forge the felicitous intersection of social and economic productivities, the union of individual and civic goals in the service of economic growth. It presented the creative economy as a model of this harmonization of social and economic goals. Its approach to culture was, moreover, consistently constructed as the way of the future: Given the inevitably of an increasingly immaterial capitalism, creativity would be an ever more important skill. Thus, synonymous with a welcome embrace of ceaseless change, creativity would also be the privileged marker of one's personal evolution toward a reflexive capitalist modernity.

Chapters 2 and 3, ranging beyond New Labour and the British context, consider how particular ideas about art and artists, especially authors and authorship, have been marshaled to promote the connection between capitalist modernity, reflexivity, and flexibility. Chapter 2 turns again to Florida's work to consider the surprising parallels between his understanding of the creative class and neo-Marxist theories of immaterial labor. What they share most notably is a fundamentally ahistorical conception of creativity as the natural expression of an innate opposition to routine and to management. They deny the contradictory and constitutive histories of artists' labor and of images of artists at work that subtend their conceptions of subjectivity. Labor theories of cultural production, which attend to the position of the producer within the marketplace and within a broader field of social relations, can provide an alternative. I outline two relevant tributaries: the development of the contradictory relationship between artists and the markets for their work; and the mainstreaming of the figure of the artist as valorized mental laborer.

Chapter 3 continues in this transnational and genealogical vein by charting what creative-economy discourse and its models of the flexible personality owe to an understanding of the creative person that extends back to the late 1950s and 1960s. This was the period when US-based psychologists like Abraham Maslow and Frank Barron began to posit creativity's importance to the optimal self and when progressive management theory, informed and informing psychologists' findings, began imagining all business culture as an outlet for and source of workers' enterprising individual self-fulfillment. This process later found one of its signal articulations in the new-economy rhetoric that celebrated "liberation management" and an idealized flexible workplace whose epitome is the dot-com paradise of jeans and sneakers and foosball tables—a rhetoric that dovetails significantly with creative-economy discourse.[11]

Little research accounts for how particular ideas about artists' work have exerted their influence—ideas about its flourishing in unstable conditions or about its relationship to economies of competition and prestige, for example. That what exert influence are not simple facts about artists but rather aspects of a discrete aesthetic ideology with its own rich and contentious history is often ignored. Chapter 3 argues that since the early 1950s influential psychologists and management theorists, mostly US based, have tended to present study of artists as straightforward evidence that the social is a form of constraint to be transcended by the effective working self. Their work has had global implications for how art is perceived and for how work is organized. They have depended upon and reinforced the notion that making art is the fundamentally insular expression of one's personally directed passionate devotion to "the task itself," "the materials at hand," or simply "the work"; and they have formed and circulated models of good work as a flexible and self-sufficient enterprise averse to social responsibility, human interdependence, and collective politics. Brian Holmes suggests that rigorously exposing, situating, and undermining mainstream celebrations of the flexible personality are part of the work of narrating new subjectivities.[12] It is part of the collective work of imagining new ideals of autonomy and authenticity to counter the old critique of massification, whose demand for liberation of a limitless human potential from all social constraint proved so useful to management discourse. These new ideals will not arise from yet another innovative discovery originating in the inherently creative intellect. They will emerge instead from old roots that need only be uncovered and valorized. In Luc Boltanski and Eve Chiapello's compelling formulation, they will stem from sensitivity to others' conditions of existence and from the incrimination of any model of the self that assumes and privileges its egoism.[13] In concert with these other theorists, I suggest we can challenge the model of the asocial or antisocial flexible individualist by stressing that she is produced by the same social circumstances she is supposed to disavow, and we can attend to socially responsive visions of human agency and identity that are evidently more relevant to many creative workers. I turn to literature to find mediation of these visions.

**

The chapters in the second part stem from the observation that, though ideas about their working lives have made them a norm-setting model, writers appear to experience making culture less an inherently fulfilling self-expression and more an encounter with heightened contradictions: between the traditional veneration of artistic autonomy and the reality of conscription into proliferating state and corporate initiatives, and between the social production of culture and the lionization of the individual creator. My focus is how literature has reflexively exemplified, internalized, and critiqued vocabularies and phenomena that are integral to our unfolding creative-economy era.

Chapter 4 takes up two novels that at once exemplify and interrogate the therapeutic imperative to use self-criticism and traumatic experiences as progressive engines through which to achieve personal contentment and career success. It begins with Aravind Adiga's 2008 acclaimed novel *The White Tiger*, which offers a thorough critique of the entrepreneurial personality and was marketed as Adiga's self-critical rejection of his own earlier work as a finance journalist. Its narrator is Balram, a once-destitute servant who decides he must kill to succeed in India's newly global economy of dot-coms and enterprise zones. The marketing story attached to the novel tapped into the creative-labor ideal: interviews and profiles praised it as a product of the author's critical self-reflection, claiming it refuted his earlier work as a mainstream finance journalist by critiquing the neoliberal rhetoric of entrepreneurial innovation. The novel suggests that this rhetoric downplays dependence on an expanding service class and requires its protagonist's antisocial conception of the flexible self as an engine of capital accumulation. The novel incorporates a further self-conscious commentary on the commercial success of narratives about the Indian economy's dark side. Highlighting how he turns his suffering into an inducement to succeed, the narrator remarks, "To break the law of his land—to turn bad news into good news—is the entrepreneur's prerogative."[14] This remark of course extends to the author as well. If his journalism involved disguising bad news as good news, his literary labor is not altogether different, since his stories of others' suffering produce his success. So if his novel is attentive to the abject and the untold, it is also worried about the service these provide to the writer's career. Self-critical gestures like these are by now an almost clichéd means for writers to negotiate the terms of their participation in the literary field. I argue, thus, that the novel, its marketing, and its reception all emerge as worried responses to the popularity of literary works that emphasize the inequities and depredations of a rapacious capitalism.

Chapter 4 compares Adiga's work to Monica Ali's 2009 novel *In the Kitchen*, homing in on its depiction of the breakdown of Gabriel, an aspiring restaurant owner who embodies many of the features of the creative worker imagined by New Labour policy. I suggest that the novel offers a deeply ambivalent take on the limitations of its protagonist's obsessive interiority. While it suggests that his tortured self-consciousness is a form of social and political paralysis, it also counsels the reader, through the example of Gabriel's employee Oona, that to perceive his foibles with sympathy is to evince the kind of fellow feeling that he himself lacks. I suggest that this ambivalence, balanced between empathy and critique, is how Ali imagines her aesthetic purpose. I relate this imagining to the hostile reception of her novel *Brick Lane* as a Trojan horse for the creative-class takeover of London's East End.

These novels' respective forms of interest in entrepreneurial protagonists who suffer from significant psychoses—psychoses inseparable from their precarious working lives—speak to a broader zeitgeist. When approaching the new world of work, many writers emphasize its troubling psychological effects, its alienating impact, and its reliance on a precarious underclass. Chapter 5 considers writers who, while partaking of the same cultural moment, focus their inquiry on the practice of making culture itself. The chapter takes as its starting point literature development initiatives that aim to ameliorate social problems and boost intellectual property production by increasing diversity within the creative industries. The best example is *decibel*, an Arts Council program that, among many other projects, partners with Penguin Books to offer prizes and publishing outlets to minority writers. Initiatives like these appear to have heightened writers' sensitivity to the idea that they need to appeal to their belonging to a specific minority niche in order to receive funding, win prizes, and ultimately find success within the market. However, as often as writers make such appeals, they are accused of lacking the authentic community connection that sells their works, and the controversies that arise from such charges tend to aid their literature's further circulation. I suggest that these fraught circumstances are encouraging minority writers to articulate agonized conceptions of their own labor.

A signal case is Daljit Nagra's poetry, in which we witness the author's staging of himself as a brand designed to address a gap in the market with the proliferating commodities united under the author's name. His self-presentation enfolds objections to his own market value but also includes his recognition that his very objections will become what his brand is made up of, contradictorily adding to the value and interest of his work. Nagra's strategies are usefully compared to Gautam Malkani's in his 2006 novel *Londonstani*. Malkani is editor of the Creative Business page at the *Financial Times*, and his controversial first novel unwittingly reveals his serious reservations about translating his own teenage years in the "rude boy" subculture, which was the subject of his novel and of his Cambridge anthropology honors thesis, into his means of entry into a privileged creative elite.

Critics of British creative-economy diversity initiatives claim that they perpetuate long-standing and often restrictive assumptions about authenticity and representation. "Ethnic" or "minority" writers and artists have often been burdened by the notion that they should articulate an ostensibly whole and organic community. Their work is understood as the innocent "outgrowth" of their belonging to that integral unity, and, as the emanation of a particular culture, their work is presumed to capture its essence.[15] Meanwhile, an existing roster or canon of texts is thought to lack diversity in a way that the inclusion of certain "representative" figures will correct, such that those writers are taken as speaking for a previously

neglected group.[16] Writers who thwart these prescriptions—as many do—
tend to find themselves accused of inauthenticity. Such charges are hardly
a straightforward problem, however. Despite the seeming naïveté of many
official cultural diversity policies, it is debate about authenticity that seems
to be particularly pressing, perhaps because contemporary readers and
writers already think routinely about how to live authentic lives in which
their relationships to family and community are honest and sincere and in
which, in Marshall Berman's terms, their "capacity for life, freedom, spontaneity, expressiveness, growth [and] self-development" is fully realized.[17]
In other words authenticity debates perhaps provide a uniquely relevant set
of terms for literary expression and discussion because we already engage
the challenges of authenticity as part of their own reflexive self- and career
development.

The focus of Chapter 6 is British writers who take up commissions
to work with property developers on urban renewal schemes. It thus
outlines some very new purposes to which the aspiration and training
to write are currently being put. Writers tend to work with developers in
two main ways. The first can be deemed a poetic function and has some
precedent, as they contribute words for public art to feature in new or
revitalized structures. The second function is a newer one, focused on
narrative, as they facilitate public storytelling about a region's history,
present character, and possible futures, before finding creative ways to
convey the gist of what they have gathered for the public to read and for
developers to consider and, at times, implement. The rise of the writer-
consultant clearly signals the use of culture as an aid to gentrification.
Yet we see in writers' own thinking about their work as consultants, and
in the various products of their commissioned labor, that they continue
to express concern about the precise relationship between art and the
official development establishment. Writers' descriptions of their commissioned work either evince some hesitant hope that they might have a
progressive impact on the renewal or urban capital or suggest that they
are content to be the sanctioned opposition to the process. Even if we
decide that their autonomy is imagined, we cannot deny that their own
faith in it informs how they engage with and understand the projects to
which they are aligned. I argue that, far from making the question of
the artist's relation to capital more passé than it already was, the work

of the writer-consultant reveals the question's ongoing salience, as its permutations are inscribed in and inseparable from writers' fulfillment of their contracts.

Use of writers and other artists as consultants appeals to developers keen to justify their work as attentive to the public interest and motivated by goals greater than profit making. Ian McEwan's 2005 novel *Saturday*, the focus of Chapter 7, pivots upon a similar sense of art's anti-instrumental impetus. The novel has received a lot of scholarly attention, perhaps because there is little agreement about the meaning of the novel's technique. For every reader who laments its insufficient distance from the focalizing consciousness of its protagonist, neurosurgeon Henry Perowne, another remarks upon its subtle revelation of the blinkered outlook of the privileged male professional living in a posh home in London. There appears to be consensus, though, about the novel's pivotal scene, in which Baxter, an underclass home intruder suffering from Huntington's disease, is moved against his intent to harm the Perownes after hearing Matthew Arnold's "Dover Beach" read aloud. The scene tends to be read as affirming art's ameliorative capacities: in the face of the aesthetic, the intending criminal retreats, his capacity to be moved by poetry proving his heretofore hidden humanity.

I argue, however, that if we attend to the novel's intensive interest in the nature of *Henry*'s consumption of art, the idea of McEwan's faith in its transformative potential becomes hard to support. I argue that *Saturday* presents the arts, especially music and the visual arts, as all too easily made into signs of its protagonist's elite status and props to his conventional modes of self-affirmation. It presents literature, the medium that Henry fails to appreciate, as holding the most potential to act as what Russell Keat calls a "meta-good," meaning a good that may cause us to reflect upon the relative value of other kinds of goods to human well-being.[18] However, it also highlights what appear to be insurmountable barriers to this potential ever being realized. I thus interpret the novel as a highly ironic treatment of New Labour's attempts to connect art to social inclusion. It suggests that, in an era in which art is asked to do much but appears to change little, the writer's task is to enumerate and scrutinize the substantial barriers to his medium's own effectiveness.

**

  This study, <u>reading the presence of the literary in creative-economy discourse against literature's own interest in the instrumentalization of culture, does not deny outright that literature can operate as a site of resistance.</u> <u>Literature can critique the excesses and inequities of neoliberal capital,</u> and its rigorous focus on the inner life can allow us to perceive anxiety, guilt, and other negative feelings hidden behind the cheery face that mainstream discourse draws for today's workers. However, in its very criticality, literature can also exemplify and internalize some of the foundational aspects of the creative-economy turn. Most formulations of creative work have a vision of autonomy from instrumental imperatives built into them. During the New Labour years in particular, policymakers, social scientists, and management theorists routinely enjoined people to <u>look within, beyond materialistic concerns,</u> as a way to uncover an <u>authentic expressive self to participate in market activity;</u> contradictorily, <u>one's faith in one's distance from market imperatives was said to make one better able to engage in work that would prove both economically and socially productive.</u>

  I suggest that <u>this emphasis on the market value of an authentic self should be read in relation to a broader social and cultural history.</u> Just as psychologists were turning to the study of creativity after World War II, psychological terminology was being popularized in unprecedented ways, and a therapeutic imperative was encouraging people to imagine themselves as constantly pursuing better versions of themselves. Indeed, <u>overlapping therapeutic and Maslovian terminologies, celebrating the self in reflexive and lifelong pursuit of its own best version, are by now culturally dominant.</u> Fomented by a widespread embrace of the value of the artistic way of life,[19] by the 1980s the individual's interior world seems to have become, in Timothy Aubry's terms, "the site of greatest importance, interest, complexity, depth, and fulfilment in the world" and "the staging ground for all the suffering, risk, trouble, and heroism that . . . continue to be perceived as necessary aspects of a meaningful life."[20] According to Nikolas Rose, individuals are now "incited to live as if making a *project* of themselves: they are to *work* on their emotional world, their domestic and conjugal pleasure, to develop a 'style' of living that will maximize the worth of their existence to themselves"; this process is, moreover, linked to the "rise of a new breed of spiritual directors"—novelists among them—who help instill a "reflexive hermeneutics which will afford self-knowledge and self-mastery."[21] Embrace of the primacy of the therapeutic self, motivated by nonmaterial or postmaterialist goals and committed to constant indeterminacy and self-evolution, converges with the neoliberal image of the flexible creative worker whose career is her primary site of self-discovery. In this light, if writers mark their own distance from art's instrumental applications, they find particularly rich material because readers of literature are themselves inclined to disavow instrumental goals as secondary to, or as inhibitors of, immaterial goods like self-knowledge, authenticity, originality, and happiness. So literature's anti-instrumental and self-critical gestures may exemplify and model larger cultural mores and may be highly marketable for precisely this reason. Instead of simply celebrating these gestures, I attend to the material conditions, informed by a broader set of sociopolitical circumstances, which make them so appealing.

I focus, in addition, on ways in which writers have themselves reacted to the palatability of many forms of critique. The writers I study cannot be said to assume the validity of routine anti-instrumental and self-critical gestures and can by no means be summarily dismissed as complicit in circulating the neoliberal model of the ideal self. Instead, each of my readings suggests more troubled and more tangled forms of self-consciousness, far distant from any celebratory self-appreciation. Among the works I consider in detail are some that reckon with the ambivalent consequences of an excessive focus on interiority and individual expressivity, some that suggest an inability to either embrace or disavow entirely the idea that art should be separate from any instrumental application, and some that attempt not simply to critique but to respond to critique's apparent exhaustion within a cultural economy so able to accommodate it. Writers have been contributing to a broader questioning of conceptions of culture that literary tradition has helped to constitute and legitimate: conceptions emphasizing a self-referencing interiority and creativity, self-expression and self-invention, freedom from constraint of any kind, and that ideal of the autonomous artwork, expressive of individual genius and innovation, that has proven so useful to neoliberal capital.[22] But this questioning cannot be celebrated in any simple terms.

It should be noted that visual artists have long been committed to affirming a fundamentally social view of their creative practice. Claire Bishop has recently discussed how the rise of "participatory art" and "relational aesthetics," in which artists collaborate with co-producing participants in the creation of social situations, has been motivated by an "ethics of authorial renunciation."[23] Yet she argues that developments in the visual arts prove that collaborative activities, often promoted regardless of their aesthetic merits and particular political purposes, are an insufficient response to the problems of the art world's complicities and incapacities. The idea that artists should be involved not only in their own career development as solo authors but also in the forwarding of social goals is one that neoliberal governments have tended to embrace; self-managed career development and commitment to social goals are promoted as entirely compatible directives, and it is hardly the case that all social practices, processes, commitments, and transformations are automatically progressive. The point then is not to suggest that singular authorship activities might or should be replaced with collaborative production of social processes and situations of whatever stripe. What matters rather is that we highlight the techniques and strategies that artists have developed as they have come to focus on the problem of the instrumentalization of their practice, including of its legacies of "negation, disruption and antagonism."[24] A key target has been the celebrification and circulation of the model of the virtuoso star producer. What has emerged to challenge this model is, sometimes, straightforward insistence on the priority of social bonds. In other instances, though, we find what I take to be more productive emphases: on the social constitution and framing of models that privilege autonomy; and on an aesthetic practice driven not by the solo author's self-definition and self-validation but rather by a constant unraveling of the ideal of her self's priority and sufficiency.

Writers join this debate belatedly and with some difficulty, in part because mainstream literature is historically inseparable from the model of unique expression protected by copyright on the grounds that it is one individual's original work. The writers I discuss in Chapter 6, who are engaged in work with communities, tend to renounce this model, if only for the sake and duration of those projects, and are akin to socially engaged visual artists in that they perceive their work as an opportunity to involve the public in participation in forwarding broader social goals. Most of the writers I study, though, are hesitantly qualifying traditional ideologies of authorship from within the tradition itself. Their takes on the idea that creativity's primary engine is a self-willed expressive force are, even when unwitting, consistently agonized and affective. Their writing suggests not a contended giving up of one's controlling position for the sake of fostering a participatory community of creators but rather a struggle against oneself, against one's own work, and against the traditions of one's medium.

To worry about the formation and circulation of the value of creativity is hardly new. This worrying has in recent years become more focused and more visible, as more and more parties to a global conversation about the creative economy have highlighted the pathologies of the ethos of individual self-management and self-referencing introspection, and have advocated an understanding of creativity not as the happily individual innovation that is the engine of enterprise but as a set of socially constituted and situated activities whose purposes and consequences—social and ethical—must be considered and judged. Where there is a willingness to continue to embrace the aesthetic as a space in which value can exist independent of capital, and to support the ideal of productive activity as an end in itself, it is tempered by awareness of the ways that these conceptions have been put to the same uses that they have often been marshaled to oppose.[25]

A brief reading of Kazuo Ishiguro's *Never Let Me Go* (2005) begins my Conclusion, in which I highlight a problem that is implicit and perhaps niggling throughout these pages—a problem that other scholars have usefully addressed and whose proper treatment would require a different kind of study than this is.[26] I am referring to the matter of how to define artistic autonomy in a way that is attuned to our contemporary moment, a moment in which, in Brian Holmes's terms, the "cultural exception becomes the productive rule."[27] My overall approach to this problem is to waver between valuing and challenging writers' claims to autonomy and to suggest that writers are often similarly caught between affirmation and refusal. This wavering—between celebration of the potential of autonomous art, and indicating all of the ways that exact celebration has been useful to neoliberalism—is precisely the critical position I support, and my Conclusion says more about why. I crystallize there what will already be evident: What might seem at first glance like a split, dividing literature as incipient critique from literature as marketable, palatable critique-*lite*, I see as an essential and united feature of our literary world. The writers I study exhibit various levels of reflexive engagement with the commercial and political aspects of their work, and I think it is important to highlight those differences. However, overall it seems that writers tend now not just to position themselves as critics but to use their work to explore the barriers to effective critique—not least, the incorporation of critique into neoliberal capitalization. A primary theme here is thus literature's engagement with the incorporation of the value of culture's autonomy from capital *into* neoliberal capital.

When Pierre Bourdieu wrote about artistic "autonomization," a process he said reached its fullest flourishing in the bohemian Paris of the nineteenth century, he claimed that writers themselves made a signal contribution to public recognition of bohemia as a "new social entity." They invented and spread the whole idea of bohemia, as they constructed its "identity, values, norms and myths." He notes as an example Honoré de Balzac's 1830 *Traité de la vie élégante*, which posited three classes of being—man who works, man who thinks, and man who does nothing—before drawing attention to the ultimate exception, the artist, whose "idleness is a form of work, and his work a rest," as he is often found "meditating a masterpiece without appearing to be occupied." To Bourdieu, schema like Balzac's helped to constitute the autonomous aesthetic realm that it claimed to be describing. "The reality designated by words in ordinary usage—writer, artist, intellectual—has been made by cultural producers," Bourdieu writes, through their normative and performative statements about what the world is and what it should be.[28] In Bourdieu's treatment, Balzac was thus a key participant in a successful movement to justify the beliefs of a social grouping of artists who valued their own autonomy from capital—a group that sought, and actually achieved, something of a monopoly hold over the production of interpretations of culture and society. My research is indebted to Bourdieu's claims because it is interested in how the social world has been shaped by the split between art and commerce that bohemia solidified and valorized. My central research focus is really the afterlife and telling persistence of the art-commerce dialectic that forms the generative heart of Bourdieu's whole scholarly endeavor.

Boltanksi and Chiapello consider how the "artistic critique" of capital—the critique that Bourdieu thought reached its zenith in an authentic bohemia—influenced the social movements of the 1960s and encouraged the transformation of the capitalist workplace into a space of self-appreciation. Jasper Bernes argues succinctly that what results are "new forms of autonomy and self-management that are really regimes of self-harrying, self-intensification, and inter-worker competition disguised as attempts to humanize the workplace and allow for freedom and self-expression in work." It isn't so much that artists have been straightforwardly determining the transformation of spheres to which they do not belong, however. It is rather that they and their working habits have been a source of answers to questions that press upon all working people and are thus woven through the social fabric. In writers' work, and in their personae, they provide terminology and discursive critique, shaping a "network of terms, practices, attitudes and values" that firmly bind the workplace to what Bernes memorably deems "the aesthetic situation."[29]

It seems that literary writers now rarely feel that they have the kind of power to construct that social imaginary that Bourdieu attributed to figures like Balzac, Flaubert, and Baudelaire. They tend rather to consider the dissipation of literature's power and the attenuation of public faith in the notion that there is any merit to the idea of an autonomous aesthetic realm. They take up the autonomization process not as an easy and assumed inheritance but as a problem in search of a solution. I hope that my approach to this problem will encourage more study of writers as cultural practitioners interested in the uses to which their work is put. Literary studies' relative inattention to matters of cultural policy and cultural work may be another sign of the trenchancy of some of the conceptions of creative expression that I explore—conceptions of its "antagonism toward counting," its inherent aversion to state intervention and to economic rationalities, or of its relative autonomy from the state and from capital.[30] As Stephen Schryer has recently argued, literary intellectuals still want to embrace the "compensatory privilege of viewing their work as an anti-instrumental antidote to the triumph of instrumentalism," even if this means papering over the distinction between instrumental service to capital and instrumental service to social goals to which capitalism is averse.[31] Hence our ongoing reluctance to cross the disciplinary divide between social science and humanities inquiry, a divide itself often fathomed as an expression of the split between instrumentalism and its countermeasures. But crossing this divide is important, in particular because a rich seam of social science and social theoretical research precisely illuminates ongoing debates over the idea of autonomous art as endless countermeasure to capital. Throughout these pages I draw upon this research for its insights into cultural workers' conceptions of their own practice in order to frame writers' persistent and pressing inquiry into the merits and limitations of conceiving of the creation of culture as a form of autonomous aesthetic production. This focus suggests ways that literature is informed by and engaged in broad debate about the status of art and uses of culture and cultural value within contemporary life. Indeed, I argue that the current struggle over the nature of creativity and the value of cultural expression, a struggle sometimes referred to as the "war over measure," is one in which literature is thoroughly involved, implicated, and interested.[32] The writers I focus on are evidently interested in collapsing distinctions between economic, political, social, and cultural forms of value; they are interested in the diverse social, political, and economic ends to which cultural practice is now being indexed. An interdisciplinary approach, balanced between literary studies and social science work in geography, sociology, and psychology, is thus a necessary response to the interests of the writing in question. One cannot fully understand how these writers conceive of and engage in the work of writing literature without paying attention to the broad political-economic movement toward neoliberalism and to the attendant transformation of cultural policy by creative-economy discourse.

1

The Creative Class
and Cultural Governance

My initial discussion of the creative-economy turn must begin with a reading of an influential social science monograph, popular with policymakers: Richard Florida's *The Rise of the Creative Class*. To understand *The Rise of the Creative Class*, we need to consider the book's rise to the status of handbook for creative-industries policymaking and the convergence of the social science research it contains and its author's own working life, as the book describes and is an instance of the merging of work and life. It combines presentation of research findings with autobiographical ruminations, it articulates a theory of creative work that makes it and its author paradigmatic, and it is written to secure its author's elite position as "thought-leader" within the creative class that it defines.[1]

Florida agrees with many scholars that in the United States work in agriculture and industry has declined. Replacing it is work in the service sector, along with a kind of work defined not by the sector in which it might be placed—finance, advertising, or the arts, for example—but instead by those who do it: the new "creative class." Defined as "people who add economic value through their creativity," according to Florida they make up 30 percent of the US workforce, and an increasing amount of power rests with them. Some belong to the creative core, among them "scientists and engineers, university professors, poets and novelists, artists, entertainers, actors, designers and architects," and some make up a lower order of "creative professionals," including those who support, disseminate, reproduce, and implement the innovations generated by the core—lab technicians and editors, for instance. Those in the core group practice what Florida calls "the highest order of creative work," which is "producing new forms or designs that are readily transferable and widely useful."[2]

Members of the creative class are said to share a set of lifestyle preferences to which governments, human resource departments, and urban developers could and should appeal. They "prefer weak ties to strong," and despite a characteristic reluctance to see themselves as belonging to any collective, they are members of a distinct class formation and share "similar tastes, desires and preferences."[3] A highly educated and mobile group of cultural professionals, they are typically city dwellers who encounter within the urban milieu the cultural and experiential diversity necessary to their self-conceptions. They are attracted not to big sports complexes or opera houses but to authentic bohemian downtowns, peppered with coffee shops, music venues, and a mix of people from diverse races and classes and with different sexual orientations. Cultural policy and urban planning should reflect these preferences. In Florida's work, as in previous attempts to establish a formula for revitalizing brownfield sites and docklands into "cultural quarters" and "enterprise zones," affluent people with high levels of human capital are appealed to as the "bearers of civility [and] good culture" who will make the city safe, clean, and prosperous again.[4] These people are also said to be "anti-establishment, anti-traditionalist and in respects highly individualistic: they prize freedom, autonomy and choice."[5] At work they fear overt forms of corporate or state-based intervention, and they tend to prefer instead the inward-looking "soft control" that operates via "new forms of self-management, peer-recognition and pressure and intrinsic forms of motivation." Primary among these intrinsic drives is the wish to "express [their] identities through work."[6] Florida counsels corporate management to respect these desires.

This argument that a creative elite is at the vanguard of post–World War II socioeconomic transformation likely sounds familiar. As early as 1959 Peter Drucker referred to the "professional specialist" in the "educated society," whose power is innovation and whose job is "to convey knowledge in usable form"; in the 1970s Daniel Bell wrote of the rise of a postindustrial middle-class meritocracy, and Erik Olin Wright, Alvin W. Gouldner, and Barbara and John Ehrenreich debated the existence and power of a "professional-managerial class," sometimes called "the new class" or "the new middle class"; in the 1980s Paul Fussell identified a "Class X"—neo-bohemian people who "belong to no one" and will only do work that they love; and in the early 1990s Robert Reich described "symbolic analysts." Closer still to Florida's work are the proliferating UK creative-industries task force publications of the late 1990s, to which I return later, as well as Paul H. Ray and Sherry Ruth Anderson's *The Cultural Creatives* and John Howkins's *The Creative Economy.*[7]

Florida's limited attention to his contemporaries and forebears is significant to his book's form, argument, and success. The fact that *The Rise of the Creative Class* is not overly burdened by excessive citations, by an extensive review of existing research, or by belabored attempts to distinguish itself from what came before helps to ensure its broad appeal. Unaccompanied by substantial methodological claims or by attempts to position the work within a larger body of scholarship, Florida's approach is instead grounded in the language of direct empirical observation. He and his co-researchers developed and implemented a series of patented measures, such as a "Creativity Index," a "Bohemian Index," and a "Gay Index," designed to quantify the relationship between an urban location's level of lifestyle diversity and its success in attracting creative professionals. *The Rise of the Creative Class* appeared when Florida was already a well-regarded and established academic, so its data have credentials. He was teaching at Carnegie Mellon University; he had written one book about the international application of Japanese industrial practices and co-edited another about the economic benefits of US- and Japanese-based university research. Presented in a way that was designed for widespread dissemination, the metrics that he and his team devised were a safe and concrete option for planners looking to conceive, implement, and measure practical revitalization strategies. Not long after its publication, supported by a global speaking tour, *The Rise of the Creative Class* became a bestseller and a "public-policy phenomenon,"[8] securing its author's rise to guru status as globetrotting government adviser, corporate consultant, and think-tank founder.

He is now professor of business and creativity in the Rotman School of Management at the University of Toronto, from whence he directs the Martin Prosperity Institute, which studies the role of "location, place and city-regions" in "global economic prosperity,"[9] and runs his own consultancy firm, the Creative Class Group, which offers a range of services from corporate advising ("research, strategy and marketing techniques that allow companies to reach the creative class consumer") to tools for creative communities (helping "emerging leaders . . . generate greater economic prosperity in their regions").[10] The group was recently paid $2.2 million by the Ontario government for a study that concludes, not surprisingly, that creative workers will be the key to the province's future economy. He offers his services to corporate clients as well, including Citigroup and Goldman Sachs. His current salary is $346,000, his speaker's fee is $35,000, and his wife is his manager.

The Rise of the Creative Class, the book that made his career, epitomizes its own definition of essential core creativity, for which careful distinction between Florida's own writing and other research is quite unimportant. What matters rather is rendering of "ideas" and "innovations" from any source into material that is "readily transferable and widely useful," a rendering that in this case took the form of empirical measures protected by patent law and described in a straightforward, even aphoristic and anecdotal style. So if for Florida the creative class includes anyone who works to "add economic value through creativity," such that the creative moment *is* the addition of economic value, this definition exists in supportive accord with his own mode of research articulation. The content of his argument and the form of its presentation are harmonized, and *The Rise of the Creative Class* trumpets what it is: work designed to cross over readily from an academic context into the public milieu and corporate application.

By its own definition, the object meant for global market circulation—a book, but along with it a set of data and a codified means of collecting the data, and a persona and career—matters to the creative economy insofar as it endeavors to render certain information amenable to market circulation. It is precisely this rendering that is, by its own lights, its originality or creative genius spark; thus, the very definition of innovation becomes inseparable from marketability, which is proven by wide-scale dissemination. Florida's definition of creativity makes the language of the market and the language of individual expressivity inextricable, and it reimagines the original genius of Romantic ideology as one who has found the ideal commercial outlet for a given innovation. It believes that everyone is creative but that only some people—people like him—devote their lives to finding ways to market new ideas and, along with them, the career-selves that emit them.

Many factors matter in achieving such marketability. I have noted that the book is the work of a respected professional backed by a prestigious university, the arguments are presented in an accessible style, and they are supported by what appear to be concrete measures recommended for direct implementation. We might also notice that Florida enjoys the limelight; he is a photogenic and dynamic public speaker who is as comfortable with an audience of CEOs as he is at an academic conference. It helps, too, that his book devotes some pages to chronicling his own life history, an act that attaches his biographical personality to the book from the beginning, as Florida intersperses presentation of data with tales of growing up in Newark, New Jersey, where he witnessed a period of urban decay followed by a revitalization that he attributes to creative professionals. When he talks about what the creative class desires, he often appeals to his own experience as proof; health and fitness is a recurring motif, for instance, as he describes his passion for bicycling and his sense that extreme leisure makes him a better thinker. That its anecdotal evidence about the leisure preferences of the creative elite is based in part in his own self-image and that its publication and dissemination secure his position within the class that it describes make *The Rise of the Creative Class* at once a partial autobiography and a prop to and end point in its author's own development.

Though his arguments have parallels or precedents in other scholarship and many people were involved in developing and conducting the research he presents as support for his claims, as the cover's lone author and as a biographical presence in the book Florida becomes its embodiment and its spokesperson—both in a relatively untroubled fashion. Florida's take on the creative class's economic importance is not meant to track the history of the various political arrangements and market mechanisms that make it operative, and it does not pretend to account for any social totality that might be said to produce the charismatic "thought-leader" he has himself become. Instead, Florida is content with a book that makes him synonymous with the creative class. He becomes its voice and its paradigmatic figure, so much so that his personal website is www.

creativeclass.com/. This collapse of Florida's life into Florida's work is part of what he notices and recommends, as he suggests that the creative class has forsaken distinctions between work and life.

The Rise of the Creative Class, more recent works like *The Flight of the Creative Class* and *Who's Your City?*, which largely continue its themes, along with his global travels to talk about his work, and his role as adviser to governments and corporations all work to foster new connections between culture, capitalism, and government. Translation of Florida's message into new policies and practices disseminates and legitimates the biography of this particular member of the creative elite. The extensive circulation of the book is the only real measure of the value of the information and ideas it puts forward. It hardly matters if cities that attempt to apply his ideas to build a more "diverse" downtown are not in fact more likely to attract the creative class, if the creative class is interested in diversity only as a kind of consumer spectacle, if his work never establishes the existence of a coherent class, instead only proving again what Edward Glaeser's work on human capital has already established—the higher the level of educational attainment in a city, the higher the level of growth there[11]—or if attempting to plan and build a "creative quarter" betrays the requirement that an authentically edgy urban milieu develop spontaneously.[12] Florida's words, backed by his guru status, are used to justify new blueprints or policy provisions for development of urban spaces and workplaces, and the lionization of this particular author figure continues to perpetuate the conditions he both recommends and exemplifies.

Though Florida mentions it only briefly, *The Rise of the Creative Class* is informed by some early British policy research about the creative industries and creative economy; Florida's work in turn accords with and shapes how the creative economy has been posited, defined, and discussed in the UK and globally. The particular vocabulary of creativity he helps foster, highlighting the economic impact of culture and the arts, gained popularity after Tony Blair's government began to promote the idea that creative expertise would secure the postindustrial UK's viability within the global economy.[13] The Department for Culture, Media and Sport (DCMS) was established in 1997, and it soon designated a Creative Industries Task Force to define and measure the creative industries' nature and value.[14] Its early findings estimated that cultural pursuits employed

982,000 across the UK, generating £50 billion in revenue and £6.9 billion in export earnings each year.[15] In 2006 the DCMS reported that the creative industries "contributed 8% of the UK's Gross Value Added" in 2004 and were responsible for one-fifth of the jobs in London.[16] In 2007 it boasted that "creative employment [including jobs in the creative industries and 'creative jobs' in other fields] increased from 1.6m in 1997 to 1.9m in 2006," an average growth of 2 percent per annum, doubling the figure for the economy overall.[17] That same year, then DCMS head Tessa Jowell wrote that the "size of the creative industries is comparable to the financial services sector. They now make up 7.3 per cent of the economy, and are growing at 5 per cent per year (almost twice the rate of the rest of the economy)."[18]

Meanwhile, in 2005 the DCMS initiated and backed an overarching Creative Economy Programme (CEP), designed to ensure that, in the words of the then creative industries minister James Purnell, the UK would become the whole world's "creative hub."[19] The CEP was tasked with formulating a strategy to unite government, schools, think tanks, and the private sector in pursuit of a shared goal: continued production of sufficient labor for the creative economy. Both the DCMS and the CEP consistently describe creativity as an engine to generate new wealth; both Purnell and Jowell stress that the creative economy will be key to ensuring the UK is able to compete in a global marketplace for highly skilled employees. Its flourishing creative industries will ensure that the UK is branded as the place to work in a creative profession and shop in the marketplace for creative goods and services. More than that, though, its creative expertise will expand into the economy as a whole: culture and design trades will make the UK a place to go to "add value" to any product or service; arts education will help the next generation develop the creativity to fend off the "competitive threat" that countries like India and China present to what remains of its hold over high-skill trades.[20] In a speech Blair gave at the Tate Modern in March 2007, he presented the creative economy as a sector peopled by those who appreciate their own human capital: "The more it is developed, the better we are. Modern goods and services require high value added input. . . . Much of it comes from people—their ability to innovate, to think anew, to be creative."[21]

It is this seemingly straightforward understanding of the creative industries as a source of wealth and competitive advantage that circulates most extensively in the media and in policy circles. But as in the case of reference to the creative class, to refer to the creative industries and creative economy is more than an innocent way to signal the economic value of the practices, institutions, and products protected by the intellectual property regime. Measuring the creative industries is a task often undertaken by its advocates, and claims to identify their importance help constitute and promote what they enumerate and quantify. Because the vocabulary of creativity helps forge and solidify the circumstances that it claims to identify and quantify, what its advocates put forward is quite simply socially consequent. New blueprints for creative-economy development, backed and disseminated by think tanks, government officials, and academics, have a direct and observable impact on how the future will unfold.

It matters then that the new vocabulary of creativity frames relations between corporations, government, and citizens in a way that achieves specific political mandates. In the UK case, reference to the creative industries, which may have found its original force as a tactical means for the DCMS to secure funding for culture, soon became for the Blair government an effective way to brand itself as having a new, reform-minded, forward-looking approach to provision of government services, distinct from the approaches of previous Labour and Conservative governments.[22] As Justin O'Connor argues, New Labour's emphasis on the economic importance of culture was well rehearsed in an extensive 1980s and 1990s literature on the cultural industries. What came to matter under New Labour was "the brand value of the term 'creative industries' when embraced by a high profile government and successfully . . . exported around the globe."[23] In a pamphlet written for the Progressive Governance Network, Blair writes of the need to rebrand progressive politics and advocates "restructuring and reform to build more diverse, individually tailored services built around the needs of the modern consumer," along with the forging of closer links "with the more exciting and dynamic intellectual currents in economics, management theory and social policy."[24] He established the Government Information Service to help develop and target "key messages" and "improve co-ordination from the centre, so as to get across consistently the Government's key policy themes and messages."[25] Creative-industries discourse provided one of these key policy narratives, a narrative constructed by a closely linked network of government officials, industry personnel, and think tanks like Demos and the Institute for Public Policy Research.[26] For instance, Charles Leadbeater, management consultant and self-styled expert on matters of creativity and innovation, was a policy adviser to the Blair government while working as an associate at Demos, where he helped author several of its core pamphlets. He is cited as an expert in several government studies, including the first DCMS Mapping Document. Blair so admired his insights that he wrote a blurb for Leadbeater's 1999 study of the knowledge economy, *Living on Thin Air*, a book that argues that New Labour had thus far been too timid in its modernization program. It promotes a more aggressive turn to public-private partnerships and advocates the creation of a "venture capital or innovation fund" to encourage "a much more active market for money to flow to people with talent and ideas in the public sector."[27]

Blair's willingness to register respect for Leadbeater's views intimates the link between creative-economy policymaking and the broader political transformation. Continuing what was started by Margaret Thatcher and John Major, who had emphasized that the "users" of government deserve the "consumer choice" said to result from private-sector competition for public contracts,[28] New Labour courted private investment and welcomed blurred distinction between public and private mandates. It helped to construct and then acquiesced to the demand that the government should meet market criteria of efficiency. It invested authority in management consultants and other experts contracted to perform studies and make recommendations. It encouraged workplace reforms that would promote individual responsibility and undermine unions or other collectivities.[29] The 1999 white paper *Modernising Government* speaks of improving the provision of public services "to match the best of the private sector." It promotes a series of "creative" approaches to improvement, which include financial incentives or rewards for staff members who "identify financial savings or service improvements." "Distinctions between services delivered by the public and the private sector are breaking down in many areas," we read, "opening the way to new ideas, partnerships and opportunities for devising and delivering what the public wants." Throughout this document, the word "creative" is interchangeable with "reform" and with "modernisation"; each term is used to indicate a willingness to entertain market-based approaches to provision of government services. Government regulation is referred to almost exclusively as restrictive and as a "burden" to business; citizens appear uniformly as "consumers"; and we read that "in the private sector, service standards and service delivery have improved. . . . People are now rightly demanding a better service . . . from the public sector too." New Labour is thus "looking hard—but not dogmatically—at what services government can best provide itself, what should be contracted to the private sector, and what should be done in partnership."[30]

A few broad conclusions can be drawn here. To begin with, it is evident that creative-economy discourse was the means by which a more systemic program privileging private-sector modalities and economic ends was made relevant to culture and the arts in the UK. It was the way government set about transforming its relationship to the arts into one determined by the ostensibly inevitable necessity of securing future economic development. Hence, creative-economy discourse is friendly to private enterprise and wary of public subsidy, and friendly to a flexibly self-sufficient and self-managing workforce and hostile to collective politics and workers' interdependence.[31] It construes the cultural sector as something of legitimate concern to government and as something it understands and has a handle on, while providing its politicians with a platform for promotion of commercially driven initiatives and values. Presenting creativity as something everyone possesses, and culture and the arts as things to which all should have access, appears to be democratic and egalitarian. Yet certain forms of arts provision and funding were nonetheless privileged by New Labour, and certain images of cultural producers were more common than others. Regions now tend to compete with one another for limited resources by claiming to possess creative potential, personnel, and facilities. Funding for cultural producers, services, and infrastructure has tended to overlook less profitable activities to privilege a few urban enclaves where marketable expressions of creativity are concentrated, such as Hackney as it prepared for the 2012 Olympics and attendant Cultural Olympiad. Creative-industries policies have been rapidly embraced as an inexpensive way to brand one's city or region or nation as friendly to private enterprise and to investment and development. As Andrew Ross notes, attracting major manufacturing firms and large corporations requires tax breaks, infrastructure support, and the risk of great loss, while appealing to creative labor requires only setting up a few coffee shops and some loft-like work-life spaces and renaming some areas "creative quarters."[32]

Meanwhile, government and government-linked think-tank statements about creative work, along with training programs for those aspiring to creative careers, were encouraging people to conceive of themselves as self-managed entrepreneurs of the self.[33] Low-level service work may be pushed to the boundaries of this environment, but it hardly disappears. The expressive mental labor of the urban elite, exploited via long hours and a devoted dissolution of work-life boundaries, depends upon a core of flexible service workers to whom ostensibly noncreative tasks can be outsourced. The class stratification is both global and local: a new T-shirt design is born and patented in the creative economy and then assembled for pittance wages in an export processing zone; the creative class moves into and helps gentrify neighborhoods whose residents were dispossessed when manufacturing jobs moved overseas. Old abandoned warehouses become posh lofts and work spaces; the defunct fire station, a restaurant-café.

Since 2010, as the Conservative / Liberal Democratic government has reduced funding for the arts, the treatment of culture as an adjunct to urban revitalization, as a competitive regional or national advantage, as worthy of subsidy in a diminishing array of circumstances, and as the work of happily self-managing individualists, has continued apace. If anything, the current government's response to the aftermath of the 2008 economic crisis has entailed an even more conscious use of culture to attempt to shape a society suited to neoliberal capital. Prime Minister David Cameron has urged people to understand the economic crisis as a fundamentally cultural matter, by claiming that it was caused by the welfare state's imposition of supports that deprived people of the impetus to create a just world on their own. In his view, if people are simply told to limit neoliberal markets, they will never do it. Instead, only the absence of an imposed regulatory framework will create the conditions in which people will uncover their integral fellow feeling and create solutions to social problems like rapacious greed.

The "Big Society" concept that anchored the *Conservative Manifesto 2010*—a document billed as "an invitation to join the government of Britain"—featured the antiestablishment rhetoric of self-determination ("be your own boss") and community power ("sack your MP"). It expressed views that Cameron had often articulated elsewhere: for example, that people should be motivated by their integral culture rather than by an imposed power—so, by affection rather than procedure, by authentic connection rather than by the seeking of reward or the fear of punishment. He claims to want a "connected society" and states that what will produce such a thing is not the state but rather autochthonous culture and creativity. He claims that expansion of the state served to suppress natural "human kindness, generosity and imagination." Human creativity is thus, in Cameron's conception, anathema to bureaucracy. It follows that Cameronite government policy, which does not want to impose top-down regulatory measures, does not want to stifle creativity, does not want to intervene in the natural formation of affective bonds that are also good business networks, aims instead at cultural disposition, at creating a commonsense way of thinking about the self and society. Instead of regulating, it prefers to "nudge."[34]

So when we look at how the current British government has understood the causes of the economic crisis, we see everywhere its application of the various theses of the Big Society. What produced the crash were immoral actions of individuals not persuaded enough of their social responsibility, committed only to rampant individualism, belonging to no authentic communities, ignorant of the way their interests need to be balanced by spiritual pursuits, by goodness, by charity, by right action. These moral failings are all attributed to "big government" public services and supports. In Cameron's words, state control via bureaucracy had replaced "moral choice and personal responsibility." By taking power and responsibility away from individuals, government has only, he says, "served to individuate them."[35] So less state, rather than more, is the only proper response. The Big Society will correct the ills that led to the crash by encouraging individuals to take the responsibility to be the protectors of the integrity of society rather than expecting the state to play that role; it will also remake businesses as responsible social agents with the civic duty to engage in charity and volunteerism.

As Alan Finlayson points out, the Big Society thus proposes to operate contradictorily: it promotes "withdrawal of the state from various

areas in order to make way for the vibrant energies of voluntary society";
but "pro-social behaviours" will not simply appear magically.[36] Rather,
in Cameron's words, "we need strong and concerted government action
to make it happen. We need to use the state to remake society."[37] So the
Cameronite state must be engaged in an endless self-denying self-perpet-
uation. It has to exist and work constantly to ensure that people do not
in fact need it. Its major function will be in a real sense an aesthetic one:
devising ways to create a compelling, aesthetically rich, and culturally persuasive commonsense narrative about the right way to act "pro-socially,"
the right way to balance one's self-interested investment in one's own
human capital with a commitment to society and to shared capabilities,
talents, capacities. What we find, thus, after the economic crisis, is the
neoliberal state as "nudging" storyteller, as a source and center of meaning
that is also strangely absent. This is not quite the creative-industries or
creative-economy theses of the New Labour era, which related the making and appreciating of culture to social and individual well-being and a
whole host of other laudable outcomes. It certainly isn't in any simplistic
way about the old Thatcherite focus on the contribution of culture to the
economy, although that remains crucial of course. It is about the state as
the primary and generative engine of stories about what sort of economic
agent I should strive to be—curious, open, humane, aesthetically inclined,
participating, producing, visionary but not antisocial, an innovator but
not against capital. I should be, above all, committed to remaining free—
or, as Matt Stahl would have, bereft—of actual state support.[38]

   The continuation of these processes after New Labour suggests their
basis in a broader neoliberal politics, while, symbiotically, the spread of
neoliberal ideology owes something to the success of New Labour's mes-
saging about cultural governance. At the same time that the creative-economy turn worked to enshrine private-sector concerns with capital accumulation as the focus of government's interest in culture, New Labour
used creative-economy discourse as a means to market its own political
program and seek legitimacy for it. It used the culture that it highlighted
and rewarded, which was culture that could be shown to be both economically viable and socially consequential, as a barometer and symbol
of its entire enterprise. Culture *was* what New Labour's Third Way rhetoric claimed to be able to forge: the felicitous intersection of social and

economic productivities, the union of individual and civic goals in the service of economic growth. The founder of Demos had claimed that the "wider culture" is "the centre of the agenda for government reform, because we know from the findings of a wide range of recent research that culture is perhaps the most important determinant of a combination of long-run economic success and social cohesion."[39] New Labour's creative-economy turn, which Demos worked assiduously to back, examine, and reimagine, was an expression of this conception of culture's centrality.

New Labour was remarkably successful in marketing itself as the party in tune with the future society. This society was characterized by what Anthony Giddens, one of the government's premier intellectual backers, helped to dub our "reflexive modernity," in which there are no constants except a mutable capitalism, and in which openness to ceaseless change is the privileged marker of one's personal evolution. More than that, though, New Labour succeeded in selling the idea that it is the task of any government to attempt to encourage people to accommodate themselves to the inevitability of capitalist modernity and to envision culture as a crucial tool to be put to this purpose. The celebration of the successful creative-economy worker as the ideal subject of our reflexive modernity might be read as an instance of this placement of culture in service to government. The next two chapters pull back from the specific case of New Labour governance to consider in more detail the nature of the parallels—parallels the government drew upon and cemented—between the creative-economy worker and the subject of reflexive modernity. The core theme of these chapters is how ideas about art and artists, in particular about authors and authorship, have been deployed by those who have worked to foster connections between modernity, reflexivity, and flexibility.

2

Work as Art / Art as Life

This is my life. I plan to make it count. I plan to make it memorable. I plan to
give it my all. I plan to . . . **make art** . . . in accounting . . . or information systems; in sales . . . or customer service. I am Brand You. I am Performing Artist.
—Tom Peters, *The Brand You 50*

Of course, artists have always seen their work as an expression of themselves, and
society has accepted this more readily for them than for other sorts of worker. It
is easy to accept a new sculpture as a work of self-expression; harder to see a new
spreadsheet in the same light. But they are essentially the same. Both are expressions of our abilities, interests and imagination.
—Richard Reeves, *Happy Mondays*

This chapter examines in more detail some recent conceptions of
creative labor by considering the surprising resonance between Richard
Florida's definition of the creative class and the definition of immaterial
labor put forward by theorists linked to the radical neo-Marxist autonomia movement.

Florida and the autonomists broadly agree that over the past few
decades more work has become comparable to artists' work. For Florida
this is a positive development. For the autonomists it is ambivalent, but
they state with little equivocation that the kind of aesthetic expression
subsumed within capitalist production is not real creativity but rather
creativity's codified and corrupted appearance in commodity form. Still,
both camps imagine creativity as located within individuals' uncontain-
able experimental energies and self-expressive capacities. In Florida's

work these capacities are often facilitated and liberated by development of one's career within an expanding marketplace for creative work. The autonomists are instead threatened by such incorporation. Indeed, they are quashed by the sheer process of individuation, since that, too, has by now been thoroughly subsumed into capitalist relations, until only a "monad" of pure "potential," existing somehow before incorporation or even socialization, can be the source of real creativity.

Nevertheless, this potential, which is an inherent germ available for development, is for the autonomists also crucial to capitalism's demise. For both them and for Florida new currents in capitalist production may feed the universal germ of autonomous creativity. They part ways, though, when the autonomists state these currents trigger the rise of "the multitude," which may, will, or should mean the end of capitalism and the fruition of something resembling Marx's "social individual": the worker who does tasks that a thing cannot do, whose work is so satisfying it will be done for its own sake, under no distant compulsion or direct domination[1]—thus, again, the worker as romanticized "artist," in this case imagined on the other side of capitalism's demise. For Florida, this worker already exists; he is one himself.

Florida's research accords with, and has influenced, government policy and mainstream social science and management literature, in which individuals appear as born innovators, the origins of enterprise, naturally predisposed to be against what exists and to try to perfect it through invention, while the economy discovers this preexisting tendency and then nurtures it into an engine for ceaseless renewal of capitalism. The autonomists' theories of a resistant subjectivity that is at once subsumed within, outside, and the source of liberation from capitalism are not equivalent to Florida's. Nevertheless, they are likewise more symptoms than diagnoses of the pervasive vocabulary that fathoms creative expression as an essence of experimentation emanating from an internal, natural, or biological source and that finds one of its models in idealized apprehension of artists' resistance to routine, to management, to standardization, and to commodification.

For Florida, the fact that this vocabulary is one that contemporary capitalism clearly requires and reinforces is not a problem: his imagined creative subject is the fruit of the progress of modernization, of the spread of self-reflexivity and freedom. The autonomists' case is more difficult. They themselves tend to lament that the expressive self-realization at the core of their theory is the same one nurtured and expropriated by capital, yet they do not offer any alternative to this conception of human desire and behavior. Their immaterial producer, her character assumed rather than interpreted, appears in a largely naturalized form, destitute of any significant history.

Before considering their differences, it helps to place both camps in opposition to Daniel Bell's account of postindustrialism, which he began to articulate in the late 1960s. "Postindustrial" is Bell's label for an economy ruled by scientific management of mental laborers tasked with tracking and producing reams of paper rather than objects. Most simply, Bell claimed knowledge would replace labor and capital as the main factor in production. He heralded the arrival of an era of prosperity for all and with it the demise of the embattled worker. But he also lamented the persistence of some cultural contradictions, a "disjunction of realms" that seemed to be slowing the coming future's arrival. While noting scientific and technical rationalization of the production process, he claimed it was in tension with a widespread embrace of "norms of self-realization" and self-fulfillment, as more and more people wished to unearth and respect not their inner technocrat but their "whole person." Captivated by the 1960s counterculture, which constellated narcissistic adversarial artist-types who were celebrants of the "free creative spirit" at war with repression, people everywhere wished to shirk the roles they were asked to perform at work, so as to uncover the authentic self, necessarily unique and irreducible, "free of the contrivances and conventions, the masks and hypocrisies." As a result, the "principles of the economic realm and those of the culture now lead people in contrary directions."[2] On the surface, supporters of the idea of a creative class, and theorists of immaterial labor, offer the same basic revision of a view like Bell's. If capitalism and the "free creative spirit" were ever really at odds, they have now been united. The figure of the resisting, elite-aesthete artist-author, a source of inspiration for Bell's authenticity seekers, plays a key role in each camp's conception of this novel integration.

For Florida, under capitalism's benevolent watch the ideal of nonalienated labor, performed by the "whole person" en route to self-development, has passed out of the realm of utopian fantasy and into the workplace. In Florida's notion, which references David Brooks's related idea of the elite bourgeois-bohemian "Bo-Bo," the once tenable distinction between bourgeois and bohemian values has collapsed into the "shared work and lifestyle ethic" that Florida calls "the creative ethos." Florida claims that, like bohemians before them, members of the creative class value diversity, openness, and noncon-formity, eschewing "organizational or institutional directives" and embracing city living as freedom from the constraints of society and tradition. However, like the bourgeoisie, they are also happily willing to connect self-worth to career success, meritocracy, hard work, challenge, stimulation, and "goal-set-ting and achievement." In general, they feel little "distaste for material things," not because they wish to grow rich through work per se but because they are living in an era of "post-scarcity." Whereas the bohemian artist suffered for her work, the new "creative," or the "Bo-Bo," taps into creativity precisely to the extent that she is free from the constraint of having to worry about pov-erty.[3] Indeed, a successful creative career is important because it means one is granted the kind of respect that translates into additional freedoms: most important perhaps, the freedom to pursue one's creative inclinations without too much concern for market necessities.

To argue that it is now common to possess a relatively content, united, bourgeois-bohemian subjectivity is in its way quite novel. What accounts of the history of bohemia present as more typical is a certain worry about the possibility that a person could be at once bourgeois and bohemian. Pierre Bourdieu describes a Parisian bohemian lifestyle as having been "elaborated as much against the dutiful existence of official painters and sculptors as against the routines of bourgeois life."[4] If one becomes famous and pursues success while affiliated with bohemia, is one then no longer a true bohemian? To qualify as bohemian, how committed need you be to a critique of bourgeois values like safety, stability, and the pursuit of material wealth? And aren't the values integral to bohemia—rejection of cant, personal freedom, self-expression—in some ways deeply compatible with bourgeois liberalism? None of these questions can be answered straightforwardly. There has never been a purely authentic and self-constituting bohemia. Members of bohemian movements have given their communities coherence by outing fakes and frauds, while, inversely, the idea of the bourgeoisie itself became clearer after bohemian enclaves targeted bourgeois mores.[5] There is, moreover, a long tradition of critique of the relatively privileged individual who is attracted to the mere image of destitution or simply wants to be associated with the aura of freedom and nonconformity attached to bohemian life. Guy de Maupassant wrote of "cette petite bourgeoise bohème" in his 1885 novel *Bel-Ami*, and Wyndham Lewis pointedly mocked what he called "bourgeois bohemians" in *Tarr* (1918). And was Bloomsbury not a bourgeois bohemia?

In Bourdieu's terms, the bohemians of nineteenth-century Paris accomplished "progressive affirmation of the autonomy of writers" by articulating their "moral indignation against all forms of submission to the forces of power or to the market."[6] As César Graña memorably put it, in her "burning and doomed enthusiasm for the life of the spirit, the daily battle against the powers of the modern world," the bohemian castigated a bourgeoisie imagined as the embodiment of those very powers in all their blithe domination.[7] In doing so, she tended to emphasize the possibility that bohemia's borders might be breached, that its modes of authentic self-articulation and nonconformity might be offered up to an outside world—whether for appropriation by the undeserving or for indiscriminate sale. So what is novel about Florida's vision is the way he conceives what was once a field of intense struggle as a realm of harmonious accord. For Florida the authenticity-seeking bohemian is no longer threatened by the possibility that her inner bourgeois will be revealed or that her community of like-minded creatives will be infiltrated. He claims that, instead, materialistic motivations exist in tandem rather than tension with the desire for self-expression, personal development, and eclecticism and states that the wish to do creative work and identify with a community of creative people is perfectly reconcilable with the desire to live in prosperity.

In celebrating this reconciliation, Florida's work exemplifies neoliberal ideologies. Whereas classical liberal doxa assumes that what we are and what we own must not be confused—presupposing, Michel Feher states, "that we do not grow spiritually rich in the same way that we acquire material wealth"—neoliberals question "the alleged heterogeneity between the aspirations of the authentic self and the kind of optimizing calculations required by the business world."[8] Florida's work positions the creative class as the vanguard instance of this union of economic rationality and authenticity, this perfect marriage between the bohemian and what had been her bourgeois other. Hence, in his view, we must simply let the creative process be organized in such a way that its essential indivisibility is respected rather than scientifically managed and rationalized. Subsequent stages of production, for example, the implementation of design ideas or the securing of intellectual property rights, may be subject to rationalization and control, but the creative process should be set apart, its autonomy assumed and structured into the workplace. In Florida's theory, in sum, tapping into the endless mental reserves of the worker becomes the source for the material organization of the industry—for the design of office space and working time, for example—and finding novel ways to arrange work around worker-artists' limitless creative potential is synonymous with finding new modes of capital expansion.

Turning now to the autonomists, the terms seem quite different: in the theory of immaterial labor, defined in part as the incorporation of information into production, but mainly as the postfactory work that "produces the informational and cultural content of the commodity," capital is busily orchestrating the incorporation of creativity into itself.[9] It is doing this by treating all of social experience as a factory in which the universal human inclination toward creative play and invention becomes a laboratory from which new products emerge. The personality and subjectivity of the worker, including the desire for variety and self-expression, are made "susceptible to organization and command." Thus, when we are all enjoined to explore our own subjectivity, that by no means does away with the "antagonism" between "autonomy and command"; instead, it simply "re-poses the antagonism at a higher level, because it both mobilizes and clashes with the very personality of the individual worker."[10] The shifting world of available ideas, which the autonomists call "the mass intellect," is something capital is always trying to access and capture, so it creates spaces where novel agglomerations of those ideas will emerge and be accessible. In this the "struggle against work" is simply useful. Immaterial production "nurtures, exploits, and exhausts" its labor force by ongoing affective social production of self-sacrificing and self-motivated workers, people who freely offer their labor because it is experienced as nonlaborious pleasure or as moral compulsion.[11] Key here is capital's desire for a worker-subject in whom "command" simply "resides": in short, workers disobey command, but disobedience is a prerequisite for productivity.[12]

For the autonomists, the essential Floridean mistake would be seeing this commingling of capitalism and unstructured work as an unquestionably benign or even ideal realization of the end of soul-destroying waged employment.[13] It represents instead its intensification, particularly ambivalent because it is experienced as the opposite and emerges precisely through a critique of work. Postfactory labor, especially in its tendency toward valorization of the enterprising self, finds its legitimacy in the struggle against work. Hence, in a structuring tension, the struggle against work becomes something that the best work entails.

In tandem, as the distinction between work and leisure is eroded, what one experiences and consumes "outside" labor time becomes part of the production of commodities.[14] As immaterial labor is a matter of social relationships, and its economic value stems from this fact, for the autonomists the consumer, too, "is inscribed in the manufacturing of the product from its conception."[15] Consumption does not just "realize" the product. It is itself the product, as at once the tracked assumption behind the product's creation and the desired outcome of it. Thus, the material reworked by immaterial labor is the general world of subjectivity and the environment in which it is produced; the content of immaterial labor's commodities is the general social milieu. Immaterial workers satisfy a demand and produce it at the same time. The social world, as the factory, is the space in which the worker is reproduced; all the culture that is consumed works to infect and influence and re-create the consumer's situation. The consumer is in simplest terms a productive force. More exactly, the person traditionally construed as the consumer—the reader, the viewer—is thoroughly incorporated into the cycle of production, and the cultural producer is herself conceived as a consumer, as the member of a class defined by the accoutrements of lifestyle and leisure, and as one whose habits of consumption do so much to define her and whose experiences as a consumer are what generate the ideas that are later codified in rights to intellectual property. The process of immaterial production is thus cyclical and all pervasive, very nearly incorporating everyone.

Having painted such a troubling picture, the autonomists are nevertheless careful to theorize the mass intellect as something that cannot be fully incorporated into capital. In trying to explain why this is so, Virno latches onto Marx's mention of a general intellect, especially as articulated in the "Fragment on Machines," where, in Virno's terms, Marx argues that abstract knowledge "begins to become, precisely by virtue of its autonomy from production, nothing less than the principal productive force, relegating parcelized and repetitive labor to a peripheral and residual position."[16] Rather than conclude that immaterial labor substantiates what can be read in the "Fragment on Machines" as a warning that workers might become, basically, slaves controlled by a superhuman intellect, Virno prefers another of this short text's possible implications: it is perverse to consider knowledge and the worker existing independently of one another, because the general intellect is the mutual interrelation of living labor and machinery, which is the fixed capital in which abstracted knowledge about working processes is embedded. In Virno's conception, the knowledge held by the general intellect "cannot be reduced to fixed capital" because it is "inseparable from the interaction of a plurality of living subjects."[17]

"Mass intellectuality is the composite group of Postfordist living labor," Virno writes, and it "cannot be objectified in machinery."[18] As the general intellect is constantly recombined and reconstituted within the wide expanse of living labor, whenever it is translated into fixed capital, a conflict emerges. Capital's constant struggle to fix knowledge is met by living labor's lack of willingness to have its knowledge abstracted. For Virno the general intellect is, exactly, "the intellect in general": it is the basic human ability to think and process information; it is the inherent creativity possessed by everyone, "rather than the works produced by thought." Postindustrial modes of accumulation depend upon and tap this unending resource; its ability to operate requires the inexhaustible resource potential of the creative impulse, grounded fundamentally in the "potential of labor to execute contingent and unrepeatable statements."[19] This is a social knowledge that is the opposite of that possessed by the new "labour aristocracy." It is the "immeasurable" site of "heterogeneous effective possibilities." It arises from the faculties for thinking, perceptions, language, memory, feelings, all part of the "fundamental biological configuration" that distinguishes the human animal.[20] It is a never-ending potentiality—in the autonomists' vocabulary, a "virtuality."[21] It is this that capital attempts to transform into productive labor, and that Hardt and Negri have located at the utopian center of the political promise of "the multitude."

It is in understanding the relationship between this potentiality and its transformation through immaterial labor that the autonomists tend to invoke aesthetic models. Virno prefers to figure innovation as the "virtuosity" of the live performer, whose activity "finds its own fulfillment (that is, its own purpose) in itself, without objectifying itself into an end product, without settling into a 'finished product,' or into an object which would survive the performance."[22] It would seem then that real creativity cannot survive transformation into "product" or "object"; its rightful aura cannot be preserved or accessed by others outside a singular moment of its own expression, interpreted as "its own purpose."

For his part, Lazzarato applies the literary circuit of "the author, reproduction, and reception." He positions the author as a consumer who puts together a unique amalgam of materials available within mass intellectuality and then offers up that assemblage of her labor to capital. That offering up is the crucial thing; in its absence one remains and continues to perform as living labor or "virtuoso," capital's ceaseless countermeasure, the thing that it will never fully "subordinate it to its own values." To engage in immaterial production is to author something, which inevitably means to work in a way that "distorts or deflects the social imaginary that is produced in the forms of life." At the same time, though, those forms of life are the ultimate and final source of innovation—in the simple process of being alive, ideas occur, so the actual production of immaterial commodities is ultimately dependent and secondary. Everything is, of course, socially authored, since it is "the whole of the social relation," embodied in the author-work-audience relationship, that brings any kind of meaning "into play." But through the author of immaterial products, who possesses what Lazzarato calls autonomous "synergies," capital will "attempt to control" and "subordinate" these irreducible energies to itself.[23]

So in the work of immaterial labor theorists, as in the work of the creative class's enthusiasts, ideas about the status and work of the elite artist-author shape how they understand contemporary labor. For the latter it seems that the old ideal of the artist's aversion to market success no longer holds. The artist has been subsumed into the creative class, bohemian values persist only as lifestyle choices, and creativity and market circulation are synonymous and unfold in tandem. The authenticity and subjectivity of the creative act are in no way threatened by market circulation; indeed, they are protected by it. For the former, the artist is the model for the absorption of subjectivity into the market. She is the figure for any worker who "originates" the authored and authorized discourse that is inseparable from capitalism but separate from something else it cannot contain: inherent human creativity, understood as the variability of the infinite potential for recombination.

The Floridean and autonomian viewpoints are thus similar in their assumption that creativity and capital have by now been merged in some novel ways, as the production of various kinds of symbolic content— information, knowledge, entertainment, art—have become economically dominant and as the artists' vaunted resistance to routine work has helped transform the total organization of elite labor. However, their worries about the process mean that the autonomists end up somewhere distinct. Their wish seems to be to preserve the space between what they conceive as the mass intellect and an individual and entrepreneurial appropriation of its products for personal gain. Their concern is to highlight what occurs when, from the general world of social production of the commodity, an author like Florida extracts a small bit and becomes its authorized owner.

Thus, as they maintain these theories of virtuosity and virtuality, constantly returning to what authorized speech cannot capture through immaterial production of intellectual property, they actually continue, rather than attenuate, Daniel Bell's sense that there is some pressing contradiction between creative expression and work. Though they are not entirely critical of what immaterial labor represents, their writings evince a clear wish to maintain a sublime mass that is at once outside property relations and the source of everything available for transposition into them. This wish is perhaps most evident in their continual return to oppositions that are resonantly ethical: quantities are pitted against the unquantifiable; actual products are pitted against future potential for the creation of anything; the model of the solo author is pitted against the collective intelligence that is actually held by everyone and merely appropriated for the author's use; writing and codification are pitted against the universal possession of language and its ability to be constantly redeployed, reformulated, and recombined; intellectual property rights are pitted against "the commons" and the multitude; and measure and all it implies about quantification and exchange are pitted against immeasure, figured as the endless fecundity of social knowledge and its irreducibility to exchange relations or as its unavailability for abstraction in machinery.

At its most extreme, this logic holds that to act artistically is to construct "new being" and to oppose death, and it is only the multitude that can do this, through its constant "proliferation of vital experiences that have in common the negation of death, the rejection and definitive refusal of that which stalls the life process."[24] The universal multitude is to the "global world" (closed, entropic, exhausted) as the working class is to capital, or as living labor is to dead labor; in this polarized conception, art is the "ferocious struggle against death" that gives birth to—and is—the multitude.[25] While introducing a recent translation of Virno's work, Sylvère Lotringer cautiously supports Hardt and Negri's tendency to pit "love and community" against an Evil Empire figured as "a giant with clay-fleet, vicious, abusive, controlling, a predator always engaged in 'an operation of absolute violence.'"[26] Empire as system becomes an "abstract and empty unification" and a "parasitical machine" that lives off the vitality of a simple and innocent multitude while also, mysteriously, endangering itself.[27] Virno's own work is run through with a similarly Manichean "will to be against."[28]

Thus, where Florida and the autonomists concur, we find an image of an economy in which individual human creativity has become the vanguard driving force and key productive engine. Where they diverge, we glimpse continued conflict over what it means that so much labor is now being called creative or that respect for the productive powers of creative impulses has been incorporated into the system of capital expansion. For Florida and his students and allies, artists are models of successful and fulfilling work within the marketplace, while noncreatives are simply a problem. It is not that they have nothing to offer—like the autonomists, Florida states that everyone is basically creative—but that, because they are trapped in deadening work, their potential is not being accessed, which means "wasting that great reservoir of our creative capital."[29] This represents a problem both for them and for the businesses that might trade in their creativity.

In marked contrast, for the theorists of immaterial labor, these noncreatives are actually where true creativity resides, because their ceaseless ability to combine and recombine is the source of all knowledge. Their approach is to transmogrify those who don't author—or those who "refuse"—into the only source of resistance to capital, a resistance that capital always does and does not incorporate. That is, whereas Florida positions creativity as the market meeting minds, for the autonomists it can only be minds as they meet outside market logic. Thus, the author becomes any figure whose thinking being is exploited by capital, and also, quite simply, capital itself. Both the figure and the system require that whole social world to remain outside authorship or authored experience, to be the source of potential that cannot be reduced to labor value. Once your labor has become available for this reduction to product, by expropriating potentiality, you have become an author. Because the agent of immaterial production makes property, and that property is the stuff of her self and her personality, she is in the worst possible situation. She is inseparable from capital; to maintain her irreducibility to it would be ridiculous. Yet there is a nonauthor, in possession of a nonmarket mass intellect, who possesses that kind of irreducibility.

**

The construction of contemporary labor as a form of creative self-expression and self-realization, and the activation of images of expressive artist-figures in defining what that means, have often been critiqued. Critics have, for example, examined the pernicious psychic effects of the use in the workplace of romantically aesthetic models of selfhood, pointing out that management has aided and benefited from the mainstreaming of the artist's aura, as it acclimates people to lives of instability and flux, to inadequate or irregular remuneration, to the rhetoric of collective purpose and the reality of a competitive star system, to the fetish of authenticity and the reality of managed output catered to market demands, and so on.[30] At its most extreme, the merging of work and life in the "self-work ethos"[31] finds people contradictorily enjoined to "look within" to discover their true selves—who they are irrespective of markets and of society—but precisely as a means to develop their human capital, as part of their enterprising self-appreciation.[32] Recurring institutional investment in the idea that we should all be engaged in self-referencing introspection has led to despair, depression, mental collapse, reliance on therapists, and medication dependency.[33]

Others have objected that to insist too much that the driving force of our economy is knowledge, ideas, information, culture, et cetera, or to state that all work has become somehow akin to the work of creative self-expression, is to paper over a number of pressing realities. Most of the world's work is still in agriculture and heavy industry, and it may be that a condition for elite creative labor is the outsourcing of so-called noncreative tasks to a growing service sector and underclass industrial and migrant workforce.[34] Florida's definition of what constitutes a creative profession is itself so capacious that his statements about a vanguard creative-class takeover seem like the product of statistical maneuvering.[35] He will admit that a service class, those who perform low-end, low-wage, low-autonomy, and low-skill work, grows along with the creative one, especially as the elite's long and unpredictable hours make them disinclined to handle mundane tasks that can be assigned to others paid to do them. He writes that statistics "point to a real divide in terms of what people do with their lives—with the economic positions and lifestyle choices of some people driving and perpetuating the types of choices available to others."[36] Still, ostensibly noncreative jobs appear in his work as a challenge to be overcome rather than as a structural necessity: the goal should be to make all labor into creative labor, doing away with the persistent split between elite, fulfilling mental work and the banal, meaningless manual tasks performed by service workers and production lines flexibly contracted to bring any innovative new designs to fruition.

In the case of the autonomists, their "factory without walls"—labeling the incorporation of all of life into capitalist production, the blurring of production and consumption, or leisure and work, as labor time takes over all time and the factory becomes the whole social matrix—may not be overly new. Capitalism has long needed not just bodies in factories but social reproduction of laborers, work for which women and other unpaid people are usually most responsible.[37] In its early years the Italian New Left advocated a social wage to acknowledge precisely this point. Since then, however, the theorists of immaterial labor, best known among those who emerged from the original movement, have insisted upon the radical extension of social reproduction via capital's creeping logic, as it moves, in Jason Read's terms, "deeper into the social networks that produce and reproduce life" until "subjectivity ceases to be a supplement to capitalist production, both necessary and exterior," migrating instead "into the center of production itself."[38] Critics have queried how general this creep is or how overstated its effects might be. They have wondered how different it is from previous forms of subsumption and how useful it is to label what comes of it "immaterial."[39]

Finally, both camps can be charged with solipsism. As I suggested earlier, Florida's management image of a creative class may be an idealized representation of his own working life. For their part, the autonomists transform their ties to a historic antiwork movement into a transhistorical framework that understands all work to be resistance to itself and, ideally, overcoming of itself. Their works could be said, thus, to self-valorize, but not at all in the sense that workerism once celebrated. To speak of self-valorization was after all once to speak of workers' recognition of their own power to control and constrain capitalism. This was a key aspect of the original movement's insistent inversion of the labor-capital relation-ships: its early spokespeople posited capital's absolute dependence upon labor and on a working class resistant to its own absorption into the logic of capital.

In Mario Tronti's foundational articulation of the "strategy of refusal," capital knows it is subordinate to worker-producers; the history of capital is the sequence of its attempts to extricate itself from this depen-dence. That capital then "seeks to use the workers' antagonistic will-to-struggle as a motor of its own development" does not mean it succeeds.[40] Workers' self-valorization cannot be absorbed into capital; it only ever destructures—never restructures—capital. In Tronti's and others' early writings we find a working class that has to struggle against its own exis-tence as labor. As Harry Cleaver puts it, that is what the working class is; that is what its work is.[41] As we have seen, appraisals of contemporary labor take much from this tradition; we find an early model for the autonomists' faith in a romanticized resistant creative force in Tronti's take on capitalist power as vacant but pervasive, "empty but efficacious," always a "logical vacuity" and a parasite, always the negative term, always a response to the authentic verve, potency, and fullness of the working-class opposition from which all true meaning flows.[42]

Still, in the turn to post-workerism, we find theorists engaged, more simply, in valorizing themselves. Though they speak for the multitude and against Virno's "labour aristocracy," their analyses tend to construct their own theoretical and activist work as labor's vanguard. The theory of

immaterial production brings the movement's earlier ideas about workers' resistance to their own labor into contemporary relevance, while
also stressing the Italian New Left's own role as an agent of historical
change. If workerism was itself a reaction against the midcentury accel-
eration of Fordist routine, Taylorist scientific organization, and Keynes-
ian management of economic crises, it is meant to have then forced the
crises in capitalist production that brought on post-Fordism, a rearguard
action to eliminate workers or to appease their hostility toward routin-
ized and monotonous workplaces.[43] In Lotringer's account, it was "the
Italian workers' resistance to the Fordist rationalization of work, and not
mere technological innovation, that forced capital to make a leap into
the post-Fordist era of immaterial work. . . . Autonomia was a defeated
revolution, to which the post-Fordist paradigm was the answer."[44] The
theory of immaterial labor then posits itself as the name for what results
from these same shifts, as the factory gives way to the thinking, knowing, living monad as agent of production, an agent who finds new ways
to object to her own incorporation but keeps finding her rejection, sadly,
incorporated.

　　This is not the dialectic as endless tragedy, however. Instead, for the
autonomists it is precisely now that liberation from capitalism is actually
more possible than ever before, after the development of key productive
capacities: the communications technologies through which individual
self-expressive agents will come together to share their collective knowledge and agglomerate into the multitude that is just on the horizon—or
actually, surprisingly enough, already around us.[45] As Hardt and Negri
put it, through "expression of its own creative energies, immaterial labour
thus seems to provide the potential for a kind of spontaneous and elemen-
tary communism."[46] This is Virno's "communism of capitalism," a formulation that is perhaps a logical extension of the thinking that Michael
Ryan deems, in a sympathetic but also worried critique of Negri's early
work, "realization of communism as self-expression."[47]

　　This last charge is a serious one and warrants elaboration. Ryan
writes that Negri's valorization of "expressive subjectivity" depends
upon omission of the "instrumental and contextual factors" that are its
actual conditions of possibility. He laments this as an "absolutism of the
subject," wherein subjectivity is imagined as an "origin of expression"

whose potential "precedes and exceeds social mediation."[48] For Ryan, the individual Negri imagines as embodiment of irreducible difference and potential, and source of ceaseless experimentation, is continuous with the liberal subject as the site of personal choices and self-referencing, atomistic desires.[49] Since the 1980s, when Ryan's appraisal appeared, these charges have not been answered. Instead, theories of immaterial production have tended to extend and generalize the approach to subjectivity that Ryan faulted.

This is quite evident in the current of their work that I follow in the previous discussion: its activation of figures of artist-authors in analysis of what immaterial labor means. Literary scholars have shown how indispensable formulations of the subject as "origin of expression" have been to the history of capitalist cultural markets and to the formation of private rights to intellectual property.[50] The continued life of these formulations involves a confluence of social and economic forces that are of precious little interest to Florida or to the autonomists, whose theories tend instead to remove the subject they assume from historical comprehension. Lost in both sets of analyses is, thus, any sense of the contradictory, material, constitutive histories of artists' labor and of images of artists at work that subtend the conception of subjectivity they depend upon and prop up. Labor theories of aesthetic production, as part of a broader political economy of culture, can provide an alternative. Here I will mention just two relevant tributaries: the development of the contradictory relationship between artists and the markets for their work; and the mainstreaming of the figure of the artist as valorized mental laborer.

Even very brief attention to elite cultural markets suggests that ideals of originality, introspective expression, and experimentation are contradictory effects of artists' commodification as much as markers of their resistance to it. The names of individual expressive artists are continually circulated as signs of quality and originality. In Bill Ryan's terms, objects of art "must appear as the product of recognisable persons," such that the concrete, branded, named labor of the artist is accorded special importance and carefully guarded. Artists' named concrete labor is a necessity of their particular form of employment, as the act of creation is widely thought to depend on talents that are "indivisible from the particular individuals" who express them. The objects artists put their work into must appear to be original, as embodiments of "singular concrete labour," and artists themselves must seem like possessors of "inimitable capacities," of a self-generated means of production that "cannot be alienated and instilled in an apparatus."[51] Thus, the circulation of the unique author's indivisible identity and style signals the distinction of the product within the market, and the value that thereby attaches to the author's name continues to be the major source of the value of the product in general, benefiting everyone within the circuit to varying degrees. The category and value of elite production are protected when the concrete expressive priority of the individual creator is protected.

We can pause for a moment on the example of literary production. Many people are involved in making literature. Those who operate the presses that produce copies of books go home at the end of the day and may very well forget about the printing company that employs them, pays them, and differentiates so markedly between their labor and that of the author who writes the words that fill the book. In contrast, the author provides a source text that remains singularly her own and that derives its market value and claim to copyright protection from its integral connection to her indivisible subjectivity. Part of what is distinct about aesthetic production as a form of labor may be precisely this: rather than disguise the labor that goes into the production of the object, commodity fetishism in the literary field obfuscates the realities of the making of the product by channeling our attention toward the author as the singular creator whose work is in a crucial sense irreducible, that is, nonreproducibly original. The work is made available for purchase, derives value, and achieves success because of the ostensible singularity of the expression it contains, an expression attached not only to the writer's body, to the eyes, brain, and hands most obviously engaged in the act of writing, but to her being as a person, to her emotional and intellectual life and much else.

What is commodified is in this crucial sense the author's very laboring self, since to buy her work is to purchase illusory access to the being whose identity is so often used to sell the product. Literary authors may work with others to co-produce ownable literary products, but their labor power derives mainly from the value attached to their names and to the ideologies of authorship that make literary expression interesting to audiences and that secure it as copyright. In this sense there is little separation between the thing for sale and the working body behind it. Simply put, artists' social function has been constituted in such a way that they "appear to capital as the antithesis of labor-power, antagonistic to incorporation." The artist has to appear as that person who is not quite amenable to her own participation in "the process of valorization," while her resistance to it is precisely what makes her work valuable.[52]

So much faith in the true artist's irreducible authorship is also in another sense a problem. The field is shaped by a need to counteract the variable and contingent nature of artistic labor, which is unreliable to the point that it can challenge profitability.[53] One can offset the unpredictability of artists' work through gatekeeping at the management or editorial levels. Or one can invest in the creation of reputation, devoting marketing budgets to ensuring that the creator and her works are subject to effective celebrification. In some cultural arenas—television production, for instance—design of cultural goods can in fact be managed quite easily, with creation bound to the organization's "rationality."[54] More elite fields, though, are more problematic, since they incorporate into their operations substantial resentment of obviously managed and commodified works and of any degradation of the creative stage of production.

This is precisely the resentment that the autonomists take part in; even Florida does, in his valorization of the creative individual's need for that new, unique, original production outside control. In this light, the autonomists continue what Luc Boltanski and Eve Chiapello describe as the "artistic critique" of capitalism as massification. Throughout their writings we find evidence of "the denunciation of artifice as opposed to the spontaneous, the mechanical in contrast to the living, the sincere in contrast to the strategic, and hence genuine emotion, which arises unintentionally, as opposed to its simulated imitation." Authentic expressive acts are deemed to have occurred only "without a secondary strategic intention" or "without any other intention than making [them]."[55] Florida simply turns the artistic critique on its head by celebrating the desire for authentic creativity as a progressive help and corrective to capitalism, as a source of creative exploration of possibilities for formation of new institutional arrangements and new intellectual properties. Neither camp departs from the elite cultural field's own dominant self-image: the idea of the artist's special position vis-à-vis capitalist value has been structured into the field and by now thoroughly permeates all its parts; whether that uniqueness is thought to be honored by or annihilated in capitalist production, it remains largely intact.

Indeed, it seems to have flourished alongside the mainstreaming of the idea that artists' introspective, self-managing, self-referencing work is a universal model for human behavior. At the start of this chapter I mentioned that Daniel Bell lamented this mainstreaming when he wrote about the cultural barriers to efficient management of a postindustrial workforce in the 1960s. One of the sources he cites for information on the general embrace of artistic values is César Graña's 1964 book on bohemia. In Graña's reading, the original bohemian was antibourgeois because she defected from or disdained the middle class and wanted to create a new order of value that would be "worthy of [her] approval." One means of articulating this desire was adherence to socialist or communist politics. Another, more common, was the creation of works of art—works of art in which we find not political involvement but "inner strife, extremes of subjective experience, and storms of personal expression," where one's "capacity" for suffering and expressivity is what separates the creative soul from "the prudence and pragmatism of the bourgeoisie."[56]

For Graña, it was in this insistent break with bourgeois mores that we find important origins of the idea of self-expression as "the most important purpose in life," of the appreciation for artistic freedom and creative genius, of the rejection of rationalism, of the embrace of social alienation as an idealized condition, of hostility toward a world that is itself positioned as hostile to talent and "sensitivity," and of a certain world weariness, a feeling that daily life is "an intolerable burden" that only art can placate.[57] Celebration of the literary sensibility is thus, for him, part of an embrace of the expressive individual, centered on an image of the ideal person as a rule breaker who is wholly averse to boundaries and barriers of any kind. As Marshall Berman wrote in support of this image in 1970, "Each individual now, in order to maximize his happiness, required freedom to discover or to create a happiness that would be uniquely and fully *his own*."[58] Through writers' and artists' insistence on a particularly bohemian, literary, artistic sensibility, and through public recognition of this sensibility, it became possible to conceive honorable work as the autonomists and Florida do, as necessarily free, unique, and individual, whereas dishonorable work, often associated with women's labor, could mean service, routine, impersonality, and the social. In Graña's terms, for the bohemian artist regular work was "the lot of the undifferentiated masses," and freedom from it made one peculiar, indivisible, and "incomparable." The artwork was put forward as a model result of this freedom: "It is of a piece," Graña writes. "It has integrity."[59]

Symbiotically, while Graña saw the origins of much of the modern artistic sensibility in the splitting off of the literary class from the bourgeoisie, Bell claimed that this sensibility inspired the culture of self-expression that positioned itself against bureaucratic control. As Gustav Flaubert wrote of his own politically disenchanted practice, "For us the only way is to shut ourselves up and keep our noses to our work, like moles."[60] What has become increasingly apparent, though, is that the divide between self-expression and control is no longer so easily imagined. The artist's individualism, especially when set against a more avowedly political antibourgeois collectivism, was never entirely incompatible with the individualization of goals in bourgeois modernity, and the artistic critique of mass or standardized culture and administration proved to be highly amenable to capitalist incorporation. Graña's study of bohemia admitted that artistic activity was itself trapped between aesthetics and commerce, self-expression and conformity. Bohemia had no easy integrity. If the nineteenth-century writers affiliated with bohemia were "touchy" about the "momentousness and dignity" of their trade and began "to speak reverentially of the natural gap between the creator and the layman,"[61] their touchiness reflected their fear that literature's antithetical purpose could be absorbed into whatever thing it positioned itself against. This touchiness has spread. What could have once justly been called an important and generative divide between the bourgeois and the bohemian has become less and less commonly maintained or appealed to.

In a sense, autonomous bohemia disappeared with its generalization. A romanticized image of the artist's oppositional work has become an attractive model for general self-fashioning. More leisure time, wealth, education, and social and geographical mobility for some people; desire for meaningful and authentic experiences;[62] personal identity perceived as a matter of "experimental self-discovery,"[63] often radically nonconformist or even antisocial; life as a matter of successive shots at "experimental realization of [our] own personalities,"[64] as a process of artistic invention and creation; and a neoliberal capitalism that makes *homo economicus* its model agent, self-reflexive investor in her own human capital, enterprise for herself:[65] in light of forces like these, it is little wonder that artists' work might seem, in Charles Taylor's words, like "the paradigm mode in which people can come to self-definition," making the artist, moreover, "the paradigm case of the human being, as agent of original self-definition."[66]

The artist-author, herself subject to market control and rational planning, has been for some time now a profitable, pervasive, regulated symbol of autonomy from routine, standardized, mechanized production hostile to individuals and devoted to what Lazzarato laments as "the formatting of subjectivity."[67] To persist in presenting individuals as agents of expressive and experimental self-realization is to fail to place the formation of this kind of character in any fundamental, contradictory, structuring relation to capitalism, which appears to activate figures of "sovereign, freely experimenting, hybrid subjects" as much as it appropriates any preexisting vital, though virtual, potential.[68] For Florida, of course, capitalism and aesthetic impulses are pretty much simpatico; no substantive contradictions exist. Whereas Bell pitted the culture of self-expression against the fetish for efficiency, routine, and bureaucracy, for the autonomists the relevant tension is between creative potentiality and authored discourse, as the author as capital and the potentiality of creativity exist in a fundamental and structuring vacillation. Yet while they perceive a tension between real aesthetic acts and their incorporation as immaterial production, authentic aesthetic productivity remains mysteriously protected, unique, and untouchable by the same market mechanisms that constantly fabricate and deploy its image.

More research is needed to account for the particularity, historicity, emergence, and spread of the vocabulary that makes contemporary labor an aesthetic act of self-exploration, self-expression, and self-realization. The brief glimpses I have provided here, of circumstances that feed into but are occluded by Florida's work and that of the autonomists, already trouble claims that people are simply now working as artists work, or that new labor socializes the artist's special status and thereby carries within it the possibility of capitalism's overcoming. A more accurate claim is that a historically and materially determined notion of artists' work has been stripped of this history and then generalized and institutionalized as a partner to the vocabulary that makes human subjectivity expressive, self-defining, self-referencing, autonomous, flexible, experimental, and enterprising. To continue to remove this vocabulary from any determining historical emergence is to leave intact this rather poor, small, uncomplicated subject whose only reference is itself. In the next chapter I continue to reconstruct some of the history of this vocabulary by charting in some detail the nature and influence of post–World War II psychologists' turn to the study of creativity as a crucial feature of superior human personalities.

3

The Psychology of Creativity

The idea that work should be an outlet for and source of enterprising and expressive self-fulfillment has a multifaceted history. One strand of this history first involves psychologists and then those influenced by the extensive circulation of their views, celebrating insecurity as a sign of personal strength—of optimal being. Literary writers and other artists have been involved in this celebration in a variety of ways, sometimes studied as actual research subjects and sometimes referenced as generic models. Their ostensible working lives, construed as manifestations of their natural inclinations, have been presented as typifying those whose superior creativity is supposed to make them privilege opportunities to express themselves at work over secure long-term employment situations.

This chapter argues that for decades influential psychologists and management theorists have tended to present study of artists as straightforward evidence that the social is a form of constraint to be transcended by the effective working self. Their work has had implications for how art is perceived and for how work is organized. They have depended upon and reinforced the notion that making art is the fundamentally insular expression of one's personally directed passionate devotion to "the task itself," "the materials at hand," or simply "the work"; and they have formed and circulated models of good work as a flexible and self-sufficient enterprise averse to social responsibility, human interdependence, and collective politics.

In the late 1940s US-based psychologists, influenced by their research on World War II military personnel and citing anxieties about America's place in the world, first began in earnest to specify the attributes of the kind of creative individual who would help secure future prosperity. This work flourished throughout the 1960s and 1970s when, steeped in the countercultural ethos, it morphed into a celebration of the nonconformist as the ideal creative personality. It was at this time that influential thinker Abraham Maslow, who had put forward his theory of the "hierarchy of human needs" in 1943, increasingly emphasized that the "self-actualization" perched atop it involved an against-the-grain creativity that was the key means to—and ends of—proper human development.

In Maslow's work, as in the writing of his fellow humanistic psychologists, nonconforming creativity was not about social commitment or an interest in revolutionary change. It was instead figured as an innate tendency to oppose the mundane, the taken-for-granted, the common and banal, formed less by political will than by an inherent tendency toward self-exploration and self-expression. But by the 1960s, inspired by the application of his ideas within management theory, Maslow was arguing that the creativity possessed by the self-actualizing person was potentially as important to business innovation as it was to individual self-development. He suggested that the self-actualizing person would, artistlike, lose the ability to distinguish between her work and her person, as the self and the social merged in the subject whose happiness was inseparable from devotion to a kind of work that was simultaneously selfless and self-interested. The actual purpose of that work was irrelevant. One could achieve self-actualization as a corporate executive, professor, or artist, so long as one's work was a fulfillment of one's ideal self. The good society was, meanwhile, one in which self-actualizers were allowed to develop as they saw fit.

In the 1980s and 1990s Maslow's psychology—particularly his theories of the hierarchy of human needs and of self-actualization—was perfect fodder for organizational psychologists and management theorists who were beginning to romanticize self-managing employees who could overcome the divide between self and work, who could find success in the material world precisely by seeking personal "liberation" from it, or, to use a parlance common to this work, who could achieve "extrinsic" reward precisely by following "intrinsic" directives. More broadly, Maslovian thinking, echoed, supported, and developed by many scholars since its first articulation in the 1940s, has now been used to evaluate the health not just of the individual or the firm but of entire societies. For instance, in Ronald Inglehart's influential work, whole populations are measured for their commitment to self-exploration and to transcendence of materiality. These measurements are then used to evaluate their level of modernization.

Inglehart's sociology of modernity, which expands and circulates an elaborate Maslovian characterology, has in turn informed in both direct and subtle ways the tendency of creative-economy boosters to treat people comfortable with insecurity as an elite cadre that is more modern or more evolved—more willing to take risks, more willing to stand alone, more committed to self-actualization and self-development—than those who ostensibly bemoan their lack of security. In cruder celebrations of the creative personality as the fruit of effective modernization, represented in this chapter by management guru Tom Peters's work and Richard Reeves's research for The Work Foundation, a UK-based think tank—but Richard Florida's oeuvre is again equally relevant—the character of the self-reflexive, expressive, and exploratory self is understood to be both economically useful and morally correct. Those who would prefer more stability are thought simply to lack the healthy desire to embrace the art of life, seemingly predisposed by disposition to long for the nanny state or the paternalistic daddy corporation.

**

A first instance of psychologists' interest in defining and measuring creative thinking was J. P. Guilford's presidential address to the 1949 convention of the American Psychological Association, in which he discussed his own research program, supported by the US Office of Naval Research, on the "aptitudes of high-level personnel." Noting that the "enormous economic value of new ideas" is already recognized in the business world and that the US government, itself a major employer of scientific and technical personnel, is clearly interested in identifying people with "inventive potentialities," Guilford concludes that psychologists are falling woefully behind—a particularly urgent problem because, in his view, new "thinking machines" are threatening to replace human labor. Creativity has two responsive roles in such a context: it will take creative thinking to develop a new economic order in which sufficient employment will remain after machines do "much of men's thinking," and the only remaining "economic value of brains" will be their ability to think creatively, as all other forms of knowledge—notably the kinds of memorized materials and rote skills charted by IQ tests—will be easily covered by machine intelligence. His definition of creativity is rudimentary here, though for him creative thinking clearly entails particular "high-level" "aptitudes" for new and inventive ideas, and in order to properly study it, psychologists will need to abandon the conventional notion that it is simply subsumed within one's general intelligence, fostered by mass education, and measured by standardized IQ tests.[1] He suggests several methods to test people's capacity to think creatively: for instance, they can be asked to list the consequences if people were all suddenly born with six fingers, or to list all the white edible things they can think of, to name all conceivable uses for a brick. These tests would measure the fluency, flexibility, and originality of one's thought, three characteristics essential to what Guilford would soon characterize as "divergent thinking," the kind of thinking common to creative people.[2]

Guilford's address coincided with the founding in 1949 of a research center where psychologists were elaborating similar ideas to his and beginning to define creativity and study it in some depth. The Institute for Personality Assessment and Research (IPAR), on the Berkeley campus of the University of California, was supported at first by the Carnegie Corporation and run by D. W. MacKinnon. During World War II, MacKinnon had headed a station of the OSS Selection Service dedicated to determining if candidates for special military operations had the requisite resourcefulness, flexibility, and courage. The IPAR began as an extension of this research into individuals' "effective functioning," but the relationship between personal "effectiveness" and creativity soon became its primary concern.[3] IPAR's approach to assessing its subjects was uniquely immersive. Test subjects and psychologists were housed together for days at a time, sharing informal activities like meals and casual conversation in addition to the usual formal observation and testing. Because MacKinnon preferred subjects who "had already demonstrated a high level of creative work," he chose to study creative writers, architects, and mathematicians as well as people engaged in industrial research, the physical sciences, and engineering. He was particularly fond of architects and wrote that the truly creative ones are thorough nonconformists, motivated by productive internal tensions—they are, for instance, at once supremely self-confident and prone to self-critique.[4]

Frank Barron joined IPAR as a graduate student in its early days and went on to become one of its most influential scholars. Study of artists and creative writers, as well as observation of subjects' verbal aptitudes and reactions to art images, were all integral to his research conclusions.[5] For instance, in the Barron-Welsh Art Scale (BWAS), designed as a measure of subjects' dispositions toward originality, artists and nonartists were asked to like or dislike a series of black-and-white designs on three- by five-inch cards. Barron found that artists "*liked* figures which were highly complex, asymmetrical, free-hand rather than ruled, and rather restless and moving in their general effect." In contrast, "figures which were *liked* by people in general . . . were relatively simple, often bilaterally symmetrical, and regularly predictable, following some cardinal principle which could be educed at a glance."[6] These same figures that were liked by people in general were described by artists as dull and uninteresting.

In a similar measure, the Painting Preference test, Barron and his team showed subjects color postcard reproductions of European paintings and then sorted them into groups according to their preferences for particular items. He claimed that the results of the test could be correlated to subjects' self-perceptions. In one group, the relatively noncreative group, the preference was for "themes involving religion, authority, aristocracy, and tradition," and its members tended to describe themselves as "moderate, modest, responsible, foresighted [and] conscientious." In the second group, made up of relatively creative people, preference was for complex and irregular forms and for radically experimental, sensual, esoteric, sensational, and primitive themes; these people tended to describe themselves as pessimistic, bitter, dissatisfied, emotional, unstable, demanding, anxious, and temperamental.[7]

Barron perceived writers as distinctly appropriate research subjects because they engage in widespread communication of "creative interpretations of experience." He maintained that creative writing, defined as work that "communicates a single individual's interpretation of experience in an original manner," had a social impact and that creative writers' use of language, as "an expression of culture," could provide insight into "creative forces in the culture itself."[8] Thus, at one point in his research he chose a test group of fifty-six professional creative writers and ten student writers, their names largely obtained through consultation with faculty in English and in drama at the University of California. His subjects were asked to respond to the usual roster of tests and interviews, which by now included the BWAS, the Painting Preference Test, and another he had devised called the Symbolic Equivalence Test.

The Symbolic Equivalence Test was itself inspired by a writer. Barron had seen Cecil Day-Lewis give the Clark Lectures on "The Poetic Image" at Cambridge in 1946, where, in Barron's words, he "spoke to a point that was to become a central concern for me in the psychology of creativity . . . the problem of gestalt transformation in memory."[9] In the published version of his lectures Day-Lewis describes one instance of this "gestalt transformation"—the transmutation of an image from one domain into another—which Barron soon deemed an aptitude for thinking of (or thinking in) metaphors:

The poet was looking out of his window in blitzed London. A searchlight practice was on. The beams swung about the sky, then leaned together like the framework of a wigwam, and at the apex an aircraft could be seen, silver, moth-like, flying slowly, found, lost, found again by the searchlights. It was a common enough sight just then . . . but this time the poet saw it differently, as a dramatic paradox; it seemed to him that candle-beams were desireously searching for the moth.[10]

With this account in mind, Barron devised a test in which people were asked to think of three metaphors, "or symbolically equivalent images," for each in a set of ten stimulus images. They were scored for their number of "admissible" responses and for their number of "original" responses; admissible responses were scored for aptness on a scale of 1 to 3; original responses were scored for their degree of originality on a scale of 1 to 5. So, for instance, given the stimulus image of "Sitting alone in a dark room," respondents would provide equivalents such as these: lying awake at night (scored 1); an unborn child (2); a stone under water (3); a king lying in a coffin (4); or Milton (5). Barron explains that to be "highly original, or to get the highest rating," the response necessarily "grabs you, it surprises you, it gives you a chill as a great line of poetry can do."[11]

Barron extended his findings to argue that high scores on the Symbolic Equivalence Test, as on the BWAS, were significantly correlated with high scores on other tests devised to measure independence of judgment and complexity of outlook.[12] They were also correlated to low scores on tests to measure socialization, indicating a significant "resistance to acculturation" or to a socialization process that they perceived as "demand for the sacrifice of . . . individuality," which, Barron judges, "it often is." He notes as well a correlation to low scores on tests to measure one's adherence to "economic values." Writers' scores put them at the apex of those personality types who were not "playing" for financial "stakes."[13] Indeed, the writers included in Barron's studies "topped all groups" in scoring across the range of tests, becoming models for the kind of iconoclastic and creative self-articulation Barron himself valued and sought to valorize in his research.[14]

That Barron's research was slowly elaborating a model healthy self is quite apparent: all of his tests, and the correlated self-descriptions of his subjects, were eventually formalized into measures distinguishing the Complex from the Simple Person. Barron argued that an appreciation for complexity is what allows the healthy individual to experience seemingly contradictory states of being with no real difficulty: she is healthier than others because she has experienced and worked through psychological problems; she "regress[es] with confidence," because she can return to her mature self with ease; she is free to use her powers of imagination because she can also "discern reality accurately"; because the distinction between self and object is most secure, it can be allowed "to disappear temporarily," thus freeing the mind for creative exploration. It is writers who best model the Complex Person for Barron, because they are "as a class significantly more independent, flexible, and original than most people." They are also more comfortable with ambiguity, balancing dualisms within themselves; they are, for instance, at once sicker and healthier than average, as "they are much more troubled psychologically, but they also have far greater resources with which to deal with their troubles."[15]

The construction of this model was, in addition, a notably solipsistic endeavor: in isolating creativity for study, and clearly valuing particular forms of self-articulation and social functioning over others, Barron and his colleagues were themselves creatively deviating from existing ways of thinking about human intelligence and motivation. Barron's studies were, in this sense, a version of what they aimed to assess, as was much of the research going on under IPAR's auspices. His approach and his findings can be read as a social science expression of the 1960s countercultural ethos, in this case manifest as a reaction against the limitations of traditional psychology—against, for instance, its conformist acceptance of IQ testing, which connected genius-level intellect to repetition of "existing public knowledge," and worked against the romantic idea that creative geniuses are emotionally unstable and socially maladjusted.[16] Like J. P. Guilford, who found that success on standardized tests is evidence of "convergent" thinking whereas original thinking is necessarily "divergent," Barron and his colleagues found that the traits correlated with creativity would not necessarily relate to attaining high scores on traditional tests administered for mass education. These traits were instead thrillingly "alien or threatening to values dominant in psychology and the society at the time,"[17] and they could not be measured by any assessment based upon one's absorption of existing accepted knowledge. Dominant values included a desire for predictability and for "repetition and compulsive discharging of duties," a respect for popularity and for external authority, and an addiction to "fixed social patterns."[18] The divergent values associated with creative thinking involved, in contrast, an insistence on the freedom of one's thinking and one's choices from social constraint of any kind. What matters to the genealogy I am constructing here is the way that this model of nonconformity tended to align society at large not with any necessary community or ethics but with conformity and predictability, with a respect for popularity and authority, and with an unhealthy addiction to tradition. The divergent values associated with creative thinking involved, in contrast, an insistence on the freedom of one's thinking from social constraint of any kind—including, importantly, the constraint of social responsibility or political engagement.

Barron expresses occasional awareness that business organizations might be interested in understanding how creative people operate, but he is rarely concerned with specifying in any detailed way the applicability of his findings to the workplace.[19] In this he differed from Abraham Maslow, the premier theorist of the human potential movement to which Barron informally belonged.[20] Maslow actively turned his own conclusions about creative thinking, which are similar in many ways to Barron's, into management principles. His work in turn informed the ostensible transformation of organizational culture from an authoritarian to a democratic one designed to respect employees' individual needs for self-fulfillment.

Before the 1960s Maslow wrote of his surprise at being "plucked at" by corporations. He was unsure if his work could be useful to organizations or if he was instead too much concerned with "the lone wolf," someone dissatisfied with what exists and apt to work alone in a corner and be perceived as "a bum or a Bohemian" by coworkers and bosses.[21] Nor did he need to appeal to corporations in order to secure his professional standing. His academic star had been rising steadily since he put forward his 1943 theory of the "hierarchy of human needs," an account of the dynamic evolution of human motivations. According to this theory, until certain basic physiological and safety needs are met, there is no room for worry about whether or not one is respected by others or a member of a functional family. Until one has achieved respect and familial contentment, one cannot pursue the highest need, the need for "self-actualization," whose pursuit involves an array of "higher" values Maslow worked throughout his life to specify. The self-actualized person is the ideal person, the model to which all should aspire, and his needs are as inherent, inborn, or "biological" as what we typically take to be primary needs like food and shelter. This "higher" biology is simply repressed when unfulfilled primary needs get in the way. Maslow refers to these higher needs as B-Values (or Being-Values), and they include a combination of intangible and tangible qualities, including truth, beauty, newness, uniqueness, goodness, neatness, elegance, cleanliness, order, unity, justice, lawfulness, and completion.

In the early 1960s Maslow's description of the self-actualizing person motivated by B-Values dovetailed significantly with his conception of the creative person. He writes in 1962 that "it is as if" creativity "were almost synonymous with, or a *sine qua non* aspect of, or a defining characteristic of, essential humanness."[22] In 1963 he notes that "the concept of creativeness and the concept of the healthy, self-actualizing, full human person seem to be coming closer and closer together, and may perhaps turn out to be the same thing."[23] Around the same time he began to conduct his studies from within business organizations. He spent the summer of 1962 at Non-Linear Systems, Inc., a digital voltmeter factory in Del Mar, California. He took an extended leave from Brandeis University in 1969 and started a four-year fellowship at the Saga Corporation, funded by businessman William McLaughlin. It is no surprise then that he was beginning to see his findings about self-actualization and creativity as important ones for business management and for the future of the nation. At this stage in his thinking the most fully developed, self-actualized human being, the creative person, and the ideal worker-citizen began to converge, making his work a prescient forecasting of the way that, in Nikolas Rose's terms, "work has become an essential element in the path to self-realization, and the strivings of the autonomous self have become essential allies in the path to economic success."[24]

Non-Linear's president Andrew Kay had invited Maslow to visit the company. Kay had been using books by two progressive management theorists, Douglas MacGregor and Peter Drucker, as guides to how to structure the company, and he was impressed by the overlap between these studies and Maslow's research. Maslow, too, was excited by the fellowship in part because he noticed that, though working as a management consultant, Drucker had reached conclusions about human nature that were similar to his own, insisting in *The Practice of Management* that employees thrived when they perceived themselves to be respected by their bosses—that is, in Maslow's term, when their B-Value desire to be respected was met, a point that Elton Mayo had made decades before. Douglas MacGregor's 1960 study, *The Human Side of Enterprise*, derived much from Maslow's theories, as he wrote against what he labeled "Theory X Management," the authoritarian approach found in most workplaces, which "assumes that the average human being dislikes work, and because of this he must be coerced, controlled, directed, and even threatened by punishment in order to get the job done." MacGregor proposed "Theory Y Management" instead, arguing that a person "will exercise self-direction and self-control in the service of objectives to which he is committed." The organization's objectives should be attuned to workers' own needs, such as the need for self-respect or for "satisfaction of ego."[25] Rather than attempt to control workers through authority, organizations will, in MacGregor's words, succeed through "the creation of conditions such that the members of the organization can achieve their own goals best by directing their efforts toward the success of the enterprise."[26]

Maslow's work at Non-Linear built upon MacGregor's and Drucker's respective approaches. Maslow goes much further than they had, though, in arguing for the veritable absorption of the worker's subjectivity into organizational directives and in creating a fantastic image of the magical transcendence of divisions between self and society, in which the self in pursuit of its own authentic self-realization will lead inevitably to utopia. He called the book that resulted from his time there *Eupsychian Management*, incorporating his own neologism for a utopian community called "Eupsychia," defined as "the culture that would be generated by 1,000 self-actualizing people on some sheltered island where they would not be interfered with." His overarching point in *Eupsychian Management* is that managers interested in more democratic workplaces should support more intensive study of "the psychodynamics of creativeness,"[27] since it is within the creative personality that one will locate human desire and ability to transcend authoritarian structures of all kinds.

Maslow argues that ideal work is "psychotherapeutic, psychogogic (making well people grow toward self-actualization)," and that self-actualizing or "highly evolved" people "assimilate their work into the identity, into the self," so that "work actually becomes part of the self." Thus, "proper management of the work lives of human beings, of the way in which they earn their living, can improve them and improve the world and in this sense be a utopian or revolutionary technique." He was concerned, however, to emphasize that the pursuit of self-fulfillment was not purely selfish; rather, the self-actualizing person would achieve a kind of selflessness; the dichotomy between selfishness and unselfishness would be resolved in a new synergy between inner and outer motivations, as one's work is "introjected," made a part of the self. An ideal society would be arranged in such a way that producing one's individual ends would not be opposed to "helping other people"; rather, this conventional dichotomy would be "resolved and transcended and formed into a new higher unity."[28] Maslow notes elsewhere a general tendency toward "resolution of dichotomies" in self-actualizing people: their selfishness is ultimately unselfish; their duty is their pleasure; their work is play; they are childlike and mature; they regress without being neurotic; they are strong egos but also self-transcending.[29] In them opposites are resolved and integrated. They are, in a word, whole.

Maslow uses artists as models of the kind of wholeness of being that he recommends. Artists become for him particularly important figures because of what he construes as their thriving in insecure conditions and their motivation by internal directives. Importantly, echoing Barron's suggestions that creative people are better able to apprehend reality, the self-actualizing person is also able to perceive things "as they are," which involves getting beyond petty motivations like material gain. Having what Maslow called "peak-experiences" means seeing a thing, an event, a situation in and for itself, "detached from relations, usefulness, expediency."[30] To clarify, this is true during the primary phase of mystical creativeness, which is distinct from the secondary "working out" phase. The primary phase involves "the process itself" and is unconcerned about the products of one's work or "the climax in obvious triumph and success." Subjects tend to describe it as a "loss of self or of ego," as transcendence, as integration of self with nonself. It is a kind of "nakedness" in the situation, or an innocence before a task; it operates without a priori "expectations . . . fashions, fads, dogmas, habits." In its pursuit we become free of concern for other people and external judgment; we become "much more ourselves, our Real Selves," "our authentic selves, our real identity." Alienation from these real selves is the product of "neurotic involvement with other people." Realization of these selves requires that we forget any audience, so "we cease to be actors" and become, for the moment, unneurotic, unanxious, "not sick." He finds a parallel for this attitude in the "artist's respect for his materials" and attention to the "matter-in-hand." The artist is said to treat her work as "an end, something *per se*, with its own right to be, rather than as a means to some end other than itself." Thus, her behavior is a model to the extent that it is "noninstrumental," suggesting a "lack of willful 'trying,' a lack of effortful striving or straining, a lack of interference with the flow of the impulses and the free 'radiating' expression of the deep person."[31]

Maslow acknowledged that secondary processes are necessary. He claimed healthy individuals should be capable of being both poet and engineer. Deliberation must follow spontaneity. Hard work and control must follow regression into our inner beings and receptiveness of inspiration. At some point, instead of being subject to an experience, we make a product *our* subject. Nevertheless, according to Maslow primary processes are where the deepest human values are realized. The willing "regression into our depths" ends; in place of the "passivity and receptivity of inspiration" come "activity, control, and hard work." Instead of being subject to an experience, we make a product *our* subject.[32] It is through primary processes that the healthy self expresses itself, and it is through them that what the self requires can coincide with what the world requires. For example, though secondary processes are needed for one to receive financial compensation for one's work, increasing one's wealth cannot be the goal of a self-actualizing person. Instead, "B-work" or "work at the level of being"—which is only possible once one's basic needs are met—is its own intrinsic reward; the paycheck is a "byproduct, an epiphenomenon." Ideal, self-actualizing work is one's intrinsic values incarnate; it is pursuit of these values, and not work per se, that the healthy person loves.[33]

Maslow's take on the primary phase of creativity, the phase that is clearly key to self-actualization, thus consistently validates insecurity. He argues that "creativeness is correlated with the ability to withstand the lack of structure, the lack of future, lack of predictability, of control, the tolerance for ambiguity, for planlessness;" it is akin for him to the ability to "loaf," to float for a time in a purposeless void without a distinct future.[34] Neurotic people are uncreative because they have no confidence in themselves; they feel that something or someone is overcoming them and controlling them. Creative people, self-actualizing people, in contrast, thrive precisely when conditions seem most threatening; "attracted to mystery, to novelty, change, flux," the creative person feels able to "manage" the world, think of himself as "a prime mover, as the responsible one, as autonomous, the determiner of his own fate."[35] Moreover, anticipating later sociological applications of his work, Maslow argues that any thriving society would need to commit itself to producing precisely this kind of person: a person able "to live in a world which changes perpetually, which doesn't stand still"; a person "comfortable with change, who enjoys change, who is able to improvise, who is able to face with the confidence, strength, and courage a situation of which he has absolutely no forewarning."[36] Unhealthy selves need to "staticize" the world, to "freeze it and make it stable"; they need, pathetically, to "do what their daddies did."

Healthy people, self-actualizing, creative people are instead "able confidently to face tomorrow not knowing what's going to come," and it is only societies that produce such people that will survive.[37]

For Maslow, as a result, it should be a concern of policymakers to ensure that the cultivation of creative citizens—"a race of improvisers"—is a Cold War priority. The healthy person is a "political necessity."[38] What America should thus be doing is turning out "a better type of human being than the Russians,"[39] and this will mean ensuring that workplaces are devoted to workers' psychological well-being. Maslow's articulation of the qualities of this "better type of human being" became more and more stark and disturbing as the Vietnam War raged on, as he became concerned with correcting countercultural appropriation of his ideas that supported antiestablishment and antiauthoritarian political positions. He insisted that "liberalism" was a form of weakness and, sounding very much like Ayn Rand, stated that "no society can function very successfully—especially not in a world of separate, sovereign nation-states—unless there is a built-in arrangement whereby the aggridants [biologically superior members of a species], innovators, geniuses, and trailblazers of all types and in all fields are admired and valued and are not torn apart by those seething with Nietzschean resentment, impotent envy, and weakling *counter-valuing*."[40]

More recent organizational psychology and management theory appear to have absorbed wholesale Maslow's arguments about the ideal person's motivations at work. This absorption is clear evidence for Luc Boltanski and Eve Chiapello's claim that the artistic critique of capital so palpable by the 1960s, a critique positioning authenticity and autonomy against routine, management, and monotony, was rigorously stripped of any political impetus and turned into fodder for new models of capitalist accumulation. Teresa Amabile's influential recommendations to business organizations about how to nurture creativity are a good example. Her early work was not primary directed at corporations, but the updated 1996 edition of *The Social Psychology of Creativity*, renamed *Creativity in Context*, is revised with applicability to business organizations in mind. She notes that a number of concrete traits of creative people have already been "revealed" in repeated research. These include self-discipline, an ability to delay gratification, perseverance in the face of frustration, independence of judgment, tolerance for ambiguity, a high degree of autonomy, an internal locus of control, a rejection of conventional norms, and a propensity for risk taking and self-initiated striving for excellence.[41] Adding to this work, Amabile's "social psychology of creativity" is meant to "identify particular social and environmental conditions that can positively or negatively influence the creativity of most individuals."[42]

Despite its claims to uniqueness, her work wholly affirms the conceptions of the innate tendencies of the creative person that had been circulating in the psychology community since the late 1940s. She states, for example, that she is interested in the influence of social factors on creativity, social factors that include "a concern with evaluation expectation and actual evaluation; a desire for external recognition; a focus on competition and external reward; a reaction against time pressures; a deliberate rejection of society's demands; and a preference for internal control and intrinsic motivation."[43] Hence, social factors are for her primarily negative barriers to the natural inclination of the creative person to desire freedom from the social. What matters to Amabile's conclusions is the various ways the contextual factors she identifies are rejected by creative people, such that creativity is once again overwhelmingly presented as a reaction against any determinants that might influence one's natural internal directedness. Creative "in context" turns out to be creativity that is free to reject context.

Taking up Barron's and Maslow's mantles, Amabile, too, supplements her lab research with case studies of writers' biographies, in this case deriving psychological truths from her reading about the lives of Anne Sexton, Sylvia Plath, and Thomas Wolfe, among others. She argues, for example, that Sexton struggled with extrinsic motivations and was self-conscious about her own concern with making money and achieving external recognition for her work. However, because she worked against these tendencies in herself and learned to function instead as "her own worst critic," she was able to achieve despite herself the higher state of intrinsic motivation, finding in her work a positive outlet for her introspective worrying. Plath fares less well, as Amabile reads her "excessive concern with recognition" and her tendency to compare her own success with that of other writers as a crippling encumbrance. Wolfe is said to have suffered a related paralysis, due in particular to the phenomenal success of his first novel; the external expectations that were put upon him were too much for him to handle.[44]

These studies of writers, coupled with her more conventional lab findings, lead her to conclude that extrinsic motivation is detrimental to creativity[45]—a claim she later revised to acknowledge the possibility of some productive synergy between internal and external drives but that has nonetheless continued to be cited in encyclopedias, handbooks, and surveys of the field as a major finding for the study of organizational behavior. Her intrinsic motivation hypothesis resonates profoundly with Maslow's work: it holds that creativity involves an "absence of conformity in thinking and dependence on social approval," an ability to engage in an activity for its own sake, and "any motivation that arises from the individual's positive reaction to qualities of the task itself."[46]

Amabile's research has been a signal contribution to organizational psychology, and it and the larger body of scholarship to which it belongs inform the way that new-economy and now creative-economy discourse construe work. Equally important to this discourse, and equally indebted to humanistic psychology in general and to Maslow's work in particular, is Ronald Inglehart's positivist sociology of modernity and postmodernity, in which dispositions are respectively deemed modern (that is, attending modernization, which is synonymous with industrialism) or postmodern (so, attending postmodernization, synonymous with postindustrialism). Mining the World Values Survey, under way since 1970 and claiming by 2008 to cover 70 percent of the world's population in forty-three countries, Inglehart uses the data he extracts to place discrete groups somewhere on the path to full development. Accepting that the most developed subject is one for whom economic wealth must be secured before it can be transcended, and for whom transcendence of material security is the key to successful self-realization, Inglehart then calculates how many people within a given society identify as materialist or "postmaterialist," among other measures. He uses the results to measure that society's level of development, postmaterialist postmodern societies being of course the most developed. He thus generalizes and globalizes Maslovian psychology, providing what one expert on workplace reform reads as "empirically-grounded confirmation of the Maslovian vision."[47]

In a telling phrase, Inglehart compares the global sociological land-scape to "a cross section of the earth's surface," which "sometimes reveals neatly ordered geological layers, with the oldest stratum of rock lowest and the newest strata located above the older ones."[48] According to his logic, all societies are inexorably progressing toward the highest stratum, which is the model established by advanced industrial societies. As lead-ers, these advanced nations have already passed through modernization and all its attendant processes and are now moving at last into a freer postmodern phase, in which the legacies of modernization are soberly, reflexively assessed. Like Maslow's, Inglehart's theories are premised upon the notion that an innate human need for safety and comfort must be met before people are capable of even beginning to think about aiming for goals higher than materialist aspiration; and like Maslow's hierarchy of human needs, Inglehart's hierarchy of human societies opposes materialist (modernist) to postmaterialist (postmodernist) motivations and has at its apex the self-realizing and self-actualizing individual who can maturely consider all the social and cultural inheritances she finds in her world and her person and reject or embrace them at will.

According to Inglehart, the modernization phase "involves the familiar *syndrome* of industrialization, occupational specialization, bureaucratization, centralization, rising educational levels, and beliefs and values that support high rates of economic growth," as well as the spread of mass literacy, secularization, and the rise of the entrepreneurial ethos and of mass production. In contrast, with diminished insecurity, in the postmodernizing phase under way in advanced industrial societies, maximizing economic growth becomes less important than maximizing personal growth or "subjective well-being," as "there is rising emphasis on the quality of life and democratic political institutions." Production becomes less a matter of "tangible things that contribute directly to sur-vival" and more a matter of intangibles whose value is "subjective," as people become more concerned about the meaning and purpose of their lives.[49] Thus, an important part of the overall shift he describes is a gradual change in what motivates people to work. When societies are in the modernization phase, primacy is accorded to "maximizing one's income and job security"; movement toward postmodernization entails "a growing insistence on interesting and meaningful work," coupled with "a growing insistence on more collegial and participatory styles of management."[50]

These shifts do not reflect a rejection of capitalist rationality, however. Rather, according to Inglehart, people are more and more likely to accept capitalism and "market principles," to reject the idea that the government might provide solutions to workplace problems, and to prefer flexible employment because they look inward to their own individuality as a source of values and direction. This is presented as positive social change and as nothing less than the realization of human desires unfolding in a natural and proper progression. According to Steve Overell's summary, in a study of the rise of "inwardness" in the workplace, Inglehart's findings confirm what Maslow suggested: "the insistence on identity and meaningful work flow from the evolution of social values as societies become more advanced."[51]

Maslow's understanding of insecurity as essential to creativity, and of creativity as at once a personal and economic necessity, and Inglehart's celebration of the self-reflexive, self-actualizing postmodern subject who wins at work by not caring about winning, merge to find popular expression in the work of management guru Tom Peters. A highly sought-after speaker and consultant, Peters has been emphasizing the moral superiority of embracing insecurity since the early 1980s in terms that associate acceptance of it with maturity and personal strength. Early on Peters directed his remarks toward management, while in more recent years he has been addressing employees and encouraging them to be their own branded self-managers. This shift reflects the way the corporation itself has gradually faded away in his writings and public talks: early on the successful corporation was necessarily disorganized, deconstructed, and attuned to the needs of self-defining employees, but by now it is only a way station. It can attempt to lock in the best workers' loyalty, but the best workers are precisely those capable of loyalty to nothing but their own careers.

Peters echoed Maslovian psychology when he claimed in 1987 that "the times demand that flexibility and love of change replace our long-standing penchant for mass production and mass markets, based as it is upon a relatively predictable environment now vanished," and that the "winners of tomorrow will deal *proactively* with chaos, will look at the chaos per se as the source of market advantage, not as a problem to be got around."[52] His 1992 study *Liberation Management* is a working through of this emphasis on the wonders of chaos. It is nothing if not a celebration of Maslow's "aggridants," as evinced by his profile of a company whose proactive effort to deal with change grants it "revolutionary" status both because it has managed to cut its staff from four thousand to two hundred, and because its management knows the company needs "soul" in order to win over employees. In common with all the companies Peters profiles in this lengthy book, the employees invited to keep their jobs are enjoined to view work as the fulfillment of their own "creative ambition" and asked—as they wish to be asked—to make work their raison d'être.[53]

More broadly, like Inglehart, he links the transformations he observes in progressive workplaces to wide-scale changes in society to which all workers must adapt. Most telling, he connects his recommendations about "deconstructing the corporation" to postmodernism and its movement "beyond hierarchy" and its emphasis on "flexibility, choice, and personal responsibility." To explain the connection, he evokes the fall of the Berlin Wall, because for him the new management style and the symbolic end of communism as an active politics both signal transcendence of an era of disciplinary regimes. He cites at some length Vaclav Havel's address to business leaders at Davos, in which the collapse of the wall is aligned to the collapse of the "modern age as a whole," most notably of the "proud belief that man, as the pinnacle of everything that exists, was capable of objectively describing, explaining and controlling everything that exists." We inhabit now, instead, an age of postmodern chaos, in which "there is no reality!" All that exists is "the perception-tinted product of our cockeyed imaginations" and a commercial world in which the "bottom line . . . is the sum total of conjured-up dramas created by our customers."[54]

Far from lamenting this scenario, Peters describes it rapturously and sees it as the essence of human freedom. In a lengthy paean to Friedrich Hayek, he celebrates the famous economist—for whom private property, market competition, and progress toward human freedom were inseparable—for having understood "fitful economic (and human) progress as a direct function of rich, volatile, unpredictable experimentation in the marketplace." Accordingly, the successful employee now has to embrace postmodern complexity and accept all its paradoxes: liberation means a lot of sleepless nights and the abandonment of certain comforts; the new kind of organization is disorganization; meanwhile, market necessities, indistinguishable from psychological necessities, mean that passionate pursuit of one's goals must lead to the equally passionate destruction of whatever one has already created.[55]

In *Liberation Management* Peters's emphasis is still on profiling particular corporations and drawing out the links between their success, their cultivation of employees' loyalty to the "soul" of the enterprise, and their embrace of the flexible chaos of modern marketplaces. By the late 1990s he had shifted his main work to motivational speaking and writing for employees wishing to perceive themselves as self-managers and, ultimately, as brands. It is in this more recent work that artist-figures have taken on particular importance, though Peters had claimed before that he would, for instance, look to see "who's reading Chekhov" when he gets on a plane and then "bet on his or her stock,"[56] since reading Chekhov is a sure sign of one's comfort with complexity. By 1999, though, he would claim that after seeing Placido Domingo perform in *Simon Boccanegra* at the Metropolitan Opera, he wondered why "a day-at-work-in-the-Purchasing Dept" couldn't be "more like Placido's evening-at-the-Met?"[57] He concludes that it can be if one is willing to embrace the right attitude and pursue the right work. All work should be like the artist's work: it is a performance rather than a job; it is an act of unbridled passion rather than "puttin' in time"; far from being "Faceless," it is the "epitome of character"; far from being predictable, it is a "plunge into the unknown"; rather than treat the customer as an afterthought, it "alters the users' universe; it is a growth experience rather than just another day that will never be retrieved.[58]

In *The Brand You 50*, Peters continues to place faceless, predictable, unartful "jobs" in an older age that emphasized security, in which "a big so-called safety net . . . suck[ed] the initiative, drive, and moxie out of millions of white collar workers."[59] In this light, pursuing "Brand You" is more than pragmatic: it is equal parts self-reliant "liberation"—according to Peters, Benjamin Franklin and Steve Jobs both knew that there is no "they"—and "self-definition." It is about figuring out what one "stands for" in order to do work that "makes a difference" and "matters."[60] *The Brand You 50* celebrates a world in which there is no loyalty to the corporation;

loyalty should instead be reserved for one's friends, one's contacts, one's network, since it is through them that the next task will appear.

Facing this reality, what "Brand You" will need to be devoted to is the creation of a salable identity. It is here that artist-figures are put to work again. Claiming to have been drawn "more and more to reading and reportage about artists of all sorts," Peters is careful to affirm that all successful employees are engaged in performance art. "Accounting" is a "Performing Art" when "It is Your B-e-i-n-g, the Presentation of You, that is under discussion." "B-e-i-n-g" here—one's very selfhood—is inseparable from the performance of one's brand distinction. Still deploying a Maslovian terminology of self-actualization, Peters collapses the process of discovering and achieving one's highest values into market rationality: "I am urging you to think—long and hard—about your I-D-E-N-T-I-T-Y. In BMW-ian terms." That is, we are all "Rapidly Depreciating Assets" and must counter the rapid decline of our human capital with "Aggressive Investment."[61] Uncovering our most deeply held values is thus quite simply a matter of marketing. Life is a matter of giving everything to the process of self-definition through work.

Peters acknowledges that cultivating your own brand takes a lot of time. It can even include, as it has in his own life, neglect of friends and family, but, he admits, "I don't know how else to do it?!" One notes a tinge of despair in this last statement, with its twinned interrogative and exclamation. This despair is briefly present elsewhere in *The Brand You 50*. Peters admits to being "gloomy" and using Prozac and discusses his dedication to his work, some years delivering a motivational speech nearly every day, as nearly pathological. Imagined in his work after all is a self easily encompassed in formulas like: "Brand You = Time *Consciousness*. Brand You = Time *Fetish*. Brand You = *Obsession* with Time," or "Project. Portfolio. **Currency**. Signature. It's w-h-a-t I a-m."[62] But any psychosis, any tendency to obsess or fetishize, and any suffering derived from the self's inseparability from market rationality, from the incessant need to perform one's branded identity and add to one's currency, is easily subsumed into the successful self. This ostensible accord between suffering and success again echoes Maslow's—and Frank Barron's—emphasis on the successful subject's ability to live with contradiction, transcending conventional distinctions between, for instance, sickness and health, happiness and suffering, selfishness and selflessness.

Peters's insistence that the ideal self is capable of reconciling the contradictions of postmodern life within itself, ultimately impervious to the real psychic stress he himself seems to have suffered, is a key theme throughout his work on self-branding. We might note here that Peters fought in the Vietnam War and invented a gun emplacement that was written about in engineering magazines; worked for several years at the consulting company McKinsey Co., which helped many firms downsize and become attuned to "flexible specialization" since the 1970s; worked for a Pentagon project to establish a naval base on Diego Garcia in the Indian Ocean; and, while working for the State Department from 1973 to 1974, spearheaded a project to eradicate the opium trade in Mexico. These are the activities that he presents as the highlights of his own working life before he became a management writer. These are the activities that he dedicated himself to with such passion. These were his self-actualizing endeavors. Yet at the very same time, his new persona—"Brand-You" is self-invented, ever-changing, and fundamentally free from the past—can recommend the constant incorporation of "cool people" like Che Guevara into his "network" and can celebrate the kind of commitment to changing others' views about what is possible evident in Lenin's devotion to Russian serfs or Martin Luther King's to African Americans.[63]

Tensions like these are not a problem for Peters. They are a constitutive feature of the new age of liberated work and self-managed workers. While "Brand You" deploys "caring, helping, empathy, listening," she does so only temporarily and can readily transfer such skills to new workplaces. Her devotion to mastery of a task is simply equal to her willingness to move on to the next thing. Identity is a matter of marketing but also a matter of the meaning of one's life. It is something one must contemplate "long and hard," but also quickly and incessantly. Peters acknowledges the tensions, calling them "an irony" or "paradox,"[64] but they are a source of personal energy rather than of psychological harm and alienation, political indifference and quiescence.

Richard Reeves's *Happy Mondays* has an aura of respectability about it that Peters's work lacks, but it echoes Peters point for point. It also reveals in particularly stark terms the implications of the approaches to work I have outlined throughout this chapter, approaches that assume a natural human expressivity that makes people wish to avoid permanence

and association and favor self-referencing self-definition.[65] Currently editor-at-large and a regular columnist at *Management Today*, Reeves wrote
Happy Mondays for The Work Foundation, a think tank that advises UK
businesses and government on both economic performance and workplace
happiness. He has been a policy adviser to the UK minister for welfare
reform, economics correspondent and Washington correspondent of the
Guardian, and a research fellow at the Institute for Public Policy Research.
Happy Mondays is Reeves's major contribution to theorizing the new world
of work. It claims to be motivated by a paradox: People are more and more
devoted to their work, but they nevertheless keep complaining about it.
Reeves's explanation is that unhappiness at work is a self-fulfilling prophecy. People cannot embrace feeling happy at work because they have inherited an "outdated rhetoric" and convinced themselves it is true, staying in
deadening jobs because they refuse to believe there is any alternative: "It
is time to call a halt to the rhetorical carpet bombing of work. It is inaccurate. The truth is that work is good. . . . People in soul-destroying jobs
accept them because they are continually told that work is not supposed
to be enjoyable."[66] They are, it seems, lacking the right characterology, the
right narrative about the self, one that would sufficiently compel them to
embrace change and try to find something better. For Reeves there are
thus two kinds of work matched to two kinds of people: a new world of
progressive employment full of purpose and meaning, peopled by self-
explorers who prefer work to other forms of sociality; and a countering
sphere, seemingly dwindling, where the old dead-end jobs continue to
trap people without the character to escape them. He writes to convince
the latter to adopt the correct attitude so they might join those who experience only "Happy Mondays."

Who would do the "soul-destroying" work that remains? The question is never posed. Nor are the global realities of outsourced factory production and precarious service work ever mentioned. Reeves's concern,
like Tom Peters's and Richard Florida's, is with an elite prospect, and in
Reeves's case that prospect is presented as a truth about all labor: "Few
people now toil under arduous or hazardous conditions. Most people work
in safe, clean environments. Modern workplaces are a long way from the
dark satanic mills of industrializing Britain." Misreading Marx's critique
of commodity fetishism as a lament about "workers existing simply as cogs

in the production process and compensating themselves with the accumulation of material objects," he summarily concludes that those days are over. Factory conditions have now been abolished, and attending that change, work should no longer be conceived as a means to consumption and leisure but should rather be a path to self-articulation, where "creativity, purpose, comfort, belonging, identity—and even love" are explored and realized.[67]

Here, artists are again models. Reeves claims that, like "Archimedes, Einstein, Shakespeare, Picasso," one in four British workers is or was happily overworking, and he mentions a cartoon in which a man says to his wife: "I'm not a workaholic! Lawyers and accountants are workaholics. Artists are *driven*." The parallel between artists and other workers has to do not with what they produce, or with how secure or remunerative their work is, but with "drive"—one of several character traits Reeves finds figured in the artist. Most important among these traits is expressivity: "artists have always seen their work as an expression of themselves," a self-conception that tends to be accepted without much questioning. The same should be true for those in other professions, Reeves maintains; both "a new sculpture" and "a new spreadsheet" should be seen in one light, as "they are essentially the same. Both are expressions of our abilities, interests and imagination." Reeves cites a speech by Nelson Mandela in which the political leader quotes activist author Marianne Williamson's warning that "your playing small doesn't serve the world" and enjoining people to allow "their own light to shine" so that they might become beacons to others. For Reeves, by extension, devoted workers should be proud to let "their own light to shine"; like artists, they should not be castigated but celebrated as examples.[68] Letting one's own light shine means embracing many of the integral features of the new workplace imagined by its boosters. The research I have just outlined reveals how social science expertise, shored up by experiments, tests, interviews, and surveys, has helped institutionalize the features that Reeves and many others celebrate.

For example, he maintains that the distinction between work and leisure must fade away. Reeves cites as support for his case Theodore Zeldin's claim in the new-economy magazine *Fast Company* that "we should abolish 'work.' . . . By that I mean abolishing the distinction between work and leisure, one of the greatest mistakes of the last century. . . . We should strive to be employed in such a way that we don't realise what we are doing is work." For Reeves, though they are at times loath to admit it, people already tend to prefer being at work to the dull drudgery of home, where one is reduced from knowledge work to being "an administrative assistant or domestic cleaner." The workplace thus grows in attractiveness as home looks duller and duller. It is at work that people find they are most inclined to be in what Mihály Csíkszentmihályi dubbed "flow," a state of total involvement in a given activity through which people experience a kind of transcendence of themselves.[69] Csíkszentmihályi's research is grounded in the social dimensions of the workplace and assumes creative production involves a setting and a context. However, in management literature his ideas are often confined to the kind of formula Reeves places them within: work is where people achieve their fullest states of happiness; work is itself that "doing something else" that people achieve when they are in flow's state of selflessness.

Moreover, we should perceive work as a performance rather than the creation of a product. Reeves rightly presents Stephen Daldry's film *Billy Elliot* as a parable of the new age. The film pits the exuberant riches of a ballet performance at Covent Garden against the misery of coal mine labor in the midst of a strike. One represents freedom; the other, the despotism of custom. Billy wants to express himself through work; he wants to transcend all his ties to place and to the hard work in the coal mines that his brother and father do, and ultimately they support him in this goal. For Reeves Billy's success thus offers a spectacular answer to the fundamental question: "Who wants to say they do a job because their Dad did it?" As in the film, we should abandon old collectivities organized against capital, because capitalism has "evolved" in such a way that "the alienation of workers from their product" is now reduced. In Reeves's terms, "A revolution has taken place with not a single shot fired. As management gurus Jonas Ridderstrale and Kjell Nordström put it, 'The workers do own the means or production; 1.3 kilograms of brain holds the key to all our futures.'" We work now with our brains, not our hands; work is not stultifying or deadening but rather "intellectually stretching and demanding."[70]

Perhaps most centrally, Reeves argues we should embrace flexibility as an expression of a natural human inclination, since, in Frank Barron's words, "There is something in the human mind that does not like things as they are."[71] Reeves is singularly hostile toward people who stay in jobs for any length of time, claiming they are unimaginative, lazy, lacking in drive. Tom Peters would agree with Reeves that to change jobs is to be engaged actively in the search for meaning—actively and willingly that is, and not under duress.[72] Similar scorn is reserved for people who insist on distinguishing between work and life. Echoing Maslow, who might accuse them of "weakling *counter-valuing*,"[73] Reeves states that such people have an unhealthy need to compartmentalize.[74]

True of the overarching psychology of insecurity profiled here, with its trumpeting of the strength and vision of its exemplars, for Reeves the working lives he describes are an expression of natural human will. People work a lot, so they must love it; people find meaning in work that they no longer find in community, family, and religion, so that must be the way they prefer things; people want to work because it is where they find meaning; indeed, they find it more there than at home, where they often feel they are less valued. Even though it is human desire that has made work what it is, some people have not yet trained themselves to acknowledge that work is now great. It is these people preventing the new reality of work from truly flourishing, and it is their stubborn persever- ance that has him declare work must be "reconfigured in our collective imagination as an intrinsic, central part of our lives rather than an annoy- ing adjunct. . . . Work has to be recognized as a defining feature of our humanity, rather than as a dilution of our 'true selves.'"[75]

Nothing about the current configuration of labor or the economy needs to be changed, then. For Reeves all that matters is the expressive subject in search of an outlet and that more potential expressive selves inculcate a fit "imagination" and become what superior people already are—appreciative of the happiness we are all already experiencing. What unhappy people lack is, in essence, a proper grasp of work's new real- ity. They are not sufficiently "complex," Frank Barron might have said. They simply have not yet figured out that work is now the most impor- tant expression of life's meaning and source of human happiness. There is a vanguard of creative people who do grasp this reality, and they are driving change. The remaining naysayers need only be advised by man- agement consultants, self-help books, and life coaches of the right kind of self-understanding to help them catch up to a more developed form of consciousness. Reeves cannot conceive complaints about work coming from any other place.[76] They can only be an expression of one's false consciousness and one's lack of development, easily treated by a change in attitude.

The history traced in this chapter subtends Reeves's ideas about how people should and should not behave at work, as it has shaped aspects of creative-economy discourse with which Reeves's work is in perfect accord: its use of artist-figures as models; its treatment of self-realization as a process that can occur in the absence of any judgment about the impact of one's work on society; its presentation of the economy as a reflection of human nature, while at the same time, contradictorily, market realities are necessities to which we must accommodate ourselves; its stigmatization of collective politics and workers' interdependence; its lionization of an elite cadre of creative innovators and sidelining or outright omission of industrial, service, and manual labor; and its insistence that the individual worker shoulder the burden of establishing a secure future. This burden can mean vacillation between unemployment and overwork and can entail ceaseless self-promotion, including presentation of oneself as a marketable brand or commodity. Yet creative-economy boosters, in the tradition of thought charted in this chapter, rarely mention increased rates of anxiety and depression or decreased rates of political participation among the elite they imagine and typically address. Nor are they troubled by evidence that people forced to move from job to job, or from fashion to fashion in their self-presentations, struggle with and against a pressing lack of permanence and coherence and find self-referencing introspection to be insufficient grounds for the establishment of a lasting sense of life's value.[77]

4

Economy and Pathology
in Aravind Adiga's *The White Tiger*
and Monica Ali's *In the Kitchen*

The previous chapter suggests that a core feature of much of the management theory written over the last several decades has been its conception of the self as an entrepreneurial engine—a being for whom career success and personal development are inseparable pursuits and for whom work should be the expressive fulfillment of an inner life that exists in a state of perpetual revolution. More than a means of understanding how elite workers perceive themselves, this image of the self is the basis for a self-work ethic that management gurus routinely position as the ideal to which all people should aspire. Management discourse has developed this ideal in concert with psychologists and other social scientists, and it in turn informs and is informed by contemporary creative-economy policy and theory that rely upon images of the expressive and autonomous self as creator of new intellectual properties.

This chapter focuses on two novels that are particularly informed by and interested in therapeutic conceptions of the self. Each protagonist has problems that clearly stem from wide-scale social and political ills, as both novels highlight the inequities of neoliberal capitalism, emphasizing disparities between rich and poor and how government countenances, ignores, and justifies them. However, each narrative also filters its protagonist's experiences through a therapeutic language of crisis and recovery, casting his troubles as internal psychic struggles to be treated not through social or political action but rather through alteration of his personal career trajectory and of his way of thinking about and narrating his life's meaning.

Eva Illouz has dubbed narratives like these, which have fictional, confessional, and hybrid forms, "therapeutic biographies." Exemplified and disseminated by Oprah Winfrey's "tentacular" empire of television, magazine, book club, and website, these popular and proliferating texts feature protagonists who perceive discontentment, ranging from mild unhappiness to considerable psychological distress, as a temporary setback to be turned into useful fuel for ongoing work toward future successes. In Illouz's terms, they combine "the moral glory of self-change" with "grue-some depictions of suffering" to construct a narrative of the self as "double hero: on account of what it has suffered from a hostile world and because it can claim ultimate victory over that world and its own self, by overcom-ing itself."[1]

Timothy Aubry examines the prevalence of these therapeutic narra-tives in contemporary American fiction as a symptom of a larger middle-class turn toward interiority as the site and source of all of life's signifi-cance and meaning. He perceives this turn through more than one lens. It is how people without serious problems learn to perceive their lives as full of drama and interest, "urgency and consequence"; it allows middle-class readers to establish affective allegiance with victims of real suffering; and—and here Illouz agrees—it is a response to the risks to middle-class prosperity brought about by the spread of market capitalism and to the stigmatization and underfunding of a public sphere that should be offer-ing respite to the distressed.[2] This chapter serves to extend Aubry's and Illouz's commentary in two ways. I suggest that incorporation of the psy-chology of the creative personality into contemporary conceptions of work shapes the therapeutic turn that they chart, and I consider how writers' reflexive apprehension of their own literary labor informs their treatment of their protagonists' introspective tendencies.

The protagonist of Aravind Adiga's *The White Tiger* certainly interprets the political sphere as its own kind of therapeutic drama, in which evil is rooted in the private venality of a cadre of abusive landlords and in which the narrator's triumph over his boss is cast in Oedipal terms. However, the novel is never a straightforward presentation of its narrator's story. Instead, it frames his narrative first as a pathological manifestation of the psychosis that makes him an exaggerated version of the entrepreneur as ruthless solo-agent. The narrator's sense that he is a model of the triumph over adversity is in fact belied by his very narration of that triumph, as his need to tell his tale, to no matter what listener, is a further symptom of self-referencing pathologies from which he never entirely recovers. Not stopping there though, Adiga frames this traumatic story once more, as his own response to his creative-economy labor, first as a finance journalist enjoined to keep the "bad news" out of his work and then as a writer of literature for whom "bad news" is meant to be the essence of his concern.

In contrast, in Monica Ali's *In the Kitchen*, in which the interior and domestic life of the protagonist is also the site of dramatic concern, the story of his descent into and recovery from mental illness is presented in a relatively straightforward fashion without any elaborate metafictional framing. The protagonist's melodramatic inflation of his own anguish is at times lightly mocked as the manufactured strife of a man whose life is otherwise singularly lacking in drama. However, it more typically appears as an understandable and legitimate response to a gaping hole at the center of his self—a hole that he begins to patch at the novel's close. Moreover, *The White Tiger* presents its narrator as a villain and its technique as a matter of the novelist's own afflicted conscience, whereas *In the Kitchen* aligns the writer with her protagonist, as the novel's free indirect discourse is near to his consciousness and shares in his guiltily ambivalent and internalizing take on the neoliberal economy. Still, Ali's novel is hardly a witless indulgence of middle-class longings and needs. Because its commitment to interiority is always guilty—always conscious of and concerned about what frames and legitimates that commitment—it is in its own way highly attentive to the complex interplay of economy and personality that defines contemporary work. Moreover, though she forgoes the kinds of metafictional techniques Adiga deploys, Ali does slyly work against her narrative's own dominant focus, as she uses the character of Oona to gesture toward a more compelling, though only shakily articulated, vision of the kind of selfless common sympathy that might counter the trends that privilege but also beset her protagonist.

"Bad News": The Entrepreneurial Ethos
in *The White Tiger*

The White Tiger was one of the big books of 2008. It won the Man
Booker Prize, and Aravind Adiga was named Borders bookstore Author
of the Year as well. It is a rags-to-riches tale and a postcolonial bildung-
sroman, a hybrid genre whose basic features Joseph Slaughter has usefully
delineated: it features the core *bildung* structure tracing a protagonist's
education and development, but it frames those features in such a way
that their political inheritances and ramifications are noted and lamented;
and it enacts a "metacritique of the literary and human rights economies
in which it is itself subsumed."[3]

The White Tiger's narrator, Balram, is a poor man from the Indian
state of Bihar, which he detests and deems "the Darkness," and with
ample reason. Despite considerable academic promise, at a young age
he is removed from school to work in a tea shop; and in a dilapidated
hospital that no doctors deign to visit, he witnesses his father's death
from tuberculosis. Longing for escape, and attracted to the uniform,
he decides to seek work as a driver, becoming a servant for the same
powerful family that lords over and impoverishes his fellow low-caste
villagers. By turns cunning and obsequious, Balram is soon selected to
move to Gurgaon with his boss, Mr. Ashok, and his boss's wife, Pinky
Madam. This is "the *modernest* suburb of Delhi," Mr. Ashok boasts, "the
most American part of the city."[4] It is full of shopping malls and posh apartment complexes, spheres of luxurious life and leisure from which Balram
is mostly excluded. There, after months of tortured introspection and
psychological decline, Balram kills his boss and steals money that was
expropriated through landlordism and political corruption. He then
departs for Bangalore, where he starts a taxi company that serves call
center employees. He hires drivers, promotes his services (their motto:
"We Drive Technology Forward!" [258]), and achieves considerable
success, all the while trying to appear blithely unconcerned about the
anticipated revenge killing of his family. In telling this story, Balram
imagines that he has as a narratee Chinese premier Wen Jiabao, who is
on a trade visit to India. He presents his autobiography as a corrective to
what he expects the premier will be told by more official sources.

Adiga appears to have little in common with his protagonist. Before he published this, his first novel, he attended Oxford and Columbia and then worked as a journalist specializing in finance. He covered US politics for the *Financial Times* until 2000, and since then Indian politics, culture, and finance for the Time International group. He has lived in Delhi and did so while writing *The White Tiger*, but he spent much of the last ten years abroad. Amitava Kumar and Sanjay Subrahmanyam, both well-known commentators on Indian literature and politics, critique Adiga's work in light of this background. Subrahmanyam is particularly unconvinced by the portrait of Balram—"This is a posh English-educated voice trying to talk dirty"[5]—and he suggests that the book's success measures two kinds of middle-class angst: within India, the novel indulges "the neocolonial imagination" of the bourgeois city dweller, for whom villages, increasingly "asphyxiated by Delhi's expansion," produce servants who threaten to morph into disgruntled and terrifying "criminal castes"; outside India, it feeds liberal objections to the country's "archaic and primitive" class relations.[6] Kumar is from Bihar, and his take on the novel is not unlike Subrahmanyam's. Responding to a scene in which Balram takes Mr. Ashok and Pinky Madam on a driving tour back through the old village, he asks:

Who is looking here? The village to which the car is returning is not only the employer's village but also [Balram]'s—he is returning to the place where he was born and grew up and has only recently left. Yet does it appear to be the account of a man who is returning home? He recognizes no landmark or person, he has no emotion, he has no relationship to the land or the people.[7]

In light of this moment and others, Kumar concludes that the novel's perspective on downtrodden Indians is inauthentic and insensitive. Aspects of Kumar's and Subrahmanyam's critiques are echoed by some of the book's other official critics,[8] as well as by a sizable number of the several hundred readers who have so far contributed reviews to amazon.com, which I will return to cautiously later. What the novel's critics tend to downplay is its basic formal conceit. It is not a naïve perpetuation of exoticizing stories but an exploration of the demented psyche of a particular teller of tales about India.

In interviews and articles Adiga has presented the novel as a manifestation of his own self-critical creative process. He has asked his readers to place *The White Tiger* in opposition to business books for aspiring elites and to the brand of finance journalism offered by the newspapers and magazines that once employed him, which boast overwhelmingly celebratory treatments of the globalization of markets and the arrival of the "new India."[9] He has also suggested that it was while writing journalistically that he gathered material for his fiction, stating that Balram's life is a composite of the many misfortunes he encountered during his travels between meetings with wealthy politicians and businessmen.[10] Balram belongs to what Adiga has in interview called the "servant-master system, the bed rock of middle-class Indian life."[11] This system, of course, long predates India's reincarnation as an "Asian tiger," but the novel presents its continuation as integral to the functioning of the "new economy." Adiga additionally claims that his treatment of Balram's labor stems from a distinction he felt forced to draw in his own career between his "official reporter's diary" and "another, secret diary" that contained what he was meant to leave out of his journalism, when his responsibility was to that "middle-class Indian" rather than to his or her servants. *The White Tiger*, a fictional rendering of the contents of Adiga's "secret diary," is meant to right this discursive imbalance. Stated precisely, it is meant to correct what the author came to perceive as mainstream journalism's elision of the reality of exploited service labor from images of India's economic boom.

We could refuse to credit this self-presentation, but entertaining it as a possibility does clarify the novel's technique, as Adiga appears to have transferred his own resistant relationship to the mainstream take on Indian entrepreneurialism onto his narrator. Early on Balram directly positions his letters to Wen Jiabao as an alternative to state propaganda and to the sorts of "American" business books, like *Ten Secrets of Business Success!* or *Become an Entrepreneur in Seven Easy Days!* (4) that one finds all over Bangalore: "I would like to insert my own 'sidebar' into the narrative of the modern entrepreneur's growth and development" (194), he states. His is a thoroughly critical insertion, a "sidebar" that refutes the main text. For example, combining pride and shame, Balram imagines telling Wen Jiabao:

Our nation, though it has no drinking water, electricity, sewage system, public transportation, sense of hygiene, discipline, courtesy, or punctuality, *does* have entrepreneurs. Thousands and thousands of them. Especially in the field of technology. And these entrepreneurs—*we* entrepreneurs—have set up all these outsourcing companies that virtually run America now. (2–3)

It is through tours like the premier's that contracts are signed and "enterprise zones" built and expanded; so, fashioning himself as a kind of anti-diplomat, Balram claims to want to ensure that no dignitaries leave the country with only the officially branded national story. All should also carry away the sorrier, sadder truth that he has to tell. He conceives his story as one that can stand in for these other sad histories, as representative of "how entrepreneurship is born, nurtured, and developed in this, the glorious twenty-first century of man" (4).

That said, the ambiguous meaning of "glorious" in these first pages, positioned uncomfortably between sincerity and sarcasm, provides an early clue that Balram is unable to settle upon a coherent message. To be sure, he might appear to be a positive specimen a visitor could study as a model case of rags-to-riches entrepreneurial acumen. It is after all Bangalore's proliferating "outsourcing companies"—Balram's shorthand for the call centers, start-ups, and dot-coms contained within Electronics City Phase 1—that secure his own future, and once he is there, he becomes one of the privileged few, in cahoots with the local police and invited to mistreat his own employees as he was once mistreated. Still, Balram cannot muster much more than confusion about these ostensible successes.

This is understandable, since often over the course of the narrative it appears to be Balram's tragedies that breed his "triumphs." Having suffered is what makes Balram want to pursue a better life, giving him something to seek to overcome. Suffering might seem to supply him with a particularly valuable property, his personal story, whose quantity of misery is what makes it worth sharing with visiting world leaders. But, of course, that sharing is not really happening. In reality he is alone in his office late at night, talking to himself, struggling to understand his personality and experiences, trying, most notably, to justify committing a crime that once seemed to him to be just the change he needed. That change required strikingly brutal violence against a man who may not have deserved to be its target, and it will result in his own family's annihilation. In attempting to rest content with these realities, Balram is not just unusual or sociopathic. Not minding about the murder of his family makes him an exaggerated version of the contemporary worker's infamous atomization. Balram is preeminently "low drag," not tied down by social commitments, willing to move anywhere for work, willing to do anything to get ahead, and he also lacks anything remotely resembling a secure future: steady employment, a livable wage, and protection from starvation and disease, for example. As he self-critically states, "Only a man who is prepared to see his family destroyed—hunted, beaten, and burned alive by the masters—can break out of the [rooster] coop. That would take no normal human being, but a freak, a pervert of nature" (150).

Thus, another major aspect of celebratory rhetoric about the new economy that the novel takes up—in addition, that is, to its elision of the reality of service labor—is the psychological harm required for conceiving of the self as a flexible, dynamic, self-regulating, entrepreneurial engine, willing to engage in constant reassessment and destruction of past beliefs and allegiances in pursuit of a more fulfilled and productive existence. Balram's story makes a mockery of this brand of biographical progress narrative, which is at once securely attached to the elite vanguard of new labor and generalized and globalized by popular tales of entrepreneurs' paired psychological and professional development. He vacillates uneasily between approaching the image of the entrepreneur with sincerity and sarcasm, between insisting upon his suffering and on his triumph over adversity, between self-celebration and self-hatred, between triumphalism and catastrophism. His radical confusion has an act of murder as its most dramatic outlet, clearly giving a pathological meaning to linkage between atomized psychic unrest, entrepreneurial endeavor, and pursuit of one's best self. Rather than assemble him into a healthily renewed whole, his conflicted account of his own life reveals fundamental fissures within the very idea of a self for whom suffering is, contradictorily, both a necessary generative motivator and relatively easily overcome, while dwelling in pain, or refusing to psychologically "deal with" the wrongs one has suffered, is "a sign of [an] undeveloped or immature identity,"[12] or of not yet having found a way to expel or excise unhappiness through self-development.

In Balram's autobiography every system of value, every place he might look for guidance in his personal "development," from the political sphere to family and religion, gradually turns into farce or fraud. He is left with no anchoring truths by which he might chart a course through his world. Balram additionally suffers an inability to imagine a collective political response to this disjuncture between rhetoric and reality. His own example suggests that it is dangerous to assume that anyone experiences untroubled submission to his or her own exploitation. Professions of loyalty are instead often paper-thin disguises of a truer discontentment, disguises that might be pierced at any moment by the revolutionary fervor they feebly conceal. Nevertheless, a pervasive source of frustration for Balram is what he sees as the complacency of the other members of his class. Having already revealed himself as one who cannot help desiring the success he castigates, he laments:

Never before in human history have so few owed so much to so many. . . . A handful of men in this country have trained the remaining 99.9 percent—as strong, as talented, as intelligent in every way—to exist in perpetual servitude; a servitude so strong that you can put the key of his emancipation in a man's hands and he will throw it back at you with a curse. (149)

The result of such thinking is that he never joins with others to combat a common condition. Abed in his basement servants' quarters he is prone to staring at "anonymous palm prints that had been pressed into the white plaster of the wall" (228); the construction workers who built the upscale apartment building left traces of their work, deliberately or otherwise, and Balram then glimpses their haunting presence, which might encourage him to identify with their labor. Yet his fixation on emblems is a symptom of a ghostly solidarity that is ultimately fruitless: he feels it but cannot articulate it or act upon it. Instead, though he is confronted with signs of the social production of his unhappiness, he ultimately only takes suffering into himself and uses it to manufacture his future biography, understanding himself as engaged in a fundamentally personal struggle of triumph over adversity.

It should thus be supremely difficult for readers to settle on interpretations of the signs and symbols we encounter in Balram's narrative. Are they really evidence of an incipient revolution, or manifestations of his troubled psyche, which has him projecting his internal struggle onto the city streets, seeing symbols of class war everywhere? Are the shadowy hands in the plaster on his bedroom walls even really there? What about the Naxalites? Balram hears talk of them from other drivers, and in the car at night he sees signs of followers' imminent revolution:

I saw men discussing and talking and reading in the night, alone or in clusters around the streetlamps. By the dim lights of Delhi, I saw hundreds that night, under trees, shrines, intersections, on benches, squinting at newspapers, holy books, journals, Communist Party pamphlets. What were they reading about? What were they talking about? But what else? Of the end of the world. (188–89)

He applies a similarly apocalyptic language to the snippets of poetry he encounters throughout his journey, which he interprets as signals to the poor that what they lack in wealth they make up for in knowledge of real beauty. Quoting Iqbal, he states early on that people "remain slaves because they can't see what is beautiful in this world" (34). Later, he claims:

The poor win a few battles (the peeing in the potted plants, the kicking of the pet dogs, etc. [Balram has partaken of both]) but of course the rich have won the war for ten thousand years. That's why, one day, some wise men, out of compassion for the poor, left them signs and symbols in poems, which appear to be about roses and pretty girls and things like that, but when understood correctly spill out secrets that allow the poorest man on earth to conclude the ten-thousand-year-old brain-war on terms favorable to himself. (217)

Here Balram reads poetry as a welcome kind of self-delusion. Through consciousness of the secrets that "spill out" from it, the less fortunate can claim creative souls and place themselves above their rulers, establishing "terms" that favor them. Balram's dim consciousness of others' anger and others' labor ultimately only contributes to the introspective machinations that end in the murder that both instantiates and secures his radical isolation.

That is, his life story, full of anger and resentment, has no real auditors, and its major act is a murder that is ultimately just a further manifestation of his individualization of his own suffering. Mr. Ashok is more sympathetic than most, but Balram has him stand in for the various radical inequalities he has faced throughout this life. In one of the book's leitmotifs, obesity is a marker of overdevelopment; it signals the structural dependence of the rich on the poor, who waste away as they are literally consumed by the system. Mr. Ashok is an exemplary case, having enough money that he is able to eat and drink more than anyone would need and then exercise excess calories away. Meanwhile, Balram has faced depredation after depredation: from massaging his boss's father's feet and picking the potatoes out of his dhosas (these are tossed aside within inches of the starving poor), to being laughed at, humiliated, and condescended to, and mocked as smelly and unclean. Mr. Ashok remains, however, less a figure of abusive authority and more a buffoonish emasculated male. In narrating his life, Balram tries to convince himself that his dead boss was the embodiment of every ill he had experienced, which would make murdering him the ultimate and appropriate expression of his triumph over tragedy. He attempts to justify his use of the stolen money in similar terms, as a just reaction to the fact that the money was earned through corruption in any case and should rightly be in the hands of those suffering classes from whom it was expropriated. Yet he never quite manages to persuade himself—or us—of anything. Instead, Balram can do little more than project onto his boss his understandable need for some singular villain against whom he can enact his revenge.

In a particularly memorable scene, he watches a black dog turning in circles, and we know what he sees is himself:

A pink patch of skin—an open wound—glistened on its left butt; and the dog had twisted on itself in an attempt to gnaw at the wound. The wound was just out of reach of its teeth, but the dog was going crazy from pain—trying to attack the wound with its slavering mouth, it kept moving in mad, precise, pointless circles. (213)

In these "mad, precise, pointless circles" we perceive the precise heart of Balram's complex characterization. The suffering that has brought him to this point makes him a figure for the precarious service class, while his mode of self-presentation and his ruthless pursuit of success make him a figure for the entrepreneurial self, who views work as the expressive fulfillment of a therapeutic destiny and turns difficulties into instigations to a ceaseless "mad" cycle of overcoming one's past self with newer, better, more productive versions. The discomfort induced by Balram's characterization is thus an integral part of the author's strategy, whether we deem the technique literary or commercial or some blend of these. On the one hand, as an embodiment of the service class, Balram can be read as a manifestation of Adiga's afflicted conscience about his work as a journalist and as a target for readers' compassion. On the other hand, as a figure for the entrepreneur whose goal is overcoming suffering en route to productive self-articulation, Balram's characterization is an unveiling of a particular model of the entrepreneurial personality and a target for readers' denunciation. As a

pathologically exaggerated embodiment of the ideal creative worker, motivated to achieve greatness by inner reserves of self-criticism and unhappiness, he is a critique of the terms of the entrepreneurial biography in which
personal success is the highest priority, and its attainment requires the self
be cut off from all connections and turn inward in pursuit of an elusive
source of meaning that will anchor one's actions. The entrepreneurial success story is, for Balram, a mitigating answer or compensation, ultimately
hollow and self-defeating, for the radical inequities and lack of stability and
secure meaning he has faced in this life. This unavoidable incongruousness,
as he unites the low-caste servant and self-celebrating change agent, has
encouraged some readers to perceive him as impossible and inauthentic. But
such is the precise point of his characterization.

Hence, if we are troubled by the fact that Adiga embodies this kind
of angst in a decidedly disadvantaged figure, a character who, critics suggest, should not have access to the vocabulary Balram sometimes uses ("now
revealing erudition an unlettered man cannot possess . . . now assuming the
pithy timbre of a suave, urban journalist interpreting India for the unfa-
miliar . . . now adopting a pedestrian voice with a limited vocabulary"[13]),
we should focus our concern in a particular way. What is so unsettling
are the contradictions that *The White Tiger* illuminates, contradictions not
just within conceptions of the infinitely entrepreneurial self but within contemporary capitalist production more generally: how it depends on a cadre
of replaceable service workers, whose efforts allow the utmost introspective
freedom to elite "immaterial" producers, while also generalizing and global-
izing the rhetoric of the free-floating agent of enterprise throughout all social
strata, disseminating it even to those for whom this particular trajectory
might seem a kind of sick joke; and how its institutions and practices "inflict
on the self a wide variety of forms of suffering," while simultaneously accen-
tuating the individual's "claim and right" to be a Balram-like aspirational
master of her own destiny, using self-work to improve her human capital
and create a life "devoid of suffering."[14]

**

Though Balram presents himself as an authoritative source of information about himself and about modern India—who could better tell the

story of his own life?—our reliance on him as a source of information is thoroughly exploded. He is never presented as our trustworthy guide to the various locations he traverses; he is, rather, a sociopath whose perception of himself and of the world around him is thoroughly suspicious. The novel's exploration of its narrator's disturbed psychology seems to be its primary purpose. The total hostility with which Balram sometimes perceives people, the way he presents the village he grew up in as a place of utter destitution and horror, the way he refuses any form of solidarity with others: all these features of his narration are inseparable from his characterization as the embodiment of an antisocial entrepreneurial ethos oriented only toward the survival and success of the lone individual who possesses it. If anything, then, the novel is a study of the murky origins of the kind of self who might become a new-style orientalist exoticizer, telling sad stories about India to visiting dignitaries.

The fact that this dimension of the novel has been overlooked may have to do with readers' suspicions about the book's extensive market circulation. Adiga's self-critical insistence upon his novel's attention to an economic underbelly has been a key plank in the most pervasive marketing narrative attached to his text,[15] one that has been authorized to ease its circulation and reception by stressing its act of uncovering part of capitalism's hidden history. A notable portion of Adiga's journalism about India already contains subtle and even not-so-subtle critiques of middle-class complicity in perpetuating poverty and inequality there,[16] often irritating, in the words of a colleague and friend, "critics of the foreign correspondent corps [who] insist we are always banging on about poverty and filth, when we should be pointing out the five-star hotels."[17] Still, by his own lights his novel is a product of his afflicted conscience, and this self-construction informs the branding story most firmly attached to the novel, as publishers and marketers, prize committees that have honored the work, and the author himself uniformly encourage readers to perceive it as a rejoinder to celebratory treatments of "Asian tiger" economics.

Krishan Chopra, editor at HarperCollins India, has said of the novel: "If one were to give just one reason why we decided to publish the book, it would be its startling originality and perspective on the new India."[18] Here, as on its cover and cover-flap blurbs, the novel is positioned as unique and marketable because it offers this "startling" insight into life experiences construed as otherwise untreated in literature. That is, though a number of well-known novels treat poverty and landlordism— Mulk Raj Anand's *Untouchable* and Rohinton Mistry's *A Fine Balance* come to mind—and though surely other works do address the particular underbelly of India's dynamic economy, in the publisher's marketing eye this wasn't yet true of any English-language work designed for large-scale global circulation.

The book's success has since been facilitated by continual emphasis on its interlocking originality and provision of neglected information that people should want to possess. We are told again and again that here is a book that shines much-needed light on the darker realities of globalization; it takes up the lives of the Indian underclass, those whose labor subtends the ascent of the "new India" but who continue to be excluded from places like elite American-style suburbs and call centers and dot-com start-up enterprise zones. Thus, when Michael Portillo, chair of the 2008 Man Booker judges, states that it won the prize for its way of "dealing with pressing social issues and significant global developments with astonishing humour," he picks up and supports the sanctioned story about the novel. He even quotes the official publicity for the book when claiming that it possesses the "enormous literary merit" of "originality," earned through its devoted presentation of "a different aspect of India."[19]

Publicity for the novel would have been hard for Portillo to ignore. Large and numerous print advertisements appeared before its release in India, the United Kingdom, and the United States. There were life-sized promotional cutouts for bookstore display. The author was profiled widely. Indian news channel CNN-IBN even aired a video book advertisement, which was soon available on YouTube. The advertisement is an instance of a new trend in book promotion. Presenting themselves as short films rather than as advertising, as cultural rather than commercial, these pieces are typically expensive to make and reserved for promotion of select lead titles released by major firms. In the case of *The White Tiger*, an animated piece depicts "a world-weary man from the village entering Delhi suburb Gurgaon and getting into an orange-coloured taxi";[20] this taxi, also appearing on the book's original cover, was the visual clue meant to tie the short film to the novel, hopefully turning viewers into readers when they encountered the image in stores or online.

Of course, the marketing story attached to a work like Adiga's, and supported by an aggressive advertising campaign, need not be embraced to be effective. On the contrary, the ideal scenario seems to be for a book to be put forward as an engine for generation of controversy. Debates about authenticity have proven particularly useful to this purpose. In Adiga's case, critics of his novel, constructing a counternarrative that also circulates with the work, as journalists mention it in profiles and readers mention it to each other, acknowledge its desire to provide new information about emerging economic realities—for Kumar, novelists do well to "explore how the news enters people's lives and indeed becomes a part of daily life"[21]—but argue its success is compromised by the distance between the author and his real-world subject matter. The very marketability of the novel encourages some of the most vituperative appraisals of it, as readers challenge the legitimacy of Adiga's hold over the voice he uses to capture the "originality" that makes the work a worthy object for extensive marketing. The core marketing story attached to the novel, which highlights Adiga's turn against journalism and his "original" treatment of a neglected reality, fails to impress readers who, at their most extreme, question his ability and "right," as a member of an elite, to produce a fictional rendering of the subjective life and pathologies of a low-caste servant.

Contributors of customer reviews to the US-based amazon.com site are perhaps the most strident in this respect. Their views cannot be cited without some skepticism. There is no guarantee that contributors to a given forum are who they say they are, or believe what they profess to, or live where they say they do, or didn't write dozens of hostile reviews under various names. That said, forum comments do allow us some insight into how a book might be interpreted, and they help circulate potential readings. They can be read as performances of, and encouragement for, possible interpretations. In the case of *The White Tiger*, hostile reviews are common but not dominant. Some celebrate the book as a straightforward story of the "liberation of a man born to be a servant of the rich,"[22] failing to notice its critique of Balram's self-fashioning. Others read it in relation to their own professedly "romanticized" notions of India: they saw it as a "land-of-meditative enlightenment,"[23] as the place to which "more and more" American jobs are now "sent,"[24] or as a credit card zone that they access through call centers.[25] For these readers, the novel offers a welcome corrective.

Those who are less enamored by it are no more uniform a group. Reviewers who claim to be located in India or part of the Indian diaspora tend to stress that Adiga's work is designed for a non-Indian audience, though the novel was aggressively promoted within India and found a sizable audience there, winning praise from several media outlets. These reviewers clearly separate themselves from this intended readership and from the kinds of cultural translation and circulation they attribute to the author. Some express clear suspicion that achieving success as an English-language writer requires some willingness to indulge a specifically Western readership's misconceptions and fantasies about India. Some imply or simply state that it is, ironically, Adiga himself who is the entrepreneurial character in this situation, enriching himself by applying a cultural calculus to determine what will sell in Europe and North America—prurient glimpses at suffering others in distant locations. Adiga, as much as Balram, becomes for them the true cynical entrepreneur ("Mr. Adiga would surely be admired by his protagonist"[26]), and his earlier work is read as continuous with his novel, or as simply good training for it, rather than as an attempt to right some of its wrongs. As one reviewer notes, "Adiga who worked as a business journalist with Time magazine in India knows what sells the best in Europe and America."[27] In other instances, while raising concerns about Adiga's success, reviewers also take the opportunity to inform others about inaccuracies and distortions in the text that might otherwise go unnoticed ("the author should have put in more effort to get all his facts right"[28]).

There is, of course, no guarantee that users of the forum will actually read these comments and be thus chastened. It may be that those who write do not much care if their words are ever read, much as Balram himself remains uninterested in how exactly his story might reach his chosen narratee. The point for Balram seems to be pursuit of an elusive catharsis through his own self-articulation, which is formed, contradictorily, at once in opposition to and in conformity with the story of entrepreneurial success within the "new economy." Amazon.com, for its part, facilitates related expressions of dissatisfaction. Particularly discernible within these expressions is significant anger about the association of India with an economic underbelly and about the ossification of these associations in the form of celebrated intellectual properties ("Is there nothing good to say about life in India today?"[29]). Present, too, is readers' hostility about the global celebrification of figures

like Adiga, a process facilitated or even necessitated by global media concentration, as powerful firms elevate writers who are willing to co-produce
themselves as translators of Indian experience for various far-flung audiences. This reading of the situation might be limited and essentializing—I
have already noted the audience for the novel within India, as an example,
and my own reading of the text is more sympathetic—but it responds to
significant social inequalities that capitalist cultural markets can perpetuate
and mirror, despite, or perhaps sometimes because of, the critiques contained within the texts they circulate.

    That is, as we have seen, Adiga's novel is marketed and then cel-
ebrated as a welcome supplement to the extant portrait of an economy
of uneven development, one that excludes an underclass from the inter-
dependent spheres of wealth accumulation and cultural representation.
Critics then object to the terms of his intervention, often situating themselves as readers whose life experiences make them more familiar with
the subject than many others would be. The curious can then turn to
the novel to assess competing claims for themselves. Amid all this the
novelist himself is wisely neutral and will appear either open-minded or
self-contradictory depending on one's feeling toward him and his project.
His task is evidently to facilitate further circulation of and conversation
about the novel, so he declares a typical reluctance to endorse the notion
that his work is a vehement critique of the situation it describes. In claiming to be engaged in a simply descriptive act, he vacillates between two
positions: first, his innocent wish is to bring true stories to light; second,
Balram is not meant to be one real man but an amalgam of many voices,
a fictional creature through and through, and an expression of his wish
to contradict or supplement other kinds of writing he has done. In this
latter mode Adiga presents himself as a filter for others' voices, a passive
receptacle listening to and learning from those he met during his travels
as a journalist.[30]

"Can you ride it, whatever it is?": Affect
and Ambivalence in *In the Kitchen*

    Like *The White Tiger*, Monica Ali's 2009 novel *In the Kitchen* charts
some of the inequities of the split between elite and service work, depends

upon a therapeutic vocabulary, and diagnoses the neuroses of the aspirational entrepreneur. Also like that of *The White Tiger*, Ali's primary subject is the new world of work, and she connects her protagonist's troubled subjectivity to the absence of a defining social milieu or overarching narrative that might lend immediate significance to his existence. Richard Sennett's *The Corrosion of Character* and Zygmunt Bauman's *The Individualized Society* are among the works Ali consulted during her research for the book. Her interest in the transition from secure lifetime employment to flexible labor, and her sense that it has involved some corrosion of character rather than the triumphantly self-defining pursuit of character as destiny, is evident throughout.

The novel could be read as a fictionalization of Sennett's and Bauman's work, depicting the reeducation of a man undone by his too-ready embrace of the new regime of flexible, self-managed labor. As Bauman's work would predict, Gabriel internalizes his social context, filtering everything through an intense awareness of his life's biographical trajectory; complementing Sennett's research, Gabriel, a head chef and aspiring restaurant owner, represents the new world of knowledge-based employment, while his father, Ted, a retired mill worker, represents the old world of factory production. Gabriel grew up in a small town dominated by the textile industry, and he positions himself against this history. He views his old town as indicative of everything outmoded in British life: a respect for authority that is actually a fear of being "what you really are";[31] and a glorification of community that is in fact an expression of racism and xenophobia. Meanwhile, for him London is a place where people respect each other's differences and just go about their business. Gabriel aspires to be a great chef, maintaining that he is motivated not by a desire for extrinsic rewards, such as Michelin stars, but rather by a passion for cooking. He is convinced of his own autonomy and free will and is persuaded that self-expression and self-discovery are goals that should motivate everyone. Gabriel's plans for his own business, and remarks about the new world of work, lead Ted to bemoan the end of community and personal character in Britain. Ted promotes doing over feeling, the material over the affective. He suggests that any breathing body could have done his job at the mill, a claim that troubles Gabriel because a sense of the superiority of mental labor is so ingrained in him. Embracing the rhetoric of the new world of work, Gabriel states that "'having character,' that was just a way of saying you did what was expected of you. It's almost the opposite of having a character, a personality, of your own. Now you've got to know yourself, what you really are" (243). Ted laments that what people now want is "pleasure without responsibility" (260) and suggests the new economy they have built is based on nothing. England is no longer the "workshop of the world" but instead a "nation of consumers" (260): "All as we've got is a few assembly plants," he points out, "most of them foreign-owned" (261). Gabriel, in contrast, avers improbably, "There's more people employed in curry houses now than in all those old industries combined" (260) and suggests that the sheer number of people eating in expensive restaurants is proof of ongoing prosperity. "It's invisibles," Gabriel says, "you know, banking and finance and advertising" (261). To Ted it is, instead, a house of cards, built on "nothing solid."

Ali's 2003 novel *Brick Lane* also featured acknowledgments of debts to academic research. It was again a work of social science that was credited, in this case Naila Kabeer's *The Power to Choose*, a study of Bangladeshi women's experiences of the labor market in London and Dhaka. Most critical treatments of *Brick Lane* overlook Ali's evident interest in using fiction as a means of mediating insights derived from social science studies of contemporary work.[32] Instead, her writing is read in relation to migration, multiculturalism, and identity—topics that have been extensively explored by sociologists, of course, but that tend to appear in treatments of Ali via postcolonial literary theory instead. Study of *In the Kitchen*, a novel so resolutely shaped by its engagement with social and political neoliberalization, may encourage a rethinking of *Brick Lane* as an exploration of the relationship between one's psyche and one's working life; after all, the transformation of the protagonist from subservient immigrant housewife to independent creative worker is the novel's core narrative. *In the Kitchen* is considerably less sanguine about the transformative potentials of the new world of flexible work, and at the close of this chapter I briefly suggest that Ali's changed tone may have to do with the eruption of a controversy over her novel *Brick Lane* that saw her cast as a privileged member of the creative class, selling stories about Brick Lane's underprivileged minority population to delighted metropolitan consumers.

According to Eva Illouz, narratives that develop their characters as therapeutic subjects will present people beset by experiences that can be mentally isolated and dealt with, and people for whom suffering is contradictorily both a necessary generative motivator and a state relatively easy to overcome. Gabriel is a perfect example: plagued by a looming sense of guilt about the world he lives in and in need of a way to move through his guilt to find happiness; troubled by tension in his relationship with his dying father and enjoined by his sister to "sort it out" and "let it go" (235). But *In the Kitchen* blends the generic conventions of the therapeutic biography with those of the "state of England" novel, connecting Gabriel's story to a national condition. He is head chef at an upscale restaurant at the Imperial Hotel, a once-glorious establishment that has lost some of its grandeur. A primary feature of the postcolonial Britain Ali observes is its transient immigrant workforce. At the Imperial Gabriel supervises an international staff that includes many who have fled political turmoil and violence. When he wants to give a rosy glow to his job, as to the nation such diversity portends, he pretends— despite the occasional fistfight, his suspicions about shady deals going on in the hotel's back regions, his hatred for the kindly Jamaican sous-chef, and the mental decline and drug dependence of his French pastry chef—that they are a kind of United Nations, happily brought together around a common cause.

The tragic event at the novel's opening rattles Gabriel's contentment: the body of Yuri, a Ukrainian kitchen worker, has just been discovered in the hotel's subterranean halls. Gabriel suspects the man did not die of natural causes, and discouraged from pursuing the matter, he has vivid dreams in which he guiltily enjoys delicious food within arm's reach of the corpse. We learn eventually that these dreams manifest a guilt he does not consciously recognize or understand, as well as a frustration at the fact that he cannot do anything about situations like this. The dreams become more vivid with the unfolding of his affair with Lena, who had been Yuri's lover, as she exposes Gabriel to tales of the underground economy in which she moves. Faced with the realities of slave labor, exploited illegal immigrants, and forced prostitution, and troubled by his apparent inability to take any positive action, he experiences a mental collapse that pivots on his ceaseless self-interrogation and, in particular, on his inability to settle on any actual qualities that might anchor his self-definition. He is confronted by a gaping void at the center of the self he had until now taken to be a self-evident agent of change in possession of free will and positive forward movement. This void is one Ali carefully connects to the new world of work and to a broader emptying out of the meaning of Britishness under neoliberal governance.

Hence, prompted by his father's illness, Gabriel returns to his small-town childhood home to find a familiar transformation: Riley's, the mill that employed his father, is now Riley's Shopping Village, which is adding a "Weaver's Time Tunnel," an industrial heritage center, as the novel closes. Meanwhile, a new housing estate has just gone up, and its predictability displeases Gabriel: "All the houses were 'individual' (to increase the price at which they could be marketed) but basically identical, sharing an architectural style—a Tudorbethan mishmash of stone cladding and fake timbering—that found favour with the upwardly mobile" (213). Gabriel also confronts his father's and his grandmother's racism and promotion of an old community ideal, an ideal that affronts his liberal multiculturalism. Nana shares old yarns about neighbors who have discovered that their attics have been overrun with Pakistanis, and she boasts that there was once a time when all the doors on the street were open and people "clubbed together" (246). For his part, Ted, insisting that "this town is dying," tells Gabriel, "We're talking about how it was, when people round here cared about each other. When you knew everyone in the street and they knew you. Not that that means anything to you" (218). To Gabriel, who has never spoken to his own neighbors, Nana and Ted are simply nostalgic for the time when their community had only white people in it: "What's the disease, Dad? Foreigners? Progress? What? . . . And, anyway, look—look out there, the new estate . . . doesn't look like death to me" (218). Ted's identification with an old world of industrial labor is signaled by his absent final joint on his left little finger, the result of a workplace accident. Staring at his own hands, Gabriel observes

the old burn marks and scars, the calluses, the blackened nail, the lump on the index finger of his knife hand, the duck's-foot webbing between the first and second finger on his left where a third-degree burn had fissured the skin and healed all wrong. When he was a kid he used to look at his father's hands. Ted's hands held an entire world, of work, of manliness, and now Gabe wanted to hold his own aloft for inspection because Dad had never realized that his son had worker's hands. (216)

These beaten-up chef's hands suggest that he shares his father's serious work ethic. Yet his scars are mostly old ones. Becoming a head chef is presented as a process of leaving the tactility of cooking behind to assume a creative role. Kitchen staff prepare the food that Gabriel dreams up, while he plans menus and schedules in his office—a division of labor he sometimes resents, as he misses the pleasure of hands-on cooking.

The novel's take on Gabriel's career is certainly an ironic meditation on the recent fascination with celebrity chefs, evident in cooking competitions like *Top Chef*, the ubiquitous popularity of shows hosted by the likes of Jamie Oliver, Nigella Lawson, Anthony Bourdain, and Gordon Ramsay, and the heavy marketing of lavish but affordable cookbooks adorned with their faces. What the dominant representation of the celebrity chef draws upon and reinforces is the valorization of work that can be made to seem definitively creative over that which is cast in contrast as overly routine and mundane. The split is highly gendered: More often than not, men are professional chefs, whereas women are cooks and amateurs. More specifically, real chefs are men who engage in creative mental labor; they are competitive and eager for celebrity. Cooks are amateurs who deploy rote manual skills; they are too social to compete effectively and are more eager for praise from family and friends than they are hungry for celebrity. This division is of course superficial. The aura of the friendly amateur also sells, guaranteeing the professional success of figures like Paula Deen and Rachael Ray. Yet the terms of the celebration of the master chef are nevertheless telling: the chef is an artist-worker possessed of a set of heightened creative talents that are agile, movable, ideal for transport from workplace to workplace, network to network. They can be exhibited readily in any kitchen and are inspired rather than hampered by limits; hence, competitors in cooking shows have been asked to cook with one hand tied behind their backs or to use a small number of ingredients that are not normally combined. They love to adapt new techniques and technologies, hence the spectacular rise of experimental cuisine and the use of molecular gastronomy as a method of food preparation. Gabriel's character notably draws upon this increasingly popular image of the master chef at work. He embraces his father's commitment to hard work, but he combines it with creativity and expressivity more precisely associated with his late mother, a housewife who suffered from bipolar disorder and who had a creative streak tellingly stifled by domesticity. The novel pits the domestic world of routine tasks against the romantic work of self-creation and self-expression and aligns Gabriel with his mother precisely because she ultimately disavowed the feminine sphere to which she found herself confined.

Prompted by Gabriel's questions about his mother's mental illness, Ted will admit that "community's good for those what's on the inside, but if there's some inside there's others what's out. I'm thinking of yer mother. Thinking of my Sally Ann" (396). Ted's waffling on the subject of community makes Gabriel wish "he'd go back to being sure of everything" (396). Here we see the stark contrast between Gabriel and Ted, maintained throughout much of the novel, beginning to break down. Ted is not entirely convinced by his own nostalgia for old times, and it seems that Gabriel longs for something solid himself, as evinced by his nostalgia for his father's old certainties, by his appreciation for the tactile elements of his job, and by his moony conception of the farm work he stumbles into near the novel's end. What drives Gabriel's breakdown is not the surface rejection of those of his father's values that he tends to express but rather an anti-Oedipal longing. Gabriel's wish that his father might rediscover his lost authority is a symptom of his deeper yearning for a source of guidance and meaning to anchor him in the world, something or someone that would help him make decisions about whom to love and how to understand himself and conduct his life. What he confronts in his father's dying face is a center not so much fading away as already absent, and their conversations about postcolonial Britain and its ills just reinforce to Gabriel that it will be difficult to transform his bigoted and backward-looking Dad into someone to look up to and respect.

The break in relations between Gabriel and his father is multifaceted, but, conforming to the therapeutic narrative of personal transformation, the novel does posit a definitive breaking point, a scene of rupture that Gabriel cannot or will not readily recall but that he must eventually revisit lest it plague him forever. The incident occurred when Gabriel was ten years old and Ted had taken his son to work with him at the mill. Left to amuse himself, Gabriel had tampered with some machinery. A small matter, but his father is inconvenienced and turns it into an opportunity to scold Gabriel and then laugh at him in front of the other millworkers, mocking him because he won't admit to having done it: "Let's hear the truth and no more said about it. Be a man. No waterworks. Tell it like it is" (333). Sensing the emotional harm he has done, Ted then tries to make it up to his son, walking him around and explaining the machinery as usual. But something has broken in Gabriel, and all he can think is "Exterminate. Exterminate" (334). Eventually, Gabriel falls asleep waiting for his father to take him home and, thinking he has been abandoned, goes back to find him mysteriously prostrate on the ground. He interprets the sight: "He saw Dad lying on the floor beneath the girder, like he'd fallen off. Mr Howarth was crouching over him. Dad wasn't moving and when Mr Howarth looked up Gabriel saw the panic in his face and decided Dad—what a bastard!—had gone ahead and died" (336). This series of events tells us much about Gabriel's character and crisis. Seeing his father lying prone appears to answer his unspoken command that his father be "exterminated." It is a visible sign of the Oedipal death he had been psychically enacting. Then, the way he flees the premises rather than express his concern about his father anticipates his characteristic tendency to at once flee affection by focusing on work and then fault himself for having done so. Gabriel attributes much significance to this particular day at the mill because it is an original moment of the self-definition that later becomes more of a burden than an escape.

In highlighting this scene, the novel turns what Gabriel presents as self-willed choice into a response to a moment of psychic stress, tempering and contextualizing Gabriel's insistence on his self-defining free will. A similar role is played by Nikolai, a one-time doctor who was forced to flee Russia and now works in the hotel kitchen. For Nikolai there are no triumphant change agents. Instead, life is determined on many levels: some people are lucky enough to have been born in the West and to have the right kind of parents, for example. Even the notion that you control your own thoughts strikes Nikolai as a fiction: "Can you decide when to think, what to think about, when not to think at all?" (373). Nikolai also speculates, against any obvious causal logic, that Gabriel dreams of Yuri because he takes some responsibility for what happened to him and, more grandly, "for the world in which we live, for the kind of world in which there will always be more Yuris, struggling to exist" (376).

Gabriel's response to this speculation is resolutely literal. Since he was not actually the immediate cause of Yuri's death, how can anyone claim he is responsible? "I didn't make the world," he tells Nikolai; "I just live in it, same as you" (376). Such protestations aside, Nikolai is clearly correct about Gabriel's deep-seated guilt. He goes on to suggest, also correctly, that the dream manifests Gabriel's fear of the insignificance of Yuri's death and will recur so long as he believes he cannot respond to it in any meaningful way.

The main voice discouraging Gabriel from doing anything about Yuri, and from feeling responsible for his death in any way, is his associate Fairweather, a New Labour politician who is backing the new restaurant. Fairweather claims that the long chain of subcontracts involved in work like Yuri's, combined with the universally accepted pressure to keep costs low, the lack of protection for workers, and the death of the "union model" (421), means that real labor reform is impossible. Gabriel's rejection of his family's old-town values, his interpretation of his self as destiny, and his political quietude, are all echoed and elaborated by Fairweather, who emerges as a mouthpiece for the Third Way politics of New Labour. Fairweather suggests, for example, that what Ted says about the house-of-cards economy is perhaps true. The British no longer make anything; the economy is a "gigantic casino spinning speculators' money, while asset-stripping vultures shred company pension schemes and turn the few remaining factories into luxury flats and shopping malls" (320). On the other hand, "It's a matter of interpretation. There is no gospel truth. . . . I could say that the financial sector is thriving or I could say that there's around a million white-collar drones inputting data and answering phones" (326) and "a pool of unemployed and virtually unemployable Brits" (321). He recommends to Gabriel that the only question he ask himself is, "Can you ride it, whatever it is?" (321).

Fairweather's insistence that *homo economicus* should rule extends to his take on multiculturalism, which he sees as an offshoot of and complement to the new economy:

Our so-called British identity is like our economy . . . deregulated in the extreme. It's a marketplace of ideas and values and cultures and none of them are privileged over the rest. Each one finds its own level depending on supply and demand. . . . We talk about the multicultural model but it's really nothing more than laissez-faire. (364)

He suggests, "What's interesting . . . is the way in which the idea of Britishness is or has become essentially about a neutral, value-free identity. It's a non-identity, if you like. A vacuum" (364). This conception of Britishness as an empty space available to be filled by freely flowing content at the will of the highest bidder is a generalized instance of the same emptiness at the heart of Gabriel's character. Before his breakdown, Gabriel's lack of political commitment is something that, while not exactly celebrated, is certainly not lamented. Later, though, shame does begin to rear its head as he comes to be troubled by the proximity in his own life of feast and famine, poverty and excess. As Gabriel wonders about the point of self-criticism, asking himself, "What was the point of all these questions? They just turned in and in on themselves in one big tangled mess" (291), his introspection merely contributes to the same "tangled mess," adding layers of negative affect to his existing self-scrutiny. Fairweather's rhetoric connects Gabriel's political apathy and inability to get beyond the "mess" of thinking and feeling to a larger emptying out of the meaning of Britishness.

Gabriel's consciousness of a lack of meaning in his life, expressed in his yearning for reconciliation with a father figure returned to an original authority, is always dimly present. When he mocks the prefab housing estate visible through his father's window, his view is clouded by "his own image peering menacingly from the dark" (218). This confrontation with his own menacing visage suggests that he sees himself, his type, in the sad appearance of the estate's pretense to individuality. Like the estate, what is marked as presence is really just absence, absence signaled here by his willingness, just expressed, to hide his real views from his father in order to make a point. This scene is echoed later in the novel when he confronts his reflection in a London shop window as a "featureless mannequin, every characteristic obliterated or obscured" (327). The word "characteristic" is chosen carefully: this man who insists on self-definition, on living a life determined by his fundamental character, apparently no longer has one.

Gabriel's crisis begins to abate properly only after he inadvertently joins a bus of new immigrants contracted to pick spring onions and opens his eyes to some of what lies behind his work as a chef. The workers beside him are paid very little, and some have even been tricked into the work, their visas confiscated so they cannot seek other employment.

While sympathetic to their plight, his main feeling while picking vegetables is relief:

> He wasn't anybody, he was just a man, digging in the soil. He let it all go and sank into a deep warm pool of calm. All those anxious days chasing his tail, scheming, scheduling, plotting, moving restlessly from one care to the next, justifying, reasoning, arguing with himself, all the tension and contradiction, the endless search to get whatever it was he wanted, although he did not know what that was. He exhaled long and hard and let go of everything. He didn't need it any more. (518)

Finding himself outside in the sun in a rural setting, London far behind him, Gabriel is said to feel, for the first time, "whole" (518). Gabriel's unhappiness is checked by his faith in the integrity and authenticity of hard work, and the experience lasts. Within a few days he has arrived at a new self-awareness and contentment. He is sobered and matured by his brief experience of psychic pain, just as he is by the brief stint as a farm worker. As Illouz would have it, his suffering is both psychologically significant—significant enough to have the appearance of a serious breakdown, as he cowers in a corner hating himself and scratching his bald spot until it bleeds—and relatively easily overcome, transformed into fodder for his progressive development as a human being.

This does not mean he is now committed to act on the ills he has come to acknowledge. He has hardly noticed his father's death. He has lost his job after that one act of irrational violence. The savings he has given to Lena he now regards as charity, and what he had invested in the failed restaurant cannot be recovered. We find Gabriel nevertheless taking some time away from work, visiting his Nana in her retirement home, admitting that his sister has not been ruined by continuing to live in their old small town, and basking in the kind of self-understanding that will allow him to settle down finally into domesticity with his longtime girlfriend, ready to give up his dreams of personal glory if achieving them would mean sacrifice of a more intimate happiness.

The novel's ambivalence is crystallized in this pat and decidedly domestic ending. *In the Kitchen* takes up the disparities between elite politicians, financiers, chefs, and their service workers and emphasizes some of the psychic perils of the transition from a generation of steady employment to one of flexible self-management. The novel opens the door to critiques of an economy in which wage slavery and forced prostitution are insufficiently regulated and in which attempts at political reform seem increasingly pointless. It presents Fairweather, an eloquent New Labour politician familiar with the criticisms levied against the new Britain, as ultimately unaffected by questions or worries, and it links his attitude to a neoliberal rhetoric that empties out the meaning of diversity and personal freedom just as it heralds them as the basis of the new British identity. In focusing on Gabriel's psychic struggle with himself, in which his experience of spiritual emptiness is intermingled with family dysfunction and a struggle with feelings of guilt and inadequacy, the novel emphasizes that his inwardness serves the economy in which it unfolds. This inwardness portends a political quietude, as it has Gabriel seeking a way to overcome his own guilt through action in the domestic rather than the political sphere.

Nevertheless, all the more troubling aspects of Gabriel's character—his dishonesty and selfishness, his lack of respect for Lena and betrayal of his girlfriend, his experience of farm work as dignified purifying labor rooted in the soil, his positioning of himself outside and against the political and instead in the domestic sphere—are simultaneously mocked and understood. He is subject to humorous appraisal but redeemed in the end by his personal recovery. Though clearly conscious of the conventionality of its concerns, the novel ultimately refuses to scorn them. Instead, though the novel presents Gabriel's confusion and ambivalence, and the individualization through which he turns his perception of social ills into feelings of guilt on which he is helpless to act, as definitively suited to neoliberal governance and market rationality, it never quite condemns the psychic and social phenomena he constantly manifests.

The novel tends to excuse Gabriel's ambivalence by suggesting that it is preferable to Fairweather's cynicism in being, at least, the guilty experience of a self in constant conflict with itself, a self as troubled by its inability to decide on a view of economic realities as it is by the inequities that it admits that economy can permit or, worse, require. Manifesting the same waffling that defines its protagonist, the novel distinguishes itself from Fairweather's conflicted analysis only because it reflexively contemplates the difficulty of knowing what to critique, how to critique it, and what to replace it with. Consider the alternatives offered: the xenophobic vision of community that Ted and Nana position against Gabriel's way of life and the yearning that Ted expresses for the old days in which a lifetime of romanticized factory work was a secure prospect for those British citizens who wanted it.

There is also, however, Oona, Gabriel's genuinely happy but hapless sous-chef, who exists only on the margins of the narrative but appears at times to be the novel's conscience. Throughout much of the novel Gabriel is close to firing her, affronted by her perennial cheerfulness, but in the end he realizes that she provides kindness offered by few others. She cooks him dinner when she can tell he is distressed, helps her troubled coworkers hold on to their jobs, and dispenses tea whenever it is needed, along with appropriate biblical wisdom: "Come unto me, all ye that labour and are heavy laden, and I will give you rest," she cites; "For what will it profit them if they gain the whole world but lose their soul?" (280). Her characterization rests on stereotypes about the Caribbean woman: chubby and cheerful, deeply pious, unaffected by stress or negative emotions, in touch with some higher power that keeps her calm no matter the pressure she is facing. The biblical verse she cites is, in addition, just another version of that old refrain about careerism, that those who are too ambitious will eventually require spiritual regeneration, so this verse anticipates Gabriel's own transformation from aspiring star to chastened family man. Her placement at the margins of the narrative is, moreover, suggestive: clearly serving the formal function of foil to Gabriel, her ways of being clarify how manic he is, and his eventual reluctant admission of her goodness indicates just how much he has been changed by his experiences.

Still, her small presence in the novel is all the evidence we find of a vision of community that is alternative to Nana's and Ted's, and an approach to work that is distinct from Fairweather's and Gabriel's. She treats her coworkers like lifetime friends rather than a transient crew, preferring kindness to competition, and she is devoted to her work not because she wants to get ahead, or needs like many of the kitchen crew simply to get by, but because she somehow manages to care deeply about the relative strangers that share her workplace. While her model is also affective rather than overtly political, based on her comportment at work and the feelings that seem to motivate it, she reminds the reader that Gabriel's ways of operating are not all that is available. Indeed, we have a sense throughout that she is slyly but also sympathetically laughing at his overdramatic perception of himself, though she always treats him with considerable regard—not because he has the power to fire her but because she treats everyone that way.

If Oona's conspiracies of kindness and solidarity are only dimly perceived within the narrative, this is precisely because they are outside Gabriel's particularly self-involved ken. Her presence thus points to the fact that the narrative's closeness to Gabriel's point of view is a matter of aesthetic choice, a matter of what Ali decided to feature as plot and subplot, as major theme and leitmotif. As a foil to Gabriel, Oona serves to remind readers that Ali's technique necessarily elides the distance between the narrator and the protagonist. It is Ali's way of subtly signaling that her free indirect discourse involves an ambivalent proximity to her protagonist and pushes a full reckoning with other possibilities to the sidelines. Importantly, it is also Oona's characterization that frames the feeling of sympathy as the proper response to Gabriel's foibles. Oona maintains her compassionate disposition in spite of Gabriel's mistreatment of her; she never takes this mistreatment personally, and it never colors her kindness. This portrait of benevolence encourages the reader, whose disposition toward Gabriel is of course unpredictable, to overcome any initial aversion by sympathizing with him, as Oona does despite his evident hostility toward her. It also again repositions the relationship between narrator and character as a matter not of the author's unwitting indulgence of Gabriel's foibles but of her deliberate aesthetic choice about narrative point of view, a choice that may be grounded in her identification with Gabriel's ambivalence about the creative economy but that may also be grounded in an Oona-like kindness.

We can reconsider, in this light, Ali's avoidance of overtly self-referencing literary techniques. Is this avoidance a sign of an effort on her part to avoid drawing attention to herself and her relation to her material? Perhaps, but Ali's tendency to eschew knowing literary devices does not mean that her work performs no self-reflexive literary labor. Her 2003 novel *Brick Lane* faced a singularly hostile reception by residents of the area the book depicts. It was caught up in the area's transformation from blighted immigrant ward to vanguard cultural quarter for new creative professionals, and its protagonist herself progresses from piecework clothing manufacture to fashion design. The novel's critics maintained that it misrepresented the Bangladeshi people who made up the area's majority population. More important, they claimed that, in writing about an area to which she had no substantial connection and in calling her novel *Brick Lane* just as the bit of London associated with that title was becoming an acceptable lifestyle destination for white and middle-class Londoners, Monica Ali was in fact exploiting the area's cultural cachet in a way that was crudely designed to serve her own career. She would be associated in the public imagination with a newly hip neighborhood, and her work would sell more as a result. The people who led the campaign against the novel—a team of local business-owning men—seemed cannily aware of the fact that the circulation of cultural products with the words "Brick Lane" attached to them would help concentrate cultural capital in the region and complete its transformation from blighted urban ghetto to new outpost of the creative class. They tried to police this transformation by objecting to Ali's work and by aligning her with the intrusive creative workforce they were now seeing opening stores and galleries in the area and flowing through the streets on evenings and weekends.[33]

If *In the Kitchen* responds to this context by taking on the psychoses of the creative elite to which her critics routinely connected her, it does so not by disavowing any connection to that elite but by presenting its foibles as culturally and economically significant and by urging its readers to approach those foibles with sympathy rather than derision. This sympathy is more than an emotive response. In the person of Oona, it is the basis for a working life that differs radically from Gabriel's because it tends toward the common rather than the exceptional—toward solidarity with other people rather than an entrepreneurial striving to which other people are only help, hindrance, or irrelevant.

**

Alan Liu has argued that art in the age of information must offer "a special, dark kind of history . . . history not of things created . . . but of things destroyed in the name of creation." It "must be about [that is, enact] the 'destruction of destruction' or, put another way, the recognition of the destructiveness in creation."[34] As it reveals the underbelly of the "Asian tiger" economy and unsettles the pathologies of the entrepreneurial character, *The White Tiger* seems to heed Liu's prescription for new art's proper project. Yet as he participates in the promotional circuit, carefully negotiating his position, Adiga is evidently quite aware of the fact that in order for new work to continue to circulate as original and innovative, people's struggles have to become writers' stories: the repressed have to return and seemingly authentic traumas have to be located and then translated into literature. In this context or, more accurately, given heightened self-consciousness about this context, what Liu calls a "dark kind of history" appears to be less what all good art should strive to be and more a material that contemporary writers annex for themselves ironically and haltingly, with increasing difficulty, or decreasing conviction and convincingness, in part because of the existence of extensive markets for texts that present themselves in this light, and in part because of pervasive critiques of the exoticizing forms of narration that these markets may invite.

In the Kitchen is not entirely different in this respect, though it is certainly less concerned to show that it knows that it is involved in the profitable business of producing literature about the underbelly of London's economy. Ali's focus is one man's growing "recognition of the destructiveness in creation," or coming to consciousness of what subtends his creative work as a head chef—the exploitation of a migrant workforce that grows the food prepared by badly paid kitchen staff with no job security and only the dimmest hopes of improving their lot. The novel's take on this "dark kind of history" is to emphasize the way knowledge of it troubles the protagonist, but it is ultimately—like him—unsure where knowledge leads. Its small measure of self-consciousness is directed not at its own marketability but rather at the limitations of its closeness to its narrator's point of view. Moreover, while Adiga's work is quite knowingly engaged in patrolling its author's own career and was deliberately sold as a refutation of his earlier writing, Ali's novel is an unwitting defense of the guiltily introspective confusion of the creative elite, motivated perhaps by the dramatically politicized way she had been cast as that elite's representative figure. Still, both novels beg to be read as, in part, manifestations of their authors' reflexive examination of their own tendencies as cultural producers. Their presentation of entrepreneurial protagonists who suffer from significant psychoses—psychoses inseparable from their precarious working lives—speaks to a broader zeitgeist. It appears to be almost impossible for writers to present the new world of work, work that their own creative practices have helped model and shape, without emphasizing its troubling psychological effects, its alienating impact, and its reliance on a precarious underclass. The split between Adiga and Ali is also characteristic of the field: there are those who tap into this zeitgeist in a knowing way, who point to the popularity of the critical gesture of opposition to the dominant narratives; and there are those who contribute to the trend but do not acknowledge having done so, either because they do not perceive the trend's existence or choose not to emphasize their awareness of it. A similar split is evident in the next chapter, which features two works concerned that the celebrification of minority writers is a means of diversifying and expanding the creative economy.

5

Economy and Authenticity in
Daljit Nagra's *Look We Have Coming to Dover!*
and Gautam Malkani's *Londonstani*

In the UK, creative-economy discourse refers regularly to the numerous benefits of cultural diversity. In one of its modes, supported by metrics like Florida's "diversity index," it correlates a city's demographic diversity to its status among the creative class and posits that supporting a diverse downtown is important to attracting the right kinds of residents. This approach tends to translate difference into a surface fetish. According to Richard Lloyd, whose book *Neo-Bohemia* studies the close relation between whiteness and gentrification, sharing the streets "with working-class and nonwhite residents" tends to be presented as integral to the creative class's "image of an authentic urban experience," even though in reality "personal interaction remains superficial."[1] In another mode, similarly fetishistic, diversity is simply another word for the difference that makes each individual authentically unique and thus uniquely able to make an original contribution to the creative economy. If people were not different, there would be no authentic individuals and thus no originality; hence, difference is always to be reified and celebrated. A third mode, most relevant here, quantifies the underrepresentation of minorities within the UK creative industries and promotes programs that might correct it.

The *decibel* program, first instituted by Arts Council England in 2003, was designed to serve this purpose. Some £5 million in Treasury funds were initially allocated to support African, Asian, or Caribbean artists and arts managers, as well as arts programs involving people of African, Asian, or Caribbean origins now living in the UK. *Decibel* has worked directly with creative businesses and arts organizations and has also channeled monies into regional arts councils to develop and reward attempts to increase awareness of or directly redress a lack of diversity in the arts sector.[2] For example, 2003–4 initiatives included a high-profile performing arts showcase and a fellowship program for promising curators. Though they were not absolute successes, on the basis of these foundational activities funding for *decibel* has continued.[3]

The program has had a number of effects specific to the literary field. Most notably it has joined with the British Book Awards and Penguin to present an annual *decibel*–Penguin Prize. In its initial instance in 2005 the prize could be awarded only to writers of Asian, African, or Caribbean background. The first winner was Hari Kunzru, and those short-listed for it had their work included in an anthology published by Penguin, *New Voices from a Diverse Culture*. A recent change, made under pressure from the Commission for Racial Equality, means that one's minority ethnicity is no longer an explicit criterion for inclusion. Instead, in 2006 any "personal stories of immigrants to the UK" could compete to win and to have their works included in *Personal Tales of Immigration to the UK*, the nonfiction follow-up to the earlier story anthology. Still, those writers labeled "BME" (black and minority ethnic) continue to be most often rewarded. Writers have expressed mixed feelings about these developments. Controversial novelist and columnist Nirpal Singh Dhaliwal has called the prize "a special pat on the head for Britain's ethnic minorities" and has deemed it "wholly patronizing."[4] Meanwhile, 2006 winner Diana Evans's more ambivalent response was that though it "helps to get ethnic minority writers in the limelight," it is the product of an unfortunate necessity.[5] In an ideal world, a world *decibel* is thought to want to create, potential readers would not need their attention specially drawn to BME authors because enough would already exist and they would encounter no difficulties in selling their works to a sizable readership.[6]

Like any literary prize, simply rewarding artists is only a small part of its purpose. The high-profile awards are also a marketing strategy designed to help the book industries attract more BME employees and secure more diverse audiences and greater revenues. These two motives are related: an increasingly diverse workforce is thought to be indispensable if publishers want to continue to access niche markets through street-level knowledge of the consumer preferences of specific communities.[7] As *decibel* seeks to increase the diversity of labor within the creative workforce, it works in tandem to foster the kinds of culture and the forms of marketing that will prove most appealing to minority populations, and thus most useful for interpolating them into roles as better, fitter, more active consumers of culture. We find the seemingly civic goal of cultural representation boldly coupled with corporate interest. Penguin advertises its brand through support of worthy causes and targets potential consumers who may be neglecting cultural forms they deem unappealing, alienating, irrelevant, or inaccessible.

It is worth noting that under New Labour, programs like these were also supported because they could be construed as servicing the social inclusion agenda. In the 1980s arts funding agencies would speak of "arts and the community" and present themselves as development agencies engaged in the politically expedient work of supporting artists who worked to address important social issues such as "disadvantage" (never economic inequality or injustice) and racism. The DCMS preferred to fund culture that could demonstrate impact, especially impact on measures of social inclusion resulting from efforts to improve access to culture and to encourage participation in cultural production and consumption as a means of community development.[8]

A recent report published by *Third Text*, the journal of Black Umbrella, an association of antiracist scholars and artists, questions the vision of cultural diversity put forward by *decibel* and related initiatives. It suggests that the tendency of such programs has been to privilege token forms of inclusion that leave untouched a more fundamental unwillingness to confront real barriers to participation and leave unacknowledged the role that minority artists have long played in shaping mainstream traditions. Contributors to the report call cultural diversity "a managerial formula, an institutional agenda, and, most pertinently, an instrument of governance."[9] They argue that recent arts policy restricts artists' range by isolating affiliation with specific underrepresented communities as the thing that licenses their access to and distinction within existing or emerging markets;[10] that the language of cultural diversity entrenches the inequality it seems to want to erase; that the hypervisibility of certain artists is coupled by a lack of any "constitutive change to art history, curating or art education at large"; and that what arts practitioners and policymakers should attend to is the "difference the promotion and inclusion of certain artists *cannot make*."[11]

A leitmotif within many of these critiques is that recent creative-economy diversity initiatives perpetuate long-standing and often restrictive assumptions about authenticity and representation. It is by no means only within the UK that "ethnic," "regional," or "minority" writers and artists have often been burdened by the notion that their job is to articulate an ostensibly whole and organic community and to embody and express its identity. Their work is understood as the innocent "outgrowth" of their belonging to that integral unity, and as the emanation of a particular culture, it is presumed to capture its essence. Meanwhile, an existing roster or canon of texts is thought to lack diversity in a way that the inclusion of certain "representative" figures will correct, such that those writers are taken as speaking for a previously neglected group.[12] Writers who thwart these prescriptions—as many do—tend to find themselves accused of inauthenticity.

Such charges are hardly a straightforward problem, however. Despite the seeming naïveté of many official cultural-diversity policies, debate about authenticity seems to be particularly pressing, perhaps because contemporary readers and writers already think routinely about how to live authentic lives in which their relationships to family and community are honest and sincere and in which their "capacity for life, freedom, spontaneity, expressiveness, growth [and] self-development" is fully realized.[13] Authenticity debates provide a uniquely relevant and familiar set of terms for literary expression, discussion, and comprehension for people who already engage the challenges of authenticity as part of their own reflexive self- and career development.

The cases of Gautam Malkani and Daljit Nagra offer telling evidence of the way literary work registers and negotiates the problem of authenticity as a set of competing claims. On the one hand is authenticity as cultural representativeness or as belonging to, emanating from, and expressing a particular community. On the other hand is authenticity as genuine self-expression, sufficiently compelling and sufficiently reflexively performed and explained. Their works register both forms of authenticity as properties that have an aesthetic dimension because they must be performed for audiences. They also register both forms of authenticity as productive absences. Both writers appear motivated by a search for a sufficiently authenticating narrative of the self; they use their works as forms of self-articulation and self-defense. Neither belongs to a community straightforwardly; both subject the idea of authentic community affiliation to scrutiny. In Nagra's case, the poet's labor is profoundly metapoetic. Made up of all of the aspects of his performance of himself as a writer, including his self-presentation in interviews and profiles, the poems in his 2007 collection *Look We Have Coming to Dover!*, and the packaging and marketing of his work, his labor is self-consciously designed to perform the writer's concern about his alienation from his purported community, a community that at once appears and is disclaimed as the source of his work's uniqueness and of its suitability for inclusion in official cultural-diversity initiatives. Gautam Malkani's 2006 novel *Londonstani* indicates related anxieties arising from the author's use of his connection to a particular minority community as his entrée into the creative economy. In Malkani's case, however, the work reveals those anxieties unwittingly. It is his paratextual attempts to constrain his work's reception that are the proliferating symptoms of the negative affect to which the literature only quietly alerts us.

Daljit Nagra's Metapoetics

Eye-catching as they are, the candy colors of the first cover of Daljit Nagra's wildly anticipated *Look We Have Coming to Dover!* are subdued compared to the packaging the poems received when they were printed for a second time. Here we encounter a random array of items normally found in a dollar store or corner shop, where eclectic collections often amass in a haphazard fashion. Included for display are a soccer ball, a stack of plastic chairs, an ironing board, fake flowers, a package

FIGURE 1. Cover of Daljit Nagra's *Look We Have Coming to Dover!*, first printing, Faber and Faber, 2007.

FIGURE 2. Cover of Daljit Nagra's *Look We Have Coming to Dover!*, second printing, Faber and Faber, 2007.

of "Wonda"-brand cleaning pads, and some water jugs. Yet their arrangement does not meet expectations about how a shopkeeper would shelve things for customers' convenience. Instead, each piece, from the training potties stacked at the bottom to the mops and brooms placed at the sides, adds to a visual composition that frames the crucial information of the name of the author and his book. Behind them, doing the work of a canvas, is what appears to be the kind of room divider often placed between office cubicles. The words of the title, sandwiched between Nagra's name and the distinctive Faber and Faber logo, seem to be spray-painted upon it in bold scarlet. Rather than offer us a natural-seeming depiction of real consumable items—which would reflect the book's interest in the lives of the poet's shopkeeper parents—the cover instead points to its own use of these everyday things as a means of grabbing the attention of a different kind of customer: the potential reader milling over the latest poetry. The screen serves to emphasize how deliberate the placement of everything around it is, so the volume itself, through the vehicles of title, publisher's logo, and author's name, becomes at once another part of this hodgepodge collection and a showcase item that is framed and highlighted by the commodities that bracket it.

The effect is remarkable. We encounter a package for a book that revels in acknowledging how important it is to the book's marketing. It simultaneously packages the product and draws attention to itself as a mediated, deliberately constructed package for what is, at least in part, yet another commodity now available to potential customers: brand Daljit Nagra. We are asked to imagine the poet's work as a kind of quintessential second-generation South Asian commodity, whether it overshadows, displaces, or merely supplements the sorts of fungibles that are factory-produced in Taiwan and sold at the stereotypical corner shop.

First collections by contemporary poets, even those published by Faber and Faber, are rarely reprinted. Achieving the sales figures that warrant a second run is just one of the ways that Nagra's emerging career has been exceptional. From the moment it was released, *Look We Have Coming To Dover!* was uniformly heralded as important work by a bold new writer. Critics agreed that he was rejuvenating English literature by mashing it up with voices drawn from his Punjabi family and from the suburban milieu to which they continue to belong. In light of the author's instant acclaim, what the packaging of the collection's second printing does is highlight his—and his co-producing publishers' and marketers'—humorous appraisal of such instant celebrification. "Look We Have Coming to Dover!" shouts the exclamatory voice of a Punjabi speaker, as the book itself declares "Look I Have Coming to Market!" Already a minor star, the author is presented to us here as a playful, fantastic, colorful character ready to enliven and diversify English verse and also as a cultural creator knowingly jockeying for position within a market glutted by more voices than can secure room in our reading lives or occupy niche positions cleared for them on bookstore shelves.

The final touch is the nature of the endorsement blurb offered by the *Guardian*'s Sarah Crown, in which she challenges us all "not to come away from this volume feeling gladdened, afflicted, revitalised." That her words are contained within the shape of a sheriff's badge is surely a sly play on the name of the *Guardian* newspaper: the gatekeepers of elite culture in the UK have policed the scene and have offered Nagra their badge of approval. This is unsurprising, since before they appeared in the book, some of the pieces, including Nagra's first widely circulated poem, which was to become the collection's title, were printed in the same paper's arts pages. With its title—"Look We Have Coming to Dover!"—and its first lines—"Stowed in the sea to invade / the lash alfresco of a diesel-breeze"[14]—it demands that its audience "Look" at the "We" arriving at England's shores—the shores docked by immigrants "Stowed in the sea to invade," but also the borders crossed by the coming of a second-generation Punjabi writer to the region of English verse. When it won the Forward Prize for best single poem in 2004, it created a thirst for Nagra's work that he waited three long years to slake.

Responding to journalist Rachel Cooke's wondering if he is worried about becoming "the media's latest Asian," Nagra states, "Well, I've set up myself for that. The book is obsessed with Asian-ness. But there hasn't been a lot of successful poetry about the Indian working classes so, to be honest, I'm happy to carry on writing it. If people label me, that's their concern. I don't even know who I am myself."[15] Here Nagra acknowledges that his verse is salable and interesting because, by locating itself in the experience of South Asian immigration, it does something that is rare in poetry. Nagra's Punjabi-inflected language—what he calls "Punglish"—is deployed in various guises and tones throughout his collection and serves as a constant index to the milieu from which the verse emerges. When using it, he partly comically mimics the nonstandard "deviations" common to new or otherwise nonstandard speakers—so, "have coming to" for "have arrived in" or "have come in to." However, just as the book's cover image refuses to appear unstaged, the writing within it makes no pretense to realism when evoking its characters' idiomatic turns of phrase. The relatively elite, college-educated voice of the England-born poet is never far from us. Thus, the title poem's first words also hint at what carries over into its remaining lines: a running engagement with Matthew Arnold, whose legibility as a literary reference is by no means restricted to London's literati. That "Dover Beach" is standard UK curriculum is something Nagra knows well, since he works as a schoolteacher.

"I'm working in a school, I'm teaching English, I'm living English and breathing English all the time," he tells Patrick Barkham. "Some part of me wants to be Indian as well. I really enjoy writing about Indian people. . . . I find that far more liberating. All that stuff you grew up with—the intensity of India—has to find its outlet somewhere. Poetry feels like a natural form." He goes on to state clearly that his aim is not attentive or accurate devotion to the telling ethnographic detail but rather an absorption of Punjabi idioms into "an artificial English voice" that he delights in reading aloud because he can adopt "an Indian voice" to "black it up, minstrelise it."[16]

Still, even while engaged in such minstrelsy, he rarely stops insisting on his significant discomfort about using his college-level English literary education to (mis)represent those closest to him. He describes his parents as people who were never "bookish." He was ashamed of their foreignness during his youth, and they did not understand why he wanted to be a poet until he became famous for it. In contrast, he describes himself as someone who always tried to be an exception to the rules of English racism, to "fit in" with the white kids, to share their ways of talking, dressing, and being in the world. He wanted to be "the OK one," the boy who was not too foreign and thus escaped being bullied by the "National Front kids."[17] Profiles of Nagra tend to focus on this tendency he has to confess his most shameful behavior, whether to the journalist or in his poetry.[18] We learn that he would not allow his school friends into his house and would

"bin letters about Parents' Evenings" to ensure that his mother's "illiter-
ate body" remained "hidden" to his peers.[19] He clearly belongs to these
parents for purposes of cultural-diversity programming or for commercial
marketing that highlights some appeal of—if not to—niche communities. In refusing to write about being a child in the Punjabi community—
a refusal that might have meant his irrelevance to the market—he makes
chaotic, parodic, and sometimes tragic invocations of its members' voices
the heart of his verse. All the while he insistently stresses that to do so is
to celebrate himself and his expressive individual voice by "booking" their
sometimes painful experiences—that is, by making a book out of them,
by undertaking their staging, or even most extremely, by filling a charge
sheet that imprisons them in his work of representation.

This process is most obviously articulated in the poem "Booking
Khan Singh Kumar." The name "Khan Singh Kumar" was Nagra's original pseudonym; it comically, implausibly combines Muslim, Sikh, and
Hindi elements, expressing Nagra's consciousness of the way cultural difference can become, in market contexts, "effluvia from an undifferentiated
British Asian whole."[20] Within the poem it labels a performer who objects
to his own clichéd role, asking, "Must I wear only masks that don't sit
for a Brit," and wondering if he should admit he has "discorded his kind
as they couldn't know it." They "couldn't know it," we presume, because
there is not much chance of their encountering the results of his depictions of them in performance or print. The poem is a long list of questions
directed many ways simultaneously: at the speaker, at the poet, and at
us. The querying phrases "Did you make me for the gap in the market /
Did I make me for the gap in the market" acknowledge the performer's
participation in his own commodification, while "Can I cream off awards
from your melting-pot phase" suggests he understands his success as, in
part, a manifestation of a temporary stage in multicultural "melting-pot"
policymaking. Meanwhile, the line "Do you medal yourselves when you
meddle with my type" intimates that the speaker's very existence as a voice
may be a way for someone else to "medal" herself, while such "meddling"
with his "type"—his kind, but also his words on the page, which convert
the experiences of "his kind" into typeface (once metal)—is a path to
self-satisfaction and also a response to the push to develop the market for
BME writers, connected here to a socially conscious, left-leaning urge to

feel good about trumpeting diverse communities' rightful access to and representation within cultural texts. Here, clearly, Nagra is prodding publicized commitments to support for artists who can be said to belong to specific minority milieus. He is pointing out that the publicity accorded his own work is part of a larger cycle of promotion that seeks to draw attention to writers like him in order to highlight and promote diversity in the field for reasons that deserve scrutiny rather than instant consent.

A more subtle but equally telling instance of this self-consciousness is "Darling & Me!," a poem that has appeared in a number of guises. It is the first piece in *Look We Have Coming to Dover!*, and Nagra read it aloud for one of Oxfam's *Life Lines* fund-raising CDs in a performance recorded for a promotional video now available via YouTube.[21] Nagra was one of more than sixty poets who read their works after being selected by Oxfam's own poet-in-residence, Todd Swift. Swift says of the project:

> Poetry has been hotly debated within the media recently, facing concerns that it is losing its mass appeal. But Oxfam believes poetry is alive—and can help save lives. In a bid to demonstrate how diverse and exciting poetry can be, and to show their support for Oxfam, the UK's leading poets have teamed up to create a CD of their most enthralling work to date.[22]

In this conception, poetry saves lives not because it persuades important people to do or not do certain things but because its "diverse and exciting" writers willingly lend their names and their personalizing voices to CDs that are sold to raise money for Oxfam's charitable works. Being able to boast creation of a product that features respected contemporary poets, meanwhile, lends Oxfam the cultural cachet that it needs to thrive as a charity that is also a major brand and, as such, a site of consumer affiliation. After all, Oxfam now markets its own series of products, sold along with other environmentally friendly, fairly traded merchandise to the socially conscious consumers who frequent its growing number of retail locations both online and across the UK and abroad. *Life Lines* is one of those responsible products. Readers may wish to listen via YouTube to Nagra's performance for it of "Darling & Me!" before proceeding. There they will encounter the monologue of a man recently married to the "Darling" of the title, whom he affectionately deems his "dimplymisses." As the poem opens, he speaks of calling her to announce that he is about to return home. When he hears the barman's "bell done dinging," he imagines how he will soon be with his new wife again, dancing once more to the sound track for *Pakeezah*, a Bollywood classic from the 1970s. *Pakeezah*'s much-noted decadent grandeur stands in notable contrast to the simple kitchen that the newlyweds "rumba" into to eat the roti that the speaker's wife so diligently prepares for him. Still, the film's story of a courtesan trapped in a set of patriarchal power struggles bears a distinct relation to the situation of the poem's silent kitchen-bound wife, whose husband, at first sweet and attentive, turns threatening with surprising— indeed jaunty!—rapidity.

Looking forward to his meal, the speaker soon begins to muse about his pub mate Jimmy John, who has his dinners delivered to him by a girl- friend envisioned as an incarnation of Hilda Ogden, *Coronation Street*'s luckless, beloved, perennially curler-headed charwoman. To our speaker, what she brings poor Jimmy is clearly bland fare: a "plate of / chicken pie and dry white / potato!" The exclamation here performs two notable func- tions (in addition, that is, to conveying some lightness of tone): it indicates the speaker's mockery of the flavorless English cuisine, and standing in for the "es" that would be at the end of the correct plural for "potato," it also draws the reader's attention to his immigrant's English in a way that adds comic irony to his sense of superiority. Soon after, in voicing the girlfriend's command that Jimmy eat his *"chuffy dinnaaah!"*—the word "chuffy" making her akin to the speaker, as her own demotic phrases reveal their shared class positioning—we encounter a double ventriloquism: the poet voices a speaker who is imagining the voice of this working-class Englishwoman delivering her boyfriend's dinner to the pub.

The shame of having one's private life infiltrate the public space of the bar in this way, as Jimmy's girlfriend emits anger about being made into his servant, is of considerable concern to the speaker. He declares that he would never think to have his wife deliver his meal to him "in public- ity," playing on the origins of the word "publicity" in the pub, a place where gossip has long been broadcast and transmitted. But if he did do so, and she advertised the fact by making an angry pronouncement about it, she would earn herself a "solo punch in di smack." The use of "publicity" instead of "public" and the description of the scene as one that involves an untoward "advertisement" are, again, partly Nagra's way of appealing to the comic potential in the difficulties of the nonnative speaker, but they are also once again more than that. When coupled with the threat of violence, the poem's market-based vocabulary serves to remind the reader that tales of immigrant South Asian men mistreating their wives have been highly visible within the UK, in part because their circulation tends to be attended by scandals that erupt when the represented community objects to its characterization.

In Nagra's Oxfam performance he voices the speaker's unusual locutions for their full effect, ensuring his upbeat tone makes a clear contrast with the sobering implications of what he is actually saying, since what begins as gallantry ends as brutality. The poem's final stanzas are tainted by the threat of violence. As we envision the couple dancing, the speaker likens their routine to an ice-dance performance by famed English Olympians Torvill and Dean. The new wife falls and is swung up dramatically, her body thoroughly subject to her husband's lead. The dance is less a coupling and more an exertion of his force over this "pirouettey" but silent being whose cooking makes such a welcome contrast to the bland English meat and potatoes. These two have been married a "whirlwind" month, and there is no mistaking why she is there: she will work to produce the "disco of drumstick in pot" that, with its chef, awaits the return of this man who works "factory-hard," tends to refer to himself in third person, and ends his monologue with that most telling of pronouns: "me."

The speaker's unsavory ideas about his wife's rightful position and potential receipt of a "punch in di smack" are the kinds of things that generated controversy when Monica Ali published *Brick Lane* (2003), a novel featuring several unsavory male characters. Ali is in fact in many ways an ideal foil for Nagra, since a source of opposition to her novel was the fact that she was herself only half Bangladeshi and belonged neither to the working-class milieu nor to the particular community that was her book's focus. The fact that it was necessary for her do research about the treatment of female garment workers, a process she discussed quite openly, became for some critics irrevocable evidence of her outsider status. Yet as a work of fiction *Brick Lane* evinces remarkably little self-conscious interest in Ali's approach to representing the kinds of traumas she unearthed through research. Nor does it pay much attention to the politics of representation that might have been expected to erupt given the difference between the author's own social location and that of her characters. In contrast, in "Darling & Me!" the speaker's mixed-up references to "publicity" and "advertising" are there precisely to remind us all that he is himself a fiction and that his characterization here, especially his working-class social location, his immigrant's English, and his by turns sentimental, patronizing, and threatening attitude toward his wife, is what allows the emergence into community-based branding of the poet who created him.

Most of Nagra's poems feature similar forms of commentary on the production and reception of the writer as a brand, staged as a complex intermingling of biographical self, textual effect, and commercial commodity. His work evinces relentless anxiety about his connection to a minoritized, but marketable, South Asian identity. It critiques the way this affiliation secures his distinction and permits his celebrification as *the* British Asian poet. In addition, his work suggests that, like brands in general, though "Daljit Nagra" is a quality manifest in particular objects that can be purchased and owned, the value of the name cannot be reduced to any one moment of direct exchange. That value is instead an expression of prestige or cultural capital that can be translated into future transactions. If the ecstatic reception of *Look We Have Coming to Dover!* is any indication, he is clearly on to something. After winning the Forward Poetry Prize for best single poem in 2004, he won for best collection in 2007, and later that year he was himself awarded the prestigious *decibel* prize. He established his own name as a web domain (www.daljitnagra.com) and started using the site to alert fans about appearances, to offer mp3s and video clips of his performances, and to provide a mailing list for those who would like to receive e-mails like this one:

> Dear Sarah
> Please find attached two recent poems
> Many thanks
> Daljit

Is this really him, or has he hired a machine that deploys first names in order to personalize his products, disguising mass production in appeals to an irreducible biographical self? That he wishes us to pose these kinds of questions is further suggested by a video of Nagra recorded by Meet the Author, a company that claims it is "bringing books to life!" by producing Internet clips in which writers, rather than their publishers' marketing departments, are found "speaking from their heart[s]—to YOU." Nagra's actual video performance slyly undermines this fiction of sincere and direct address: when he introduces himself—"Hello. My name is Daljit Nagra. I'm a poet."—his voice is subtly sarcastic, as though he is mocking the whole enterprise of labeling and selling himself.[23]

Each aspect of Nagra's work contributes in this way to the construction of an overarching metabrand. A major part of what this metabrand registers is the author's awareness of a merging of the ostensibly civic language of cultural diversity with private-sector desire to increase capital through the capture of niche markets, as arts organizations and policymakers collaborate with private capital to incorporate more diverse communities into the mainstream cultural field. Nagra's case suggests that for those who experience alienated distance from the milieus they reference for content, the market circulation of texts on the basis of some attachment to those milieus serves as a constant reminder of what is often an uncomfortable process—a process that entails appealing to the capital of a distinguishing cultural connection for the purpose of establishing market value. The very focus of the poetry is the writer indicating his alienation from the "type" he is aligned with, as he presents himself as one who ventriloquizes their voices because it serves in the construction of his particular brand identity.

In this way what distinguishes Nagra's verse is not just that he engages and enlivens English literary heritage by incorporating select Punjabi vocabulary, demotic speech patterns often presented through dramatic monologues, and references to real and imaginary products, brands, and popular culture. While all of that might be enough to guarantee him some relevance, part of why Nagra has achieved such success is his remarkable willingness to build into his oeuvre so much framing of his own valorization as an outcome of the kinds of marketing of cultural diversity recently crucial to capital's continued expansion. His work is interesting precisely because it continuously evinces suspicion about how belonging to an identifiably minoritized group becomes a means of constituting the distinction necessary to the assured growth of cultural capitalism.

As heated conversations about Arts Council England and special dispensations for BME figures have erupted, the methods and means of market expansion have become contentiously familiar for much of Nagra's core audience. Supporting and reading Nagra is one way that audiences can then emphasize their own knowingness about their participation in the solidification of the relationship between cultural-diversity policy, arts funding, and consumer capitalism. As David Harvey has argued, "Capital has ways to appropriate and extract surpluses from local differences, local cultural variations and aesthetic meanings of no matter what origin," and one of the most attractive "variations" for capitalist repurposing is anything which seems antimarket and anticommercial. To approximate too closely any pure commercialization is to risk losing the "monopolistic edge" of "non-replicable cultural claims" that Harvey deems the heart of the functioning of cultural capitalism.[24] Nagra's work—and acclaim for Nagra's work—can be read as an expression of this very tension: it offers resistance to its own reduction to a market function accorded it as authentically representative work, but in a way that is readily available for renewed commodification, becoming a form of salable distinction offered to poet and reader alike. Nagra thus achieves something additional, and wins more distinction within the literary field, through his anticapitalist or nonmarket critique of the selfsame pursuit of market distinction. This added distinction remains indistinguishable from the branding processes it is designed to register and resist.

Gautam Malkani's Authorial Paratexts

The release of Gautam Malkani's 2006 novel *Londonstani* was accompanied by a firestorm of hype, fueled by controversy over the authenticity of the connection between the author and the British-Asian "rude boys" to whose subculture the novel ostensibly gives voice. The novel's protagonist and narrator is Jas, a young man raised in Hounslow, a bit of outer London mainly occupied by middle-class families whose livelihoods are tied to Heathrow airport. When we meet him, he has recently cast off a nerdish smart-kid image (the brain) to take up instead with a gang of local thugs (the brawn) who identify with this popular "rude boy" sensibility and identity, blending hip-hop fashion, streetwise showoff masculinity, and an interest in South Asian popular music and dance. Jas's crew consider themselves the toughest gang going and earn pocket money through a small-scale mobile phone racket they have established to fill a "gap in the market."[25] Jas and his friends start out simply filling a need but soon progress to more nefarious business.

Hardjit is the group's leader, a muscle-bound tough with a penchant for street fighting and a Sikh religious symbol tattooed on his bicep. In the novel's opening scene he is physically savaging a sorry "gora" ("white kid") who may or may not have called him a "Paki." His friends look on. In addition to Jas, the spectators are Ravi, whose preoccupations are misogynistic ranting and stories of his own unearthly sexual prowess, and Amit, plagued by an angry mother who feels her family hasn't been paid due respect in the lead-up to his brother's wedding.

A large part of being man enough to belong to this gang is proving you are shallow and uninterested in schoolwork. Accordingly, these teenagers—all of whom, we understand, once maintained good grades— are collectively retaking their A-levels as the narrative unfolds. Equally important is the conspicuous consumption that proves they are living in sufficiently blinged-out style. They agree to go into business with Sanjay, a former stockbroker turned VAT-defrauding criminal who buys phones from them, because they admire the life he has made for himself in his posh London pad, whose design is inspired by an episode of MTV Cribs.

Jas is the clear outsider figure, struggling to conform to the complex rules of speech and conduct to which his new friends seem to adhere with so little effort. A major impediment is his interest in Samira, a woman they disapprove of because she is Muslim. Still, with Sanjay's guidance, Jas manages to win her over before everything unravels around him: she dumps him (he is too clingy); he loses his friends (by being more astute and culturally sensitive than they are); he implicates himself in Amit's brother's suicide (by engaging in sophisticated diatribes against authority and tradition); Sanjay forces him to steal from his own father's mobile phone warehouse; and he is trapped in a culminating scene of violence in which the store is torched and he is severely beaten by assailants who could be Samira's brothers and could be Hardjit's crew. These dramatic events leave him emotionally vulnerable, able in a last-page twist revelation to expose what we have until then been only somewhat clued in to: his recent masculine posturing is motivated by deep-seated psychological burdens that include, most notably, his shame about the fact that his parents are actually white. He is too.

The novel's defining formal elements are encapsulated in its opening sentences. It begins with a line of dialogue: "Serve him right he got his muthafuckin face fuck'd, shudn't b callin me a Paki, innit." This is Hardjit speaking—Harjit until recently, but he inserted the "d" to reflect his appreciation for his own macho physique—and he is justifying a beating that readers will now witness alongside the supporting cast of thuggish friends: "After spittin his words out Hardjit stopped for a second, like he expected us to write em down or someshit. Then he sticks in an exclamation mark by kicking the white kid in the face again" (3).

We notice right away their striking patois, a blend here of foul language, cockney slang ("innit"), and text-message shorthand ("b" for "be" and "em" for "them"), which in later pages incorporates vocabulary and locutions from a global hodgepodge of hip-hop, reggae, and South Asian street cultures. Jas's conscientious parroting of this amalgam resonates with some trends in post–World War II fiction: the use of nonstandard demotic forms of English for dialogue and narration, common to Irvine Welsh, James Kelman, and Roddy Doyle, among others; and the ironic tendency of some celebrated works, for instance, Martin Amis's *Money*, to both glory in and satirize themselves as literature's approximation of "slumming it." Also important is the ironic voice of the distant narrator, witness to a scene in which he is not quite participating. In this case his mocking appreciation of his leader's self-regard is particularly telling. The suggestion that Hardjit may wish to leave his friends the time to record his inspired utterances is our first clue that Jas can be read as a figure for Malkani himself. Through his careful use of several paratexts that closely accompanied the book's release, including his official website and a substantial article in the *Financial Times*'s weekend magazine, Malkani has stressed the fact that *Londonstani* is a fictional encapsulation of his ethnographic research about the interconnections between ethnicity and masculinity in the community of second- and third-generation British-Asians now often called "Desis." He used his own childhood friends in Hounslow as primary subjects, and his research formed the basis for a thesis he wrote for his Cambridge undergraduate degree in social and political sciences. In gathering this data, he found himself observing and recording lines of dialogue just like Hardjit's, collecting enough material to fill reams of tape and paper that he had no use for when writing up his findings. After he failed at his initial effort to use this set of materials to write a work of nonfiction, *Londonstani* was born.

Malkani completed the manuscript while still in his twenties, in the evenings, after his day job directing the Creative Business pages at the *Financial Times.* Meanwhile, he also penned articles on topics such as conglomeration in the media industries; the Desi subculture that shows like MTV Desi and the BBC's *Desi DNA* constitute as a consumer niche; the increasing relevance of the "brown pound"; and the fact that young South Asians seem to be inordinately drawn toward popular culture, new media, and consumer electronics, and not, Malkani laments, very much toward literary fiction—a situation he claims to have set out to rectify by giving *Londonstani* its particular form.[26] So far there is little evidence that the book has appeal for an untapped market of South Asian teenagers. What is clear, though, is that when the manuscript was unveiled at the Frankfurt Book Fair, it captured the feverish interest of Britain's largely white, middle-aged literati. The proverbial bidding war ensued, attracting much attention before wrapping in a two-book contract that Fourth Estate secured with an undisclosed six-figure advance. They released the novel in May 2006, and various foreign rights deals with prominent transnational publishing houses soon followed.

The attention granted this debut work has been explained in several persuasive ways. Some speculate that the book's focus on young South Asian men in Britain answered calls for insight into a community vilified after 9/11, and especially after July 2005, when a ring of aspiring terrorists had their London bomb plot foiled. The term "Londonstani" sounds an awful lot like "Londonistan," a common moniker for the new breed of young extremists living hidden lives in London's boroughs.[27] That Malkani's central characters are not Muslim but Sikh and Hindu, and not plotting terrorists but petty criminals and aspiring capitalists, would not stop potential readers from making their own connections. Malkani purportedly worried that his decision to hold on to the title might be viewed as false advertising for a book that has little to do with what most people think of when they hear it mentioned.

Others wonder if Malkani is particularly ripe for marketing as the next in a distinguished line of minority writers, each hyped as an important new voice delivering previously unheard stories to bookstore shelves. The success of figures like Monica Ali and Zadie Smith simply "spurred another energetic hunt for the latest hot ethnic minority,"[28] and Malkani was their ideal successor because, as Fourth Estate editor Nicholas Pearson opined, his work revealed "a world you've never read about in fiction."[29] Crucial here is the book's claim to be a unique cultural property covering territory as yet unknown within English prose, translating a distinct community's experiences into a solo-authored text that fills "a gap in the market" like the one that inspires Jas's gang's mobile phone tampering. In the words of Diana Evans, herself an award-winning minority figure, "Every year now there is at least one novel from a black, Asian or other 'nongora' writer that is deemed the multicultural event of the literary scene."[30] Malkani ensures himself a shot at this role because his work comprises material derived from his own identification with a specific underrepresented community and because he has established himself as an accredited member of the media elite who has niche expertise about the lifestyle choices of young South Asians.

It hardly follows, however, that Malkani was made responsible in some straightforward way for representing the group he claims to want to transform into an audience for literature and for which he has become a spokesperson. Rather, for marketing purposes it was evidently more useful for the author's authenticity—and for the relevance of such terminology—to be in question all along: to form the center of a debate that critics can then have about the work, to be an anchor for their commentary on it, and to pose a puzzle for the reader to piece together while working through the text. On the front of the first US hardcover Malkani's publisher quotes the *Observer's* praise for *Londonstani* as a "bold debut, brimming with energy and authenticity"; however, though only one critic explicitly condones the notion, nearly every major review states that it might be faulted as inauthentic, the product of its Cambridge-educated, urban anthropologist-cum-journalist author's attempts to seem "street" by aping the street slang of Desi rude boys in outer London.

Trevor Lewis of the *Sunday Times* offers the only direct condemnation in these terms, stating that Malkani is attempting "to palm off here as keeping-it-real verisimilitude" what is in fact "eight-carat phoniness" and claiming that "while the author fancies himself as a mimic of urban yoof-speak, there is a hollow ring to the Hounslow-born, Cambridge-educated, Creative Business editor of the *Financial Times* trying so self-consciously to appear, ahem, down with the kids."[31] In the *Independent on Sunday*, before concluding that the novel actually transcends such charges, Tim Martin muses:

It's marketed as a street-level transmission from elusive old multicultural Britain, that El Dorado of the publishing world that publishers claim, year after year, to have located in yet another sluggish tale of love and loss in London. . . . It's a story of teenage rudeboys on the streets of Hounslow that's written, somewhat paradoxically, by the Cambridge-educated editor of the *Financial Times* Creative Business pages.[32]

Similarly, Evans claims to have read the book with some wariness about Malkani's "suspiciously anthropological lens on a disaffected London tribe"; still, she decides that the novel manages to be better than she had worried. And finally, rather than "dismissing it all as a sub Ali-G spoof," Zoë Paxton takes the question to the kids themselves in her review for the *Times*. After reading out passages to a class of teens at a Hounslow school, she concludes that "it turns out Malkani does know what he's talking about."[33]

These reviews, along with several others making parallel claims, are quoted at length on the "Press" page of Malkani's own website, suggesting that in addition to the possibilities already mentioned—its focus on recalcitrant South Asian youth, and Malkani's suitability for market incorporation—another pressing reason for his success is precisely the way Malkani and his co-producers actively instigated authenticity debates through a series of high-profile authorized paratexts. Malkani's ready access to the mainstream press certainly helps here: *Londonstani* is unique among recent literary fiction for the clarity and extent of the interpretive framework the author has provided its readers, suggesting to them exactly what meaning to find in it and what context to consider when unraveling its larger significance. The most telling features of this guidance are persistent reminders that the book communicates the findings of Malkani's research for a Cambridge degree and repeated claims that it is less about ethnicity and more about his subjects' pursuit of sufficiently convincing masculine identities. Along these lines, he describes the twist ending, revealing that "Jas" is actually "Jason Bartholomew-Cliveden, aged nineteen, white" (331), as the starting point for the fictionalization process, since "it seemed the most effective way of making the point that this stuff's not about race or ethnicity, but about how those identities are used like tools to be more of a man."[34] A person with reason to attempt to assume a Desi rude boy persona needn't be South Asian. By paying sufficient attention to the subculture's rules and conventions, anyone can do it, even a white guy.

This possibility points to a blaring reality that has escaped the notice of other commentators: the novel is itself fundamentally interested in the problem of authenticity—specifically, the difficulty one might encounter when seeking access to and then speaking for a group to which one belongs only problematically. We have seen that *Londonstani*'s market success derives in part from its circulation as a product tainted by suspicion about the nature of the author's relationship to the subculture voiced in it, and this situation may be one that Malkani and his supporters encourage, clearly welcoming the opportunity to associate his work with a debate proven to help one enter the limelight and stay there for longer than might otherwise be possible. At the same time, the text itself works to undermine the logic behind the idea that the author might be guilty of appropriative posturing.

It would be easy to arrive at an overly simplistic conception of this process, observing that, rather than endeavoring to prove he possesses the authenticity he anticipates will be called into question, the author suggests that anything inauthentic in his own behavior finds its mirror in the performing masculinities of his characters. It is certainly true that despite their macho strutting Hardjit, Ravi, and Amit are presented as a group of wannabe gangsters rather than as actual thugs. Their expensive cars belong to their wealthy mothers, who deliver samosas and sodas to the safe suburban bedrooms their sons occupy while tampering with phones and arranging future business deals. On his website Malkani makes this point explicit, stating that "the young men in the book are supposed to be wannabe bad-boys rather than the real thing and are therefore pretty much all talk."[35] Meanwhile, in interview he declares surprise that "some sections of the British press" question his authenticity. After all, "he grew up in Hounslow and went to a local school," and, more important, he states exasperatedly, "that's what the kids in the book are doing! . . . These are not ghetto street kids. These are middle-class mama's boys. They talk about Hounslow as if it's the ghetto, but they live in five-bedroom houses in an affluent suburb."[36] In essence, if the writer cannot claim to be authentic, neither can anyone else.

This line of analysis is not without some merit. However, Malkani's way of handling the question of authenticity, in both the novel and in the paratextual discourse he has authored to attend it, is ultimately somewhat more layered. While dismantling the requirement that he accrue street credibility, he also appeals to an alternative source of validation: academic expertise. This ensures that if he cannot claim to be a rude boy himself, he still maintains some kind of grasp on "the real," granted to him because the novel's surface argument—that its characters' hard-man antics disguise emasculating social scars left by their assimilating elders' quiescence in the face of racism—is grounded in empirical research accredited by a major university and subsequently detailed in the *Financial Times*.

Malkani's repeated claims to affiliation with an institutionally based site of urban anthropology work to validate the claim of his fiction to unmask the pretenses behind the subculture to which he only had partial access. The forms of authority that signal his distance from the subculture, as he fled to Cambridge to become a member of London's creative class, are also precisely what grant him the insight—and the platform and the reason—to understand its "real" meaning. Thus, while the novel raises the question of one's access to an authentic community connection and then attempts to exempt the author from it, so that Malkani benefits from association with a known set of hype-generating controversies while avoiding being fundamentally implicated, it works simultaneously to solidify his position as an authorized first-person observer of diverse social and cultural realities translated into literature.

Relevant here is what happened when Malkani first conceived of the research that later went into the novel. For advising he approached Dr. Susan Benson, a recognized authority on the sociology of ethnicity in Britain, informing her that he wanted to study "the beef between this relatively new breed of hardcore Asian 'rudeboys' and 'coconuts'—a term of abuse for Asians who, despite their brown skin, are deemed to be 'white' on the inside because of their assimilation into mainstream British society." He states that part of his motivation was a simple desire to go back to Hounslow and hang out with his "mates"—not a legitimate scholarly purpose, it seems, since his research proposal suffered a thorough working over to ensure that it was "academically acceptable." He claims, surely half jokingly, that Dr. Benson instigated the following changes: the phrase "my mates" was replaced with "ethnographic informants"; "boundary" stepped in for "beef"; and he acquired a new subtitle, "Assertive Ethnicity, Masculinity and Identity," which was more appropriate than his own choice, "Chocolate Flavoured Coconut Milk."[37]

These purported alterations to the language of his initial proposal are more than cosmetic. Though Malkani is recasting his experience for some comic effect, his account signals his self-awareness about changes to his mode of self-presentation required for initiation into the role of apprentice anthropologist. The process continued with Dr. Benson's persuasive appeals to the value of maintaining distance from his subjects, even while acting as a participant-observer. The subjects he was attempting to study belong to a community whose codes of behavior mandate opacity and secrecy, making it particularly difficult for familiars to share any insights with one another. As the novel itself avers, part of the appeal of the rude boy lifestyle is that its modes of belonging present deliberate barriers to outsiders, who are meant to find it hard to relate to or sympathize with. How these young men talk is the best example. Their lingo makes sense only after one has been exposed to it at some length, much like the language of academic anthropology was obscure to Malkani until he became familiar with it over time. Moreover, to have any insight into one's own nature is to possess a level of self-knowledge and a propensity for introspection that the Hounslow rude boys seem to frown upon, associating self-awareness with being a "coconut" or "batty" (that is, homosexual).

Realizing the barriers this presented to his research, Malkani found that strangers were more willing to act as informants, sharing thoughts that their subculture's rules normally required them to be silent about. If he wanted to learn more than he could observe by skulking at the edges of the community, he would have no choice but to get over his initial shyness and approach these new people with direct questions. "Sure," Malkani writes, "it might make me feel like an idiot when I approached potential informants, but in the long term it would be a more efficient way of gathering insights into a community I'd presumed I already knew so well."[38]

By the lights of this apprenticeship narrative, when Malkani relied on existing relationships with his "mates," he found it difficult to learn what he needed to know about them. Having severed himself from them after leaving Hounslow, it seems that, as Dr. Benson predicted, when Malkani returned, his old friends proved reluctant to share information with a person following them around with a tape recorder, a pad of paper, and a newly acquired set of academic terminology. These barriers were erected as the author underwent the process of transforming his own former community—a place to which he remains fitfully attached—into the subject matter for his intellectual property, in the form first of academic research and then of fiction.

The fact that Malkani faced these barriers is what determined the form of the final story that *Londonstani* tells, making it a remnant of the situation of Malkani's interpolation into the role of apprentice anthropologist and, ultimately, creative labor. This interpolation required that he move beyond one "voice"—one set of social affiliations—in order to gain the authority to speak about the milieu to which he no longer quite belonged, and it led to his discovery that such authority then paradoxically secured the old voice's unavailability to him. Put slightly differently, when Malkani left behind the Hounslow rude boy milieu, located at the margins of London and of respectability, and became a member of the creative class and an authority on subcultural Desi identities, it is *Londonstani* that ushered him into the realm of mainstream success. The book is the end point of the novelist's apprenticeship to the creative class and instigation for his emergence into celebrity. It is also, however, a record of the process through which the author came to assume the authority to arrive at his act of representation, as its material and technique involve significant refraction of the politics of social location that at once trouble and legitimate that act's origins, gestation, and fruition. It might even be said to obfuscate these politics, if its attempt to constrain readers' perception of them—and ultimately of Malkani himself—was less transparent.

Malkani evidently figures himself in Jas by making him a quasi-anthropological outsider perched between conflicting modes of self-presentation and lionized for the self-reflexivity that he alone possesses. The one man apart, a spectator whose way of relating to his friends is a version of Malkani's way of interacting with those he decided to use as research subjects, Jas embodies the author's self-consciousness about what prevented him from attaining that elusive capital that might grant untroubled access to the subculture. For instance, his intelligence is a boon to him because he can use it to study the speech and mannerisms he adopts while seeking the belonging absent when he was just another white kid from outer London; but it is also precisely what he has to hide in order to get close enough to his new friends to earn their trust. As a result the line between Jas the participant-observer and Jas the genuine friend is effectively blurred, which makes it so easy for his "mates" to turn against him as the narrative unfolds.

Jas's concern about learning the rude boys' ways is mostly articulated as worry about his inability to talk "proper." His knowledge that he cannot quite achieve the right mix of words is a constant reminder that he is not "the real thing"; and "being real" is essential or even analogous to attaining the masculine prowess the characters desire. Malkani explains:

Speech patterns are the characters' main measure of manliness and virility. Mobile phones and tongues become the book's two phallic symbols. . . . Speech and phones are the tools the characters use to get away from their mothers, yet they're also the same things their mothers try to regulate them with. So they're a bit like weapons.[39]

This is clearly the source of "proper" speech's appeal for Jas, who has been shy and withdrawn from an early age. Reflecting on his former self, Jas observes: "I was a ponce, I acted an sounded like a batty, I was a skinny wimp . . . I couldn't usually talk proply an even when I did I couldn't ever say the right thing" (25–26). Hardjit proves willing to help "cure" him, and Jas finds a more confident voice only when he begins to use Hardjit as a model on which to base his aping of rude boy speech and behavior, much as Malkani himself found his academic footing in Dr. Benson's patient guidance and through careful study of work by Erving Goffman and Tariq Modood, but then found he had to shirk his Cambridge tones when trying to gather ethnographic data for this thesis research.[40]

For Jas, the road to true confidence is a ragged one, messy with false starts and embarrassing slipups. For instance, after watching his leader unleash his aggression in the book's opening scene, Jas has the sense that he is expected to chime in with some words of support. The result is that he utters haltingly: "Kill his fuckin . . . well, is fuckin, you know, him. Kill him." He then pulls back, characteristically, and critically observes this contribution by suggesting:

This was probly a bit over the top but I think I'd got the tone just right an nobody laughed at me. At least I managed to stop short a sayin, kill the pig, like the kids do in that film *Lord a the Flies*. It's a book too, but I'm trying to stop knowin shit like that. (9)

These lines could easily point to Malkani's own writing process, as the author worried about whether or not he could achieve the right tone in capturing some essence of the rude boys' speech patterns. This kind of parallel is often apparent when Jas conveys his crippling self-consciousness about the words he voices and the thoughts he entertains in the process of attempting to achieve what is required for inclusion. Indeed, the problem is all too clear to him. He needs to forget willfully what he already knows, since to reveal his learning is to distinguish himself too much from the other members of the group, who are determinedly two-dimensional and tend to call Jas "batty" whenever he says anything too "deep." As Malkani explains about Ravi, one of the novel's least-developed characters: "He views having depth of character as weak and effeminate."[41]

In these terms, the formal question of depth of characterization is explained away as the precise opposite of a flaw in the work's composition: it is a deliberately penned and important aspect of the characters' identities. Accordingly Jas has prescribed himself a steady diet of cultural materials that will help him be, in essence, a flatter character. "I swear I've watched as much MTV Base an Juggy D videos as they have," he tells us. Still, somehow, "the right level a rudeboy authenticity" (6) continues to elude him. Even if he can stop himself from vocalizing his thoughts—and often he cannot—Jas's inability to rid his mind of certain kinds of self-conscious knowledge and certain patterns of inner articulation continues to secure his outsider positioning. Ideally, he muses, "I wouldn't be using poncey words like attain an authenticity, innit. I'd be sayin I couldn't keep it real or someshit. An if I said it that way, then there'd be no need for me to say it in the first place so I wouldn't say it anyway" (6). Again, this passage clearly suggests that Jas sees his own tendency toward introspection as the surest sign that he cannot quite manage to "keep it real." He only needs to think the word "authenticity" because it is something he is worried that he does not possess, and worrying about not possessing it always means that you do not.

His introspection here, as throughout the novel, involves a metaresponse, a reflection on his own self-reflection, evincing what Sianne

Ngai has identified as the constant doubleness of negative feelings: we feel them, but also feel like we shouldn't be feeling them.[42] This is also the clear source of Jas's appeal and distinction. That his various voices are constantly jostling for position and that he is awkward, anxious, self-conscious, and ceaselessly introspective are celebrated within the course of the narrative and are meant to endear Jas to us. His predicament is a platform for celebration of the observer's anxious self-awareness; it is a welcome alternative to the other characters' unselfconscious participation in what is basically represented as a set of antisocial and self-deceiving macho postures.

The significance of the special distinction granted Jas becomes clearer when we remember the reluctance of Malkani's research subjects to reveal themselves to him. On what basis did the researcher-cum-author determine how much of what they said and did was a deliberately and self-consciously enacted performance and how much a deeply embodied identity they had no introspective awareness about? Where do deeply felt affective affiliation and deliberate ironic performance part ways in the rude boys' case? These questions, surely crucial ones for sociologists and anthropologists, are precisely what Malkani sidesteps, obfuscating his blocked access to the rude boys' interiority by settling his representation on an absence that resides *in them*, one that marks them as actors who are simultaneously inauthentic posers and woefully unaware of the psychic motivations behind their performances. What might just as well have been a product of a crucial limitation in the researcher's apprehension is construed as a sociological fact unearthed through a careful amassing of data.

In the *Financial Times* Malkani writes:

Nowadays people often have to work really hard and/or imagine really hard instead of just having their identity and life simply handed to them because of their surname or gender or class or caste or whatever. Our identities are therefore a performance (I should namecheck a famous sociologist called Erving Goffman here). The point of the twist [revealing that Jas is white], and other bits of the book, is to show the extent to which this can even be a fictionalised performance.[43]

Yet *Londonstani* itself puts pressure on this claim, as it suggests that despite the fact that our identities are "fictionalised," they may still be experienced as authentic, as things that have been "handed" to us and that we rarely contemplate. That we think we have some understanding of an aspect of our self-presentation hardly means there is no part of us that does not escape our own introspective analytical eye. The virility of Hounslow's Asian subculture is the "fictionalised performance" Malkani is referencing, but they do not have the self-awareness to know as much, and that is precisely why they are available for the satirical, flat characterization that makes them Jas's antagonists and foils. Thus, what Malkani is doing when he "namechecks" Goffman is making a claim about how people *should* experience their identities; he is positing a normative self-consciousness that celebrates the knowingly "fictional" and uses it as a standard against which other kinds of behavior should be assessed. In addition, his own intentions as a literary author are then described as a desire to unearth these performances, since the twist "and other bits of the book" are motivated by his revelation of a sociological point.

Something similar occurs when Malkani describes the patois that is so important to his aesthetic and such a focus of concern for Jas. Rather than a slice-of-life representation of actual conversations overheard during his research period, the speech given to *Londonstani*'s characters is actually a knowingly hodgepodge authorial construction. The system Malkani used to create it is so intricate that his website provides a downloadable guide explaining its logic. He writes:

What I didn't want to do was capture an exact picture of the way people talk by writing it just as I was hearing it . . . because slang changes all the time and words and phrases would've been out of date by the time the book was published (if indeed it ever got published). Creating a kind of futureproof, timeless slang— instead of taking a snapshot at any particular moment in time—basically meant taking popular words from different years that have already stood the test of time and then stitching them together. . . . So, just like every other aspect of the characters' identities, their seemingly random slang is actually carefully constructed and contrived.[44]

Malkani's reflections here on his own procedures exemplify an important aspect of *Londonstani*. The author creates a contrived version of rude boy slang because he understandably wants his book to have greater longevity and a wider readership than it might otherwise. To present a transcribed version of what he heard in the streets of Hounslow would be to encode a kind of difference posing too many problems for his potential readership, and too many barriers to his narrative's future relevance and circulation. Yet Malkani's explanation of his aesthetic decision does not rest there. Instead, he uses his discussion of the language that is such a crucial part of "the characters' identities" as a platform to make a further point about his real research subjects in Hounslow (here, those "people" he decided not to attempt to capture with "an exact picture"). In his conflating logic, it is their very identities that are "carefully constructed and contrived," and his apprehension and representation of them are simply the best means of conveying that fact.

The pressing thing about these identities is, again, how shallow they are. The subculture mandates that one should never reveal self-awareness, and it denies the outsider's desire to attain knowledge about it, making it at best difficult to determine how much of what its members do or say has to do with any "true" interiority. This set of circumstances is something that *Londonstani* and its accoutrements paper over, as the author offers his portrayal not as partial knowledge fundamentally constrained by a research situation that was troubled by complex social realities and antagonisms but as a representation of "real" data ordained by academic accreditation. His subject's lack of authenticity is depicted as something revealed and explained through real knowledge that Malkani, and now his self-reflexive and intelligent readers, has the wherewithal to possess.

Thus, where *Londonstani* makes it impossible to charge Malkani with appropriation or mimicry, because it subscribes to the notion that, universally, the self is a performance, it is nevertheless the case that rather than displace the hierarchy between the real and the false, it sets about repurposing those terms for the fight between self-conscious knowledge and unselfconscious, though performed, action. Again, what is set up as the crucial distinction between Malkani and his characters is what separates Jas from his friends: his intelligence and education and his willingness to use these things to arrive at a better understanding of something that he is at once a part of and separate from, an understanding that is necessary for some other expedient purpose—attaining a degree, or writing a hype-worthy novel, or gaining the self-confident voice that formerly eluded him.

An attentive reading of *Londonstani*'s paratexts suggests that achieving street credibility involves a series of complicated rules about what one needs to possess to achieve inclusion; and the more academic and literary credentials you accrue, the less likely it is that you will be able to follow these rules, especially if you are adhering to them to accumulate yet more distinguishing and distancing credentials. Nevertheless, the novel itself celebrates Jas's superior insight and does so as a means of abjuring the gaps in access that colored Malkani's own apprenticeship to urban anthropology—the apprenticeship that eased his entry into London's creative economy and, translated into fiction, secured his extensive circulation within the literary marketplace.

As one Hounslow teen opined after hearing *Londonstani* read aloud in her classroom, "He has got everything right. . . . But it's too exaggerated and you would never, ever, write these words down."[45] The way that Malkani delimits the drama of this division—the division between talking a certain way and deciding to seek authorization to write that speech down—is through Jas's superior self-consciousness, the thing that at once torments him and serves his purposes as he subjects his friends to careful observation in order to ape them most effectively. Thus, Malkani's encounter with the border between the two dominant definitions of culture mentioned in the previous chapter, taking culture as the sanctioned expression of individual genius or as the nonreflexive mores of a community, results in a work that reaffirms that border's bases by lionizing his own expertise and the self-reflexivity of the creative elite figured in Jas.

Malkani's treatment of his material can be said then to intimate his wish to alleviate some of his own unease about the relationship between his novel, his career, and his old community. If his experiences are encoded in Jas's, this is true in a way that he never openly acknowledges, either in the novel itself or in its extensive paratextual accoutrements. It seems unlikely that he could have been unaware of the connections between their shared struggles to capture the rude boys' voices. Still, he chose not to make Jas into an obvious or self-consciously fictional version of himself, perhaps because to do so would have been to open himself up to the charge that his work is self-defensive and solipsistic, a calculated means to police his emerging career and persona just as they begin to take shape. Jas is thus a figure for Malkani, but one that is partially disguised—still a product of the author's wish to police his own reception but meant to be more effective because it is not too obviously tied to his own identity. He is an anxious symptom, disavowed rather than misrecognized.

This suggests a rather careful procedure. The author must invoke certain dilemmas in order to displace them and do it in a way that is not so obvious as to jeopardize the overall effect. He seems to anticipate not just a discerning readership but one on the lookout for signs that the author has too keen an interest in self-justification or too keen a need to find ways to explain his decision to make the rude boys his first literary subject. And ultimately Malkani's anxiety about the novel's reception betters him, since it results in his extensive efforts to assert the novel's origins in fact-based accredited research. Once we have reckoned with these autobiographical ruminations on the novel, the connections between Jas and Malkani become clear, and the reason for his emphasis on the superiority of the narrator's self-awareness does as well. At which point, as in Nagra's work, every aspect of the novel begins to read as Malkani's means of refracted engagement with his own labor. The book at once avoids and encodes the multifaceted process through which he learned to assume a voice that would be recognized within an academic discipline; encountered barriers to access as he struggled to find footing and informants within a milieu to which he once belonged with more ease; and discovered that assuming the posture of participant-observer that brought him there to begin with was also the thing that displaced his access to the community whose foreignness to literary representation was part of what made his manuscript such an important commodity. In this light, though its apparent concern is depicting the rude boys' struggles with masculinity and ethnicity, what the book actually gives voice to is the negative affect of a new member of London's creative class. Like Jas, he is self-reflexive and introspective, by turns committed to the superiority of his own self-consciousness and unable to manage his worry that the whole thing—the degree, the book, the job at the *Financial Times*—is some kind of elaborate ruse, about to be uncovered at every moment. But so is everything else, the novel reminds us.

Authenticity and Literary Labor

There are revealing parallels between Malkani's technique, which involves raising and then displacing concerns about the depth of his access to rude boy psychology, and the terms of the novel's reception. *Londonstani*'s reviewers evidently wished to discuss the problem of authenticity in a particular way. They were careful to indicate that there might be sound reason to worry about the legitimacy of Malkani's connection to Hounslow, but then mostly agreed that his work cannot really be called inauthentic or appropriative. They raise the question and then displace any worries that attend it by stating that Malkani seems to "get it right," having produced a piece of writing that is much more than "slumming it," and more canny than it might be—but almost never was—accused of being. For most reviewers, designating Malkani's work as worthy of literary interest requires careful indication that he has a larger purpose; it might be said to be just a literary first, but it is actually more than that and therefore better than the reality of its marketability. More exactly, two particular and interlocking concerns seem to arise for commentators and then need to be displaced: Malkani's work is inauthentic, and it is nothing more than marketable. In order for the work to be redeemed and given an aesthetic purpose, the reviewer attempts to show that it does more than simply secure Malkani's entrée into the market by the simple fact of its being about a highly visible British-Asian youth subculture. Hence, the extent of the links between the writer's identity, his characters, and an anthropological reality—a major concern in Malkani's own commentary on the novel, as we have seen—tends to be mentioned early on and then downplayed, as emphasis shifts to his masterful invention of the rude boys' language and to his use of the material of their lives to present a serious message about what happens to young men when their parents fail to provide them with fitting models of male behavior. The integrity of Malkani's connection to the rude boys is thus, for most reviewers, much less important than the extent of his connection to a superior creative sensibility that is its own form of authenticity and that unites participants in the conversation while distinguishing them from others less knowing.

This tendency in Malkani's reception suggests that the competing forms of authenticity mentioned earlier—authenticity as community affiliation and authenticity as self-referencing expression—exist in a productive tension. Relevant to their intermingling is Michael Denning's recent challenge to two definitions of cultural practice dominant throughout much of the past century. One of these reads culture as "civility," and the other interprets it as "solidarity" so that it is either, after Matthew Arnold, a collection of "the best that is known and thought in the world" or, after E. B. Tylor, "the complex of values, customs, beliefs and practices which constitute the way of life of a specific group."[46] According to Denning what unites these seemingly divergent views is their mutual tendency to construe the cultural sphere as precisely that which is outside capital and is, therefore, authentic. Both deploy the term "culture" as a means "to name those places where the commodity does not yet rule," whether they are occupied by "the arts, leisure, and unproductive luxury consumption of revenues by the accumulators" or "the ways of life of so-called primitive peoples." Denning contends instead that culture is first and foremost "the product and result" of labor. Culture always involves work, because it is constituted by labor and is also "a name for that habitus that forms, subjects, disciplines, entertains, and qualifies labor power."[47] He maintains that recognizing the constitutive relationship between culture and work is a means of avoiding the division between manual and mental labor or between labor as conception and labor as execution. This is a division that is falsely and even tragically propagated within capitalism, and it is mirrored in these same broad conceptions of culture—as the best expression of individual geniuses or as the nonreflexive mores of a community—that Denning wishes definitively to displace.

Denning's approach is telling because, as the language of collectivity and community is subsumed into the workings of the creative economy, Nagra and Malkani seem to experience the labor of producing culture as a pained conversion of "collective symbolic capital," which we can read as an anthropological cultural horde or "culture as solidarity," into individual, self-distinguishing self-expression, which we can perceive as Arnoldian "best" culture or "culture as civility." For these writers the successful circulation of the output of their labor appears to depend upon its claim to having a monopoly on a particular, unique, irreducible form of expression borrowed from forms of community affiliation in which they do not entirely believe.[48] These conditions foster the writer's expressions of embarrassment about and disavowal of the affiliations he draws upon in order for his work to circulate as unique and brand-worthy cultural property. Thus, concern about an authenticating representative status and about an authenticating art of self-expressive self-definition emerges in tandem in a close though discordant synthesis.

Denning supports the common distinction between the process of simply working and the process that valorizes the products of labor or between "the material content of purposive human activity and the specific form labor takes under capitalism."[49] In the case of writers this might be reformulated as the common tension between the work of writing and the often traumatic experience of seeing one's writing turned into a freely circulating item. Yet such a divide seems at best precariously maintained, not least because authors often find material fit for transformation into literary property in the very experience of working as writers, experience that includes their fate at the hands of the processes of circulation and valorization. We might take their work as indicative of the way in which literature has been another site of the "war over measure" within creative capitalism, meaning the struggle of those engaged in immaterial, creative, cognitive work over the *"what, how, how much, why* and *who"* of a system of production that deifies individual subjectivity, feeling, emotion, intelligence, and communication, that makes them measurable and profitable, and that appears to welcome even those who work against measurement's instrumental ends.[50]

In both Malkani's and Nagra's work we find consciousness of the operations of literary value. The work imagines how it will be validated within the market as a product of the writer's labor—here, first and foremost through its connection to a community underrepresented in literature. The writer activates that connection but also indicates his ironic distance and even alienation from it. Meanwhile, the act of predicting and lamenting the constraints operative within the process of valuation, which we can read as the author's resistance to his own labor value, remains an additional source of distinct value for his work. The act of predicting and lamenting is what he adds to it to ensure its value has sources other than its attachment to a purportedly organic community underrepresented in literature and in the marketplace of consumers.

Nagra's *Look We Have Coming to Dover!*, at once a carefully packaged product and a collection of poems that is self-conscious about its marketed production, is a form of metabranding that labors against the fact that the author's access to value within the market depends upon his ability to inhabit a literary space that had not yet been occupied by any English child of Punjabi immigrants. Though less self-consciously, Malkani's *Londonstani* is motivated by related desires: by outing its characters as a group of unselfconscious performers to which the expressive literary writer owes no loyalty, it preempts an imaginary injunction to "keep it real." Thus, in either case the distinction between literary labor and its valuation within the marketplace appears to evaporate. The transformation of the writer's labor into products, products that meaningfully *embody* or simply *are* the writer's labor, becomes a problem that is continually staged and restaged within the work itself. That staging is a signal part of what the work—and the brand—is. I began this chapter by asserting that if naïve claims about a writer's intimate access to her purported community exist within government policy supporting various kinds of diversity programming, authors and audiences have been more inclined to fan the flames of controversy over the authenticity of these connections and to probe the relevance of the idea of authenticity to literary interpretation. Nagra's and Malkani's texts are particularly troubled by the notion that the writer's job is to make salable creative content out of the experiences of underprivileged or disenfranchised populations and thus to transform formerly unnoticed but newly attractive forms of collective experience into privately held intellectual property. They take on the idea that success in the creative economy requires appealing to one's relationship to a distinct, diverse, underrepresented collective, whose experiences are thus repurposed for the author's individual capture of niche-market positioning. They register frustration with the notion of a connection between their market access and their representation of an authentic street-level world of communities formerly unknown to literary treatment, where these communities are conflated with the Real, and where reference to these communities' experiences, filtered through the self-generated and self-expressive spark of original insight, becomes the grounds for the writer's copyrighted self-expression.[51] But their frustration is in fact a routine or even constitutive feature of the contemporary literary field, in which naïve notions of authenticity as cultural representativeness are more likely to be derided than upheld. With help from publishers, marketers, and the media, writers now seem deliberately to activate publicity-generating questions about how engagement with the Real is mediated by their elite social positions and educations, and about how real the Real is to begin with. In all this it is the model of authenticity as self-grounded expressivity that remains more or less intact. The priority granted reflexive concern with discovering the authentic, honest core of oneself, a core that exists apart from the community affiliations one might be assigned despite oneself and apart from the marketability of one's reflexive literary gestures, is constitutive of the literary field, so fundamental it is barely perceived.

6

The Strange Case
of the Writer-Consultant

The focus of this chapter is the phenomenon of British writers taking on commissions to consult with property developers on new buildings and area redevelopment projects. It thus outlines some very new purposes to which the aspiration and training to write are currently being put. Writers tend to work with developers in two main ways: the first can be deemed a poetic function and has some precedent, as they contribute words for public art to feature in new or revitalized structures; the second function is a newer one, focused on narrative, as they facilitate public storytelling about a region's history, present character, and possible futures before finding creative ways to convey the gist of what they have gathered for the public to read and for developers to consider and, at times, implement.

Involving a writer may appeal to developers and development agencies eager to address local residents' concerns about building projects and eager to present their work as enlightened by the public interest. Writers are for their part compelled to get involved for a number of reasons: some are genuinely committed to the work of urban renewal and see themselves as helping democratize the process; remuneration for more traditional writing for publication is poor and unpredictable; they are aware of the funding opportunities, tied to government investment in the idea of culture-led urban renewal, for artists committed to having a measurable impact; and they see commissions, which often involve collaboration and consultation with developers, other writers and artists, and the public, as source material and opportunity to develop their own literary writing.

It would be easy to argue that writers' willingness to position themselves as consultants to development schemes is evidence of the further attenuation of art's already etiolated autonomous critical relation to capital. Certainly, the rise of the writer-consultant is a manifestation of the use of culture as both an aid to gentrification and as a symptom of the unprecedented union of culture, economy, and governance to which this book responds. Yet we see in writers' own thinking about their work as consultants, and thus in the various products of their commissioned labor, the pressing fact of their concern about the precise relationship between art and what they identify as the official culture of the development establishment. Moreover, though they rarely index it directly to capital, they consistently describe this official culture in ways that acknowledge tacitly what David Harvey's *Rebel Cities* has recently claimed as its radical thesis: urban development is indivisible from the investment and renewal of surplus capital.[1] This chapter outlines how writers' descriptions of their commissioned work either evince some hesitant hope that they might play a role in reforming how the renewal of urban capital occurs or suggest that their job is to participate in ways that register opposition to the process from a resolutely marginal place within it. Even if their autonomy is imagined—and it would be as rash to argue that it is in every case as it would be to argue that it is never is—faith in it informs how writers engage with and understand the projects to which they are aligned. Far from making the question of the artist's relation to capital more passé than it already was, then, the specific work of the writer-consultant reveals the question's ongoing salience, as its permutations are inscribed in and inseparable from writers' fulfillment of their contracts.

As the most evident sign of the way the question of art's autonomy continues to press on artistic practice and on artists' self-conceptions, I focus on intimations that the value of consulting work lies in its very ineffectiveness and inexpedience or in its negation of the logic of regeneration, a negation that is thought to result, as it were naturally, from the writer's particular expertise. The writer-consultant inherits an older tradition of commissioning visual artists to create public art for property development and renewal, so she enters a world of work in which charges of gentrification are already well known. In 2004 the artists Hewitt & Jordan (Andy Hewitt and Mel Jordan) were commissioned by Public Art

FIGURE 3. Image of a 2004 billboard by Hewitt & Jordan. Courtesy Andy Hewitt and Mel Jordan.

Forum, a network of public art agencies and consultants, to make a piece for a wall in a dilapidated area of Sheffield. Their response was to erect a plain white billboard reading "The economic function of public art is to increase the value of private property."

Rather than refuse the commission, the artists ensured their response to it would do its work reluctantly, that it would contain its own commentary on the task it was assigned. The piece is thus at once the result of the commission and an assertion of autonomy from the driving rationality behind the commission's existence, that is, the rationality linking art to increased ground rents. Writers have approached working with developers in related ways, though with a difference that derives from a particular understanding of their unique medium. In what is emerging as the writer-consultant's main work, the literary author is imagined not as a singular voice of indignant opposition but as an expertly trained recorder of and vehicle for expression of the voices of those affected by the regeneration agenda.

Earlier chapters suggested that the creative-economy turn has involved an increasing tendency for policymakers to perceive and encourage the use of the arts as a gentrifying force. Once largely unwitting agents of rising property values—if they knew about them, they were loath to willingly encourage them—artists and other cultural workers will now deliberately position their own labor as worthy of government funding and corporate sponsorship precisely because of its capacity to add economic value to space. Writers' desire or willingness to imagine they have a marketable skill, to position creative writing as a public service available for commission, and training in writing as a means of investment in the self, should be conceived in relation to this broader tendency.

The London-based agency Spread the Word, a favorite of Arts Council England, is one of this tendency's clearest instances. Spread the Word organizes classes, workshops, and events to encourage reading and writing. It consistently connects its programming to the goal of revitalizing cities by fostering social inclusion and strengthening civic ties. It often targets participants from underprivileged areas of London where disenfranchised populations tend to be isolated, because it is within these communities that people are "least likely to have access to a varied cultural life."[2] Spread the Word boasts that it was one of twelve cultural organizations awarded part of the £500,000 allotted "to develop the creative skills of Londoners and increase their employment opportunities" in the lead-up the London 2012 Olympics, through the London Development Agency's 2012 London Cultural Skills Fund. In 2009 and 2010 it used this money to run a program called Encompass, described as a combination of "creative and practical training, mentoring, and hands on experience . . . developing [writers'] skills as community workshop leaders and increasing their employability in the field of creative writing."[3] This training is supposed to provide writers with the skills and opportunity to develop their own workshops for community groups across the five economically underprivileged London boroughs of Greenwich, Harrow, Croydon, Hounslow, and Waltham Forest. As Spread the Word projects often do, Encompass actively encouraged and supported applications from writers from Black, Asian and minority ethnic backgrounds and from those who are disabled.

Here we see much of the logic driving mainstream cultural practice in the UK. Terms like "skills" and "training" are constants, as are "practical," "hands on," and "participatory." To be sure, part of what arts organizations have to do in their public documents is present a face to power, and that face cannot possibly account for all the internal complexities and conflict within institutions. Still, Spread the Word's self-presentation, which is simply representative of many other arts agencies' current public faces, is itself telling. Whereas at one time it might have been permissible to state that arm's-length cultural agencies serve national public interest in a cultural sphere that is relatively autonomous from industry and politics, now their activities tend to be imagined as themselves simply facilitating culture's market potential, aiding its contribution to the stability of a national economy increasingly reliant on culture's immaterial goods. To risk stating the obvious, Spread the Word needs funding, and to secure funding, it develops projects that respond to funding protocols. Encompass imagines that it will train professional writers who will become members of a vibrant cultural workforce, integrated into a harmonious civic body rather than divided by diversities of race and class. This workforce will be dedicated to its own perpetuation, as Encompass workshops will train future workshop leaders, so the opportunities for growth are endless, so long as underprivileged communities exist. These communities are imagined as not yet fully integrated into the economy, not yet fully productive, and as able to use their innate creativity to write themselves out of their current contexts and into middle-class contentment.

Spread the Word's role in fostering urban renewal is more abstract than the direct consultative work that mostly concerns me here, but it gives us a sense of the landscape that writers need to navigate, the language they need to attend and appeal to as they work with developers, attempt to secure funds to support that work, and then sell the idea to other relevant parties as they seek further commissions. Often developers will seek public funds to support the involvement of a writer in their project, or it will be through a public-private arrangement, such as a regional development agency, that a writer is commissioned; public art consultancies, local councils, and regeneration agencies have all supported writers in this kind of work. The tasks that writer-consultants take on are similarly varied. They may be asked to write a new piece inspired by the location; this piece could be the author's own creation, or it could involve the collaboration of people who live in the area, whose views are solicited during workshops, area walks, and other forms of written and verbal survey and conversation. What results can be incorporated into the physical environment, whether permanently or temporarily, or it can appear on a website or in a publication distributed on-site or via a local newsletter.

Writers' thinking about this work is heterogeneous as well, but some main lines of justification and interest do emerge, and I suggest that each relates back to the key problematic of the nature of art's relationship to the development of urban capital. Sarah Butler is the major figure encouraging writers to consider working as consultants and providing developers with reasons to hire writers in these roles. She runs UrbanWords, the first organization to call itself a literary consultancy. Between UrbanWords and A Place for Words, an attendant Web resource for developers and a clearinghouse for writers' reflections on their work, we glimpse a compelling total picture of writer-consultants' reflexive self-conceptions.

It is understandable that Butler's take on her work should change with her prospective audience. When she is attempting to sell developers on the idea of working with writers, she cites a number of expedient ends: involving writers and artists can help "to positively engage a local community in a process of change and development"; it results in the creation of works that will attract visitors to the area; and it can help developers anchor new development in that attractive but elusive property, "a sense of place."[4] The UrbanWords website elaborates that cultivating this sense of place entails

finding ways to make connections between the past, present and future of a place in flux, to hold these often seemingly contradictory elements in tension, and by doing so to strengthen each. An area's physical, social, and cultural heritage, its ecology, and its future, offer rich seams which can be explored and embedded into the fabric and collective memory of a development. . . . Writers can work with communities to explore and capture the essence of a place, which can in turn inform and influence its physical regeneration. Well planned writing projects can enable people to discover the history of a place, and the relevance of that history to their own lives. They can help people to find their own creative responses to a place and to feel empowered to positively affect and be involved in its future. In doing so, such work helps create and preserve a unique sense of place for new developments, it honours and validates the history of a place, helps bring communities and individuals on board with change, and fosters a sense of ownership and pride which contributes to the continuing success of a place.[5]

This is an unusually idealized take on the writer-consultant's contribution to place-making, evidently meant to appeal to those in a position to commission writers. It imagines a kind of perfect communication between a writer and a relatively harmonious community, in which the writer achieves ready access to the diverse but shared experiences of this whole; it envisions developers who will be responsive to what the writer produces after consultation is completed; it imagines that they will "honour" and "validate" the history of a place in their building projects, that the community will "feel empowered" to be a part of the place's new future and will be thereby reconciled to change. Still, many of the tensions common to writer-developers' conceptions of their work are disguised only ineffectively by this particular iteration's blinkered optimism. One wonders, for example, if the writer is beholden to the public, the developer, or both. Is her task to intervene in and shape the development process itself or to help reconcile the public to its inevitability, by providing outlets for the expression of their hopes for the development and their concerns about what will become of their homes?

Having said this, I hasten to add that the majority of Butler's statements about development target other practitioners and are significantly more attentive to the widely acknowledged dark sides of the regeneration agenda. They tend to position the writer's engagement with the public as a means of witnessing the community's own opposition to the development process and of attempting to record its histories as a kind of salvage ethnography. The UrbanWords site claims that people react badly to the prospect of redevelopment because they have a "fear of the past being obliterated and a soulless development being plonked down in its place."[6] It is from developers' lack of attention to the intimate links between people and place that Butler appears to derive her own commitment to articulating their stories and then finding the most compelling ways to communicate them to decision makers. Hence, much like more polemical opponents to London's regeneration agenda, such as David Harvey, China Miéville, or Laura Oldfield Ford, Butler is concerned about the bleaching out of the diversity of public places, about the bland appearance of cappuccino-drinking sophisticates in architects' models, about erosion of public space. She claims to fear that "people who live in, and through that living create cities, are being shouldered out of this process of regeneration," while "those with the power to change our cities are too concerned with controlling and restricting our experience of place."[7]

The summary of a recent roundtable discussion on writers' involvement in urban renewal suggests Butler's concerns about gentrification and homogenization are widely shared. One discussant is reported to have asked, "If we are paid by the system, do we sacrifice our right and ability to be critical?" She further wonders whether, by willingly mediating between conflicting groups to find a "common narrative thread . . . writers become myth-makers who end up serving a dominant political or economic agenda, rather than questioning and subverting." A second discussant worries that writers might "become people who obscure and disenfranchise rather than illuminate and question" and assigns them a particular responsibility precisely because language is their foremost interest. Because "the jargon and the discourse of regeneration" will exclude and obfuscate while pretending to include and clarify, writers who get involved in regeneration have a special responsibility to point out these misuses of language and to "ensure that they look to include and explicate, rather than obscure."[8]

Writers' familiarity with the charge of gentrification appears in their discussions of the unique contribution they might make to the development process in the form of two key tensions. One tension is between a positive appraisal of regeneration as the renewal of communities and a negative critique of gentrification in the service of ground rents. The other tension is between a complacent conception of writers as superior and effective communicators who will bring developers just what they need (a willing public and locally resonant themes to repurpose as they try to cultivate a sense of place) and a critical conception of writers as outsider voices valuable precisely because they are trained to stress unresolved conflicts and to question the idea that their art has any expedient application. While we find in these discussions the idea that writers may have particular skills that suit them to regeneration work, right alongside it we encounter faith that the resonance of these skills derives from the very ways in which they put writers at odds with the development agenda.

Thus, on the one hand, in its affirmative mode, the UrbanWords site praises writers because they

can stand both within and outside of a situation; can care and yet be objective enough to see the complexities and the connections of a situation. They are well placed as commentators and facilitators, as people with a specific way of looking at the relationship between people and place. Good writing is accessible writing, and a poem or story can speak to a fifteen year old living on a housing estate as well as a property developer as well as a local councilor. It can inspire, question; spark conversation, contemplation and laughter. It can criticise without antagonising, and open up new ways of thinking and questioning.[9]

Writers are said to be the ideal creative consultants because they "look for what is not said" and "can turn messy, complicated issues into tight forms, dense with meaning and this . . . can become a powerful, transportable medium able to take the voices of the people directly affected by a process of regeneration to the people making the decisions about land use, housing density, [and] public space."[10]

On the other hand, intimating the fissures in its own affirmations, the site also notes the "real complexities and difficulties that plague communication between the breadth of partners involved." While all the interest groups are "ostensibly speaking the same language," the "communication gaps are vast and deep in places." The site carefully stresses that it does not imagine writers "will become willing and infallible conduits of information and ideas, that they will seamlessly negotiate the different agendas and personalities involved."[11] Rather,

because of their understanding of and skill in using language, a writer might be uniquely placed to find ways of communicating across these gaps. It might be they end up simply throwing the lack of communication into relief, making it visible and therefore impossible to ignore, and that at times might be enough.[12]

The idea that the writer's work might stop at the indication of the breaks in communication is important here. Butler often intimates or acknowledges outright that her work will not impact the development process itself, yet, if communication of people's relationship to the spaces they inhabit is a worthy goal in and of itself, lack of impact is not in any case a barrier. Rather, the public's sense that the writer is, like them, without a real voice may make them more willing to engage with a writer than with other types of consultants. Butler notes the temptation to see developers and development councils as "paying lip service to the idea of community consultation but not being genuinely prepared to take the ideas and needs of local people on board."[13] She states that, given this possibility, writers have a role, because even if the development process cannot be touched, people can productively develop their relationships to new places during the process and after: "When we see place as somewhere we can play in and play with, we can see it as something we have agency over; such empowerment can effect positive change for individuals, communities and places."[14] Here the writer's role is thus not to impact development but to discuss it with the public, to help individuals reconcile themselves to it by voicing their concerns, their critiques, and complaints. The writer's skills are valued not because they offer the opportunity to repair breaches and bring conflicting parties together but precisely because their routine practice leads to emphasis on how rifts cannot be breached, how the distance between points of view cannot be traversed. Hence, never far from view is the mainstream regeneration agenda to which the writer is meant to offer not a help but an alternative, in the form of a compensating outlet through which a local community can voice its concerns.

Most of the documents discussing writers' commissioned work downplay the entire goal of property development, which is mainly conceived as an inevitability to which people can be either reconciled or antagonistic. These texts tend to emphasize the writers' own practice and, most important, a community's needs, and both of these interest groups—the writers and the affected communities—are understood as existing in aversive relation to regeneration officials. Butler states that for the writer-consultant the regeneration agenda should be much less important than the highlighting and celebration of art for "what it is: art."[15] What art "is" emerges quite clearly across this work: it is that which, within the development process, is valued precisely because of its ineffectiveness, because it is resolutely ineffective according to any logic that developers and regeneration officials might recognize. Its source is never the developer's desires; it arises rather from the value the writer attaches to expertise in her own medium and from the value that communities derive from being heard by the writer and from helping shape her commissioned work.

Butler suggests that writers will not want to be involved in projects if there is no potential for their own practice to develop and states that for her the appeal to writers is obvious:

Regeneration is about change, and with change comes conflict and drama, which is the stuff of literature. I often teach creative writing, and am constantly talking about finding the conflict, upping the stakes, thinking about what change happens within story, so I see thematic links between this idea of story and Regeneration. It works on a more formal level too: metaphor is about change, and it is the writer's most powerful tool: this ability to transform one thing into another and in doing so find meaning.[16]

As an example of a writer finding new material in consultancy work, Butler discusses a 2008 project called BS1, in which she worked with public art commissioners InSite Arts to invite Donna Daley-Clarke to respond to the construction of Cabot Circus, a new retail center in downtown Bristol. Daley-Clarke and a handful of other artists were located on-site during the construction process. Daley-Clarke's commission resulted in the publication of three stories, "Dirt," "Stone," and "Glass," each one exploring the lives of the otherwise invisible construction workers. Daley-Clarke states that her interest in these pieces was the attention they afforded to the stories of "all these people involved in the construction of Cabot Circus . . . stories that would otherwise have been hidden and ignored. It was about giving a voice and a presence to a range of people."[17]

The idea that this work is about giving voice to the voiceless, and that this voice is important despite being ignored by developers, is perhaps the single most important feature of writer-consultants' self-conceptions, and it subtends in particular the preference for seeking employment not as creators of solo-authored public art but as consultants who engage with the community and produce works based on that experience. While it is worth mentioning that these kinds of consultancy roles also require longer employment periods and tend to be more generously remunerated, the writers involved claim to be motivated by a will to orchestrate the same kind of renunciation of traditional, monumental, product-based authorship and facilitation of the diffuse, process-based creativity of others that has inspired many visual artists over the past several decades.[18]

According to Linda France, a poet who has worked extensively with property developers and development agencies, her work might involve creative public consultation, community development, and communication or facilitation of interactions between the public and officials, "resulting in the creation of an artist's brief, or a hypothetical design proposal." It might also entail "the writer's preparatory work" of "locating concepts and metaphors to make sense of a space."[19] Chris Meade has described his work in the field as "making group poems with local residents," as a "'thought bubble' revealing what's going on in their minds."[20] Meade is a former executive director of the British charity Booktrust and former director of the Poetry Society, which ran the lottery-funded Poetry Places scheme during his tenure. Poetry Places' most noted commission paid Simon Armitage to be Poet-in-Residence for the New Millennium Experience Company at the Millennium Dome, resulting in his thousand-line poem, "Killing Time." Yet Meade's own work with developers is not on the model of the star poet helping to ensure cultural capital adheres to new spaces. He stresses instead that he interacts with local people to create

a style guide of colours, stories, textures and feelings to provide a source of inspiration to the developers, visual artists, designers and planners. I'm picking up on frustrations and aspirations, some of the history of the area and the preoccupations of its current inhabitants.[21]

He deploys this roster of techniques to "garner opinions on local issues and community tensions yet rise above them, developing conversations on the basis of having influence on but no ultimate control over the final scheme."[22] In these terms Meade imagines the writer as a consultant who mediates between the public and the planners, trusted by both groups because he belongs to neither. He appears committed to his lack of official control because it is necessary to his role as intermediary.

Those hired as principal artist-consultants often positioned themselves in this way, as the bridge between an official culture of renewal and the people whose locations are subject to planning intervention. For example, Rosa Ainley worked as lead artist on a regeneration plan for a neglected resort town in Kent, where she was tasked to "reinvigorate the public realm . . . and increase a sense of ownership in and pride about place." She imagines her role to have been "writing what hadn't yet been vocalised, providing spaces for articulation of wishes, and translating them into project form" while "unfixing the narrative from municipal assumptions, widening ownership beyond official channels."[23] She describes the project as

founded on the belief that arts can change your experience of where you live and so how you see your own and the wider world; that development of the community, of new relationships and interest groups and previously unheard voices underpins regeneration; and that involvement in the creative process is itself a starting point.[24]

A complex network of reasons for use of writing and the writer—and a modicum of wishful thinking, perhaps—is evident in Ainley's self-construction here. She affirms one of the fundamental assumptions behind support for public art by claiming that when a place features the arts, people will be more positively disposed to it. At the same time exposure to writing improves people, thereby changing how they perceive the wider world. Furthermore, including the public in creative writing projects, recording their stories and voices, helps build community, actually improving the thing that they perceive as better because they have themselves been made better by the art in their vicinity. Of importance here, evidently, is both the writer's elite cultural contribution and a consultant-organizer's ability to tap into the consciousness of the collective by eliciting their stories.

A recent report on a program based in Glasgow, Scotland—a self-proclaimed "mass public imagination experiment" dubbed "Glasgow 2020 'Dreaming City'"—celebrates storytelling in similar terms. While acknowledging the exhaustion of the idea of culture-led renewal and the suspicion that it is just window dressing for elite privilege, the report claims the program was "the first ever attempt anywhere to aspire to the re-imagination of a city through the idea of story." Glasgow 2020 set out to challenge the city's "Official Future" by asking residents to write about their vision of the future city. The report on the project describes the "rising stock of stories" as part of a shift away from the focus on "logical, linear, computer-like capabilities and the metaphor of the machine as an agent of change" reflecting "a growing interest in issues of meaning, values, ambiguity, fluidity and non-linear notions of thinking which give centre stage to subjectivity and context."[25] The report lays out two knowledge "paradigms" in support of its program. According to the rationality paradigm, people are rational agents who make decisions on the basis of their existing knowledge and the persuasiveness of new information and arguments. According to the story paradigm, which the report agrees is now dominant, people are storytellers who make decisions based on "good reasons," where the definition of a good reason is determined by history, culture, and character; and the world is a set of stories from which we choose, and thus constantly re-create, our lives.

The report draws an analogy between the "Dreaming City" exercise and social media, which is often trumpeted for its democratic potential by project partner Demos, a think tank linked closely with New Labour. The report calls social media "weapons of mass collaboration,"[26] giving rise to powerful new models of production based on community, collaboration, and self-organization rather than on hierarchy and control; by analogy, Glasgow 2020 sought to avoid the conventional hierarchy of the writer over the written, instead distributing the writing function to public volunteers, who, as storytellers, in effect became themselves the literary consultants.

The report acknowledges the "serious disconnect" between the public and the urban regeneration establishment,[27] as it laments that people have been left feeling that the future has been decided by officials, that it isn't something that they themselves "own" and "co-create." It presents the entire Glasgow 2020 project as premised upon indignation about the mainstream development agenda:

The space for innovation in urban governance, planning and design is debilitatingly narrow. The dominant formula of city-boosterism and culture-led regeneration is increasingly spent. Meanwhile the language of localism and devolution has yet to decisively open up any real freedom for civic urban entrepreneurship.[28]

Narrative appears here as an attempt to intervene in what is an otherwise closed process:

The stories that we tell matter because they indicate how we see the world, and whether we believe we have the power and capacity to shape it for the better. Stories are one of the main ways that we make sense of the world, and understand and interpret our lives and experiences. Stories and engaging people's imagination are potentially a powerful way to open up the futures of cities in democratic and creative ways.[29]

How the public's stories about their own desired futures might be communicated to those in a position to act, how the people of Glasgow might become "co-creators" of their future city, are questions studiously avoided in this report, perhaps because to ask them in a serious way would be to admit to all the flaws in the project's effort to valorize public storytelling as a conduit to a better future. Perhaps an unstated and unexplored awareness of the problem of the ineffectiveness of the project informs the entire way it is presented.

We can compare the way Sarah Butler explains her own preference for the kind of work that Glasgow 2020 attempted over projects that simply ask a writer to help brand a space by creating a text to appear within it. Like the authors of Glasgow 2020, Butler reserves her highest praise for writers who are able to put their egos aside and find a language that speaks to and for the community. The writer becomes not an author conventionally defined—the creator of a copyrightable work attached to a singular biographical person—but a "curator" finding "a form and a structure for text and words created by others." Butler also shares Glasgow 2020's embrace of the rhetoric of participatory culture. She is attracted to theorists like Roland Barthes and Michel de Certeau because they seem to her to treat cities and texts as "places which exist for us to use, subvert, question and create our own versions of"; she cites "post modern and particularly post colonial literary theories" as influences, too, because they "looked to represent the multiplicity of unheard voices."[30] In her analogy, the developers are akin to the controlling authors, and the local people who have to live with development are the readers who make meaning from space. On this model the goal is not for the user of a space to become its developer, for the reader to become writer. Instead, what is unfolding here, and is evident also in Glasgow 2020's report on its outcomes, is a conception of her work's compensatory function: because a future in which developers are truly responsive to public needs is a fantasy, far from the realities of development work, Butler imagines that giving over her own voice to others, channeling their otherwise hidden stories through her relatively privileged and authoritative voice, is the best available substitute.

Consider, for example, what resulted when *muf Architecture/Art* commissioned Design for London to create an exhibition to inform residents of Barking, a suburban area of East London, about the many building projects taking place in their town center. The exhibition featured a set of architects' models, and *muf*'s goal was to find a way to make those models accessible and understandable. Butler worked with a poet to run workshops with local people to find out how they imagined the various new buildings being used. The texts they co-created were then mounted next to the architects' models. A representative snippet reads:

I'd have a café with huge sofas and bottomless coffee pots, sell homemade carrot cake and chocolate chip cookies. There'd be free newspapers and old fashioned ceiling fans, books too. The staff would chat to you about politics and love, tell you that drinking coffee and dreaming are far more important than making money or worrying about what other people think. That life is short but afternoons are long, and good company is priceless.[31]

What appealed to Butler is clear: the project allowed people to imagine themselves in the space the architects had envisioned; they became readers of the text of the new development. The space appears as already authored and available to be read and made meaningful by the public. What emerges quite starkly from this example is the implication of Butler's embrace of reader-oriented criticism as a model for what most would take to be the significantly more politicized relationship between the developer and the community. The model envisions those without power as suitably compensated by the feeling that they are the ones who "read" the space, and thus give it meaning, once it has been built. The summation of the roundtable on writers and urban renewal mentioned earlier is also quite clear on this point: the public's words are valuable "on their own terms" precisely because they offer opportunity for them to "reclaim regeneration for themselves" by avoiding "analysis of a place for developers to profit from." It is noted that panel discussants were eager to stress how writers' interventions "may reveal more than 'evidence'-based reports" and "produce less obviously useful documents that might reveal some unexpected sides to regeneration."[32] Hence, again, writers are not committed to purposive impact: because of their various levels of stated and unstated awareness that they in fact have little power; and, perhaps more important, because of a sense that their practice necessarily entails avoidance of the kind of purposive impact that would align them too closely to the regeneration agenda.

In this imagining, which partakes of the venerable tradition, charted throughout this book, of conceiving the aesthetic as definitively inexpedient and anti-instrumental, writing is said to be valuable in and of itself to the precise extent that it avoids any kind of relationship to the profit-making enterprise. The literary is no longer only that which is published by certain magazines and by particular presses in a recognizable format. Many writer-consultants have made concerted efforts to escape those media, taking a multimedia approach involving blogs and audiovisual materials presented online and in real time. The literature development agency Spread the Word now trains the next generation of writer-consultants by featuring programs and workshops for writers interested in these new ways of thinking about how to present literary work. So the literary is not tied to a particular media or format. What it is tied to is a disavowal of economic rationality. I have been suggesting that those involved in the commissioning of writers to work on urban renewal projects support this work precisely because of the status of literature as a privileged space for the articulation of the disavowal of economic rationalities. For them narrative is in a sense both useful and useless; it is useful as a form of compensatory self-expression because its uselessness is positioned against an official culture of technocratic urban planning. The narrative impetus of the people is celebrated as a knowingly ineffective intervention in the official culture of urban renewal, and the people's voice is positioned against the official voice in a fairly stark way. It is as though the sheer fact that they are on the outside of the process means that what they want is good and what they remember or desire is worth recording even if it will not be heeded, precisely because their voices represent a nonpurposive, nonimpactful alternative to what will inevitably be.

To be sure, Butler and other writer-consultants are not content to abandon any claim to attempt to exert influence. However, even those case studies offered as evidence of impact suggest the writer's role is highly prescribed and likely to remain so, and they locate the writer-consultant's real value in sources outside the official regeneration process. If the artist creates a work designed to "become a portable language able to bridge the communication gap that often exists between those making decisions about places and those experiencing those places,"[33] there is little evidence this bridging leads to any truly significant concrete result. Again, though, this is not quite the kind of problem that a curious nonpractitioner might take it to be.

One result that Butler has cited more than once arose from the Council of Maidenhead, a Berkshire town not far from London, commissioning Chris Meade to create a text for its mobile library. Meade consulted with young library users, and the resulting group poem, which is featured within the library's design, reads:

I am the Breathtaker
a place where wonders
come out of words
I am an idea encourager
Homework helper
Snuggle down place,
The Brain Sparkler

Butler's take on this particular commission evidently inflates its significance, but with few concrete case studies of impact to present to prospective funders and developers, this is quite understandable. She is no doubt correct that creating the poem with Meade was a way for the children to express what they valued and wanted in the library and that the poem provided a "portable language" available to the local authority and the community. However, to call the poem a "powerful expressive and political tool" that "transformed not only how the library users viewed their service, but also how that service was viewed by the local authority" seems excessive,[34] especially given that hiring a writer to work on the redesign of a library by writing a text for it would strike many as an unsurprising gesture.

A case with a quite different outcome, also presented as evidence of impact, stems from the "Almost an Island" project that took place on Greenwich Peninsula in East London, a longtime target of regeneration. One result of the project was a temporary piece by the artist Faisal Abdu'Allah, which incorporated a poem that Butler composed with students from a local primary school. The poem, "A Walk on the Greenwich Peninsula," reads in part:

We went for a walk on the Greenwich Peninsula.
Tell me, what did you feel?
The barriers tingling our fingertips,
The concrete hard on our feet,
The breeze, the soft leaves, the smooth silver poles
The grass, a stone and a shell.
We felt warm, laughing, brilliant, happy.

Butler notes that the poem was well received by those who commissioned the work: it was published online and in *Spotlight*, the internationally distributed in-house magazine of Lend Lease, one of the peninsula's main developers. What purpose does this poem serve for Lend Lease employees, though, with its innocuous images of children enjoying a pleasant stroll, its descriptions of their sensual appreciation of grass, stone, and shell but also "barriers" and concrete? It certainly couldn't be said to be an interventionist work that attempts to direct or critique the logic of urban renewal. It is instead very much an instance of what Butler identifies as art meant to be appreciated for what it "is," and what it is is definitively, almost willfully inexpedient.

That these are two of the major cases Butler and the UrbanWords website are able to reference in explaining what impact a writer-consultant can have is telling. To state that such impact is negligible is to miss the point. Developers are rarely looking to have their work fundamentally constrained by one artist's point of view or by the results of public consultation, while the writers involved are very much inheritors of conceptions of art as anti-instrumental. Here, specifically, the aesthetic is the anti-instrumental expression of the feelings and experiences of those affected by and charged with merely "reading" development.

I conclude with a final representative case, "The Shop of Priceless Things," a project mounted in 2009 in a disused storefront in Rotherham, a town in South Yorkshire. Rotherham District Council had put out a call for ideas to revitalize an empty Burger King building in the town center. A team made up of a writer and a design firm responded with a plan to critique—though gently—the feverish shopping of the Christmas season. They spent a day talking to people in Rotherham about all the things they considered to be "priceless." They asked passersby "to share the sights and sounds they valued, evocative smells that triggered memories, things that are special to touch." These ideas became the stock of "The Shop of Priceless Things" when they were installed as texts in its windows. The poet, John Wedgwood Clarke, wrote a poem explaining the concept of the shop, but all the other highlighted texts were the words of those they interviewed. The designer, Adrian Riley, has said in interview that the project would not have had the same impact or been "an authentic artwork" if it had featured only the things that he and Clarke valued. Consistent with other writer-consultant projects, aesthetic authenticity is indexed to the shop's citation of the "genuine poetry" that "came out of people's mouths."

Riley explains that their initial plan had been to attempt to make the shop blend into the High Street with a design aesthetic that mirrored its usual bold and garish logos and signs, but they decided in the end on something more "high end," something more evidently produced by a design studio, because they wanted to avoid "cheapening" their respondents' words with a "commercial or discount visual language."[35]

One gathers from this reflection on their practice that the design studio imagines it responds to directives other than commerce, and the usual visual language of the high street is the counterweight to the "priceless things" Riley and Clarke sought to valorize in their work. The artists won the commission on the basis of a plan that would stress their own distance from commercial imperatives and their privileging of nonmarket values, and the design that resulted was envisioned as a way to help the Rotherham High Street become something other than a place in which people engage in commercial exchange. Riley makes this goal quite explicit as he negotiates a complex relation of connection to and distance from the regeneration agenda:

There's a bit of tension between putting something positive and, we hope, beautiful into the middle of town and the property remaining empty. In an ideal world the building would be put to commercial use as the town becomes more prosperous and permanent public artworks be commissioned as part of intelligent thought about urban space (or even better—artists invited to be involved in the design of urban space). Whilst I'd rather see empty shops put to creative use than just stand there unwanted and unloved, temporary projects like [ours] draw attention to a society and economy where the town centre needs to rediscover a role beyond just being a collection of shops. Town centres have to become an environment where people can also play, dream, be culturally enriched and just enjoy being a community.[36]

So commissioning public art would be good, but involving artists in the entire design process would be better. A commercial use for the space would be better than dereliction, but best of all would be the kind of shop they have themselves just designed: a shop that is in fact an anti-shop, culturally "enriching" because it reminds people there is more to life than shopping. The idea that some things are "priceless," and an attendant celebration of a residual community committed to nonmarket pleasures, emerges as one of the signal themes of much of the writing that results from commissioned work in the field of urban development. Recall that in response to the *muf* commission in Barking, one of the lines mounted beside the architects' models longed for a built environment that could acknowledge the fact that "good company is priceless." This thematic is perhaps the natural accompaniment to the value that those involved in these projects place on their own autonomy from a regeneration agenda taken as compromised and from the market-based imperatives that drive that agenda.

Writers do, nevertheless, participate, so my account of that participation has attempted to show how their self-conceptions register the tension between proximity and distance, complicity and critique, as they present writing as an artistic medium available for the voicing of a community's consciousness and as averse to the kind of purposive impact recognized by developers. The way that writers are attempting to institutionalize their ambivalent roles, to position themselves as formal consultants to an urban development process to which they are in many ways opposed, is unprecedented and deserves more study. The purpose of my own take has been not to fault writers for their engagement in this work but to look at how larger material forces inform the positioning of art in society and inform how writers in particular are balancing the ideas about literature that they have inherited against the forms of work that are now available to them. Their view of their medium is, I have been suggesting, the product of a complex interplay of agency and determining material context. It is an expression, most broadly, of writers' and other artists' ongoing interest—an interest shared by several of the authors I consider elsewhere—in the problem of their relative, mediated, beleaguered autonomy and in the challenge of arriving at compelling and socially responsive conceptions of their expertise.

7

Valuing the Arts
in Ian McEwan's *Saturday*

Ian McEwan's 2005 novel *Saturday* has occasioned starkly opposed interpretations. Some read it as a trenchant critique of the privileged perspective of its protagonist, neurosurgeon Henry Perowne, while others either praise or blame McEwan for what they see as his presentation of Henry as a positive model of an introspective and responsible individual.[1] In the novel's key scene, Baxter, the man who has been haunting Henry throughout the day, breaks into his home and threatens violence against Henry's family. He is startled out of that intent, however, after hearing Matthew Arnold's "Dover Beach" read aloud. Notwithstanding our lack of access to the complexities of Baxter's inner life, critics—otherwise disposed to disagreement—have agreed in reading the scene as an affirmation of the ameliorative capacities of art: in the face of the aesthetic, the intending criminal retreats, his capacity to be moved by poetry proving his heretofore hidden humanity. I argue, however, that if we attend to the novel's view of *Henry's* interest in the arts—a dimension of the novel critics have so far neglected—it becomes impossible to imagine that McEwan means here simply to affirm their transformative potential.

Baxter's response to "Dover Beach" and Henry's overall proclivities as a consumer of art have to be read in relation to each other, and their precise relation is clarified if we consider debates about the value of the arts that were contemporary to the novel's conception and publication. Audiences for mainstream literary fiction could be expected to be familiar with the various arguments in favor of public support for the arts: in the absence of state support, the market would prevail and variety would suffer; careful choice of location for new arts institutions can contribute to urban regeneration; with a little help starting up, many forms of art making achieve profitability and contribute to the creative economy; arts organizations are often committed to improving community integration and quality of life; and so on. Due to the creative-economy turn and to the New Labour government's highly publicized attempts to distinguish its investment in culture from what came before, existing interest in the fate of public support for the arts was heightened when McEwan was working on *Saturday*. Replacement of the Thatcher-era Department of National Heritage with the newly formed DCMS was, for example, a privileged symbol of the transition New Labour wished to posit: whereas the conservatives smiled upon established cultural institutions and stressed the glories of British heritage, New Labour would make culture a key part of its broader social inclusion agenda and support programs designed to encourage democratic access to a wide range of cultural activities and institutions because this access was perceived as essential to civic engagement and social harmony.

The government's Social Exclusion Unit, founded soon after the election, connected social exclusion to "problems such as unemployment, poor skills, low incomes, poor housing, high crime environments, bad health and family breakdown."[2] When it was asked to play a part in rectifying these problems, the official response of the DCMS was to claim that "art and sport can not only make a valuable contribution to delivering key outcomes of lower long-term unemployment, less crime, better health and better qualifications, but can also help to develop the individual pride, community spirit and capacity for responsibility that enable communities to run regeneration programmes themselves."[3] We see here several features of neoliberal governance. To be included means to be a functioning and "self-administering" consumer with no need of a welfare state.[4] As Alan Finlayson argues, the role of government is not to create the kind of programs that will ensure social inclusion but rather to attempt to create the kind of citizens "who will themselves create the conditions for their inclusion."[5] The economy is, moreover, not in need of regulation for social inclusion to be secured; rather, the economy is itself the social system in which people need to be encouraged to include themselves.

If we consider some of the terms of the discussion that attended this shift, as I do later, *Saturday*'s complex stake in it is clarified. Henry enjoys music and the visual arts, and in certain key scenes we gather they appeal to him because he can easily accommodate them to his habitual ways of thinking. In turn we come to see that it is literature, the art for which he lacks any capacity, which might be most able to instigate a change he dimly perceives he needs to make. While Baxter is, in contrast, positively propelled by his exposure to one piece of writing, it is by no means the case that, for him, being brought into the community of appreciation of literary goods is somehow equivalent to authentic social inclusion. Instead, the novel's treatment of Baxter's awakening to the literary suggests culture might be used as a means of pacifying unrest and that social inclusion might even be a class fantasy premised upon that pacification. These two figures' experiences cannot be separated: whatever limited promise resides in the moment of Baxter's experience is stymied by Henry's failure to change; so, personally transformative encounters with literature will have little meaning in the absence of broader social change, and that change is precisely what is impeded by settled inclinations, embodied in Henry, to use the arts as (self-)affirmation of what already exists. This take on the arts does not by any means pit the novel against New Labour policymaking, I should stress. Rather, the novel could be thought to imagine itself as a privileged interlocutor, affirming the official vision of the arts' progressive social purpose while emphasizing the serious challenges to its realization.

Because I suggest that the scene of Baxter's transformation cannot be read in isolation from what Theresa Winterhalter has called Henry's "need to retreat to a place that does not pressure him to change his life,"[6] we must first consider what the novel has to say about the nature of Henry's professional identity, class privilege, and habitual modes of self-reflection. As *Saturday* opens, we meet Henry waking early in his posh London townhome, sleepily drawn to a window where he soon observes what he believes to be an airplane on fire. His reaction to this vision alerts us to the infusion of his consciousness with a post-9/11 uncertainty, a fear of impending irruptions of "irrational" currents. Just before the plane appears to him, he is feeling rather euphoric and greets the city square that his bedroom overlooks by exalting modern urbanism:

The city is a success, a brilliant invention, a biological masterpiece—millions teeming around the accumulated and layered achievements of the centuries, as though around a coral reef, sleeping, working, entertaining themselves, harmonious for the most part, nearly everyone wanting it to work. And the Perownes' own corner, a triumph of congruent proportion; the perfect square laid out by Robert Adam enclosing a perfect circle of garden—an eighteenth-century dream bathed and embraced by modernity, by street light from above, and from below by fiber-optic cables, and cool fresh water coursing down pipes, and sewage borne away in an instant of forgetting.[7]

In our first moments of meeting Henry we see him assuring himself that things are just as they should be. His portion of the city practically glows, full as it is of "harmonious" people who put their faith in ceaseless "invention" and in the slow march of modern progress.

The specter of the airplane on fire, which he assumes is the result of another terrorist attack, certainly unsettles his contentment, but soon Henry's worst fears about the plane are allayed by a newscast. Admitting that the feeling of relief is in tension with his disappointment that no new political catastrophe has emerged to entertain him, he returns to bed to have sex with his beloved wife, Rosalind, an accomplished lawyer. He then departs in his prized Mercedes for his weekly squash game, finding himself mildly annoyed by the traffic diversions caused by the antiwar protest taking place that day. After the game he shops for ingredients for a fish stew he plans to make that evening, when his daughter, an accomplished poet, will be reunited with her estranged grandfather, John Grammaticus, a cantankerous fellow writer once jealous of her precocious success. He visits his mother in her nursing home and admits to himself that he feels guilty at how soon he begins to wish to escape it. From there, before returning home to prepare dinner, he travels to his son Theo's band rehearsal, marveling at having a musical prodigy for a son.

This then is a man with much to be proud of and much to look forward to: a successful career, an accomplished wife to whom he is passionately devoted, a gifted musician for a son, a prize-winning poet for a daughter, a gorgeous townhouse in a desirable neighborhood, an expensive car that gives him much pleasure, and evening plans that include a delicious meal, several bottles of good wine, and his family reunited. There is, however, the matter of a minor car accident that occurs on the way to his squash game. Even cursory familiarity with McEwan's work leads us to suspect this event will eventually threaten Henry's appearance of untouched bourgeois contentment. For the accident brings the other driver, Baxter, into Henry's life, and the life of Baxter—who is the novel's figure for the disenfranchised and unfortunate—begins to stress to Henry a number of already underlying questions about his own privilege and about his responsibility to those who do not have what he has.

In the initial encounter that follows the accident Henry's primary motivation is self-preservation. He has noticed that Baxter is suffering from Huntington's disease, a horrible, incurable, degenerative illness, and he gleans that he can disarm him by lying that he has insider knowledge about a possible breakthrough treatment. This lie comes back to haunt Henry, as Baxter trails him throughout the day, before breaking into his home for the inevitable confrontation between privileged homeowner, master and manipulator of life-or-death medical information, and his disaffected underclass other, betrayed by Henry while depending on him to dispense potentially life-altering knowledge.

Perceiving the parallels between Henry's indecision about the war and his desire to excuse himself from having to think about Baxter, some readers interpret Baxter's invasion of Henry's luxurious home as a political allegory. According to one of the novel's most strident critics,

The knife wielding Baxter and his accomplice who burst in . . . represent a version of the 9/11 hijackers. Baxter is like a suicidal terrorist: [he] is, metaphorically, an Arab extremist. His genetic defect is also, arguably, a displaced version of that popular reactionary concept, the criminal gene (which is paralleled by the poverty gene and the homelessness gene, and all those other bogus genes which offer a soothing pseudo-scientific explanation for the consequences of the inequalities of capitalist society).[8]

What should we make then of the novel's conclusion, in which Baxter is injured when he is thrown down the stairs, and it is Henry who is called in to operate on his brain? Henry is put in a position to decide if he would like to take revenge on Baxter by botching the operation, but he decides to do his job properly and attempt to save his life. If Baxter's presence in Henry's house is an allegory about Islamic terrorism, Henry's choice can be read in two ways. It may be a recommendation that we disavow revenge as a motive for action, which would give the novel in its final moments at least a hint of an antiwar valence, even if what it objects to is a rationale for the war in Iraq—revenge for 9/11—that was never particularly politically credible, though it was certainly useful to jingoists. Or it may be a fantasy about the triumph of Western liberalism, rationalism, and science over irrational and aggressive impulses at home and abroad. As Molly Clark Hillard surmises, "If this interpretation were correct, then McEwan with one stroke created a scene of richly layered chauvinism, in which the nation—rendered concomitantly as the female body shielded by male literary heritage—deflects an attack by forces rendered simultaneously as philistine, anarchist, and terrorist."[9]

These allegorical readings are ones that the novel appears to invite, though there is by no means an airtight connection between Baxter and any real Islamic terrorist. After all, his crime has no explicit political intent, and he threatens to rape Henry's daughter. But I suggest the connection between the Baxter plot and the Iraq War plot need not be so abstract. In a novel that is so much about how one privileged man perceives the world, and perceives himself perceiving the world, Henry's decision to save Baxter's life represents the promise of conclusive action, the promise of a kind of command over the material realities of life that he cannot achieve in the political realm, where he believes that his access to information is dictated by the news cycle and that his views about war are an irrelevance because he has no route to meaningful political activity.

It is in the context of his thoughts about the possible justifications for war that he encounters Baxter and has to figure out how to treat him; and in turn, deciding to use his professional expertise to save Baxter is his response to one of the main stories that he tells himself, that he is not a political agent, that he is a passive consumer of political information, so he must just devote himself to his work and content himself with the idea that through work he achieves some social good and earns his superior social status. After he has observed the plane in the novel's opening scene, Henry's response is contradictory: "He feels culpable somehow, but helpless too. These are contradictory terms, but not quite, and it's the degree of their overlap, their manner of expressing the same thing from different angles, which he needs to comprehend" (22). It is this feeling of being at once culpable and helpless that performing Baxter's surgery is meant to correct.

The pressure of these contradictory emotions has been present and even building throughout the day. Consider, for example, the reflections prompted by shopping for groceries:

> It was once convenient to think biblically, to believe we're surrounded for our benefit by edible automata on land and sea. Now it turns out that even fish feel pain. This is the growing complication of the modern condition, the expanding circle of moral sympathy. Not only distant peoples are our brothers and sisters, but foxes too, and laboratory mice, and now the fish. Perowne goes on catching and eating them, and though he'd never drop a live lobster into boiling water, he's prepared to order one in a restaurant. The trick, as always, the key to human success and domination, is to be selective in your mercies. For all the discerning talk, it's the close at hand, the visible that exerts the overpowering force. And what you don't see . . . That's why in gentle Marylebone the world seems so entirely at peace. (128)

There is much here that is representative of Henry's ways of thinking, as he carefully talks himself out of feeling any of the "moral sympathy" he claims is now requisite for modern living. He speculates that not having to kill his own food is what makes it possible for him to continue to eat what requires killing. This thought implies his acknowledgment that his own comfort rests upon some harm, but he soon retreats even from this intimation by insisting that it is simply impossible to be merciful to all beings, that one must be "selective," and it is fundamentally human to pay most attention to the "visible" and the "close at hand." The concluding line about "gentle Marylebone" places Henry's tendencies within a broader frame: in a world of war, gentle peace in this bit of London depends upon a collective effort to keep at bay the things we tell ourselves we do not see. Henry sees much that is not immediately visible and simply chooses to disavow any tendency in his thought that would betray his focus on that tiny portion of reality that is nearest to him.

Henry's attempts to talk himself out of self-criticism are not always so successful. On occasion he conceives his complacency as a reflection of his protected ease, as he and those he loves are shut away from the world behind high-tech security systems and heavy drapes made of lush, expensive fabrics that "have a way of cleanly eliminating the square and the wintery world beyond" (185–86). For those with little to fear, for whom nothing is really at stake, politics can be a game one plays at dinner parties:

Does he think that his ambivalence—if that's what it really is—excuses him from the general conformity? He's deeper in than most. His nerves, like tautened strings, vibrate obediently with each news "release." He's lost the habits of skepticism, he's becoming dim with contradictory opinion, he isn't thinking clearly, and just as bad, he senses he isn't thinking independently. (185)

While he will admit that his ambivalence may be somehow inadequate, he is expert at finding ways to excuse himself from acting on any political inclination or attempting empathy with people from whom he permits himself a comforting distance and difference. The novel's epigraph, lines from Saul Bellow's *Herzog* on "the late failure of radical hopes," is aptly chosen for this reason; it alerts us immediately to the fact that Henry's point of view has causes and repercussions. Henry is unable to entertain the possibility that there will ever be a world in which the various things he feels dimly guilty about are rectified.

Henry's only meaningful model of social action, his way of forwarding others' well-being, is clinical expertise.[10] Expertise is for Henry a "prophylactic against any sense of failure."[11] In the novel he comforts himself that he is "a man who attempts to ease the miseries of failing minds by repairing brains" (66); treating Baxter as a "case" is part of how Henry "cushion[s himself] against the grating roar of other sorts of lives being led."[12] In the description of his experience of the actual operation, we witness a man very much in what Mihály Csíkszentmihályi calls "flow." His passion for "optimal performance" temporarily removes him from the realm of personal interest and deliberation. It is the payoff for his devotion to his work, the time of elated absorption in the task itself. It ceases to matter whose life he is saving, just that he is applying his skills to the work before him:

For the past two hours he's been in a dream of absorption that has dissolved all sense of time, and all awareness of the other parts of his life. Even his awareness of his own existence has vanished. He's been delivered into a pure present, free of the weight of the past or any anxieties about the future. In retrospect, though never at the time, it feels like profound happiness. (266)

What is being described here is the essence of his desire throughout the novel. Finally he is released from his characteristic self-consciousness. Finally he is able to attain that "freedom from thought" that sport could not quite afford him. Finally the anxieties that stem from his "awareness of his own existence" are alleviated. He isn't even happy. He is simply absorbed, the feeling of happiness always only following after the fact. He is suffused with what is described as

benevolent dissociation, which seems to require difficulty, prolonged demands on concentration and skills, pressure, problems to be solved, even danger. He feels calm, and spacious, fully qualified to exist. It's a feeling of clarified emptiness, of deep, muted joy. . . . There must, he concludes as he stands to leave the theatre, be something wrong with him. (266)

Henry's calm in the operating theater, his feeling of "emptiness," his lack of any sense that maybe he is not "fully qualified to exist" of course have none of the neurotic oddity for which he gently mocks himself. There is not "something wrong with him." On the contrary, to many readers of the novel, themselves committed professionals, the feeling would be entirely familiar or even enviable. Henry is above all else utterly devoted to and infused with the merits of his profession. He sees the world through his work, and this professional perspective provides him with a way to handle challenges that emerge, including the challenge posed to him by all his sublimated concerns about his privileged social status, his luxurious home and possessions, and his relative safety from significant danger or the pressing weight of substantial need.

Saving Baxter is in my reading, most important, an opportunity for Henry to engage his professional competence. This competence is Henry's key means of transcendence of immediate realities and a conventional mechanism he uses for assuring himself that he is a good person who needn't discover any other kind of engagement with the world. Treating Baxter thus provides him with several levels of comfort: it is the kind of work that he can do to improve the world; it takes him outside himself temporarily; it is a mode of action that allows him to counter a sense of political complacency that has him faulting himself for ambivalence, indecision, and lack of any strong conviction. Baxter's identity fades in significance as Henry simply does what he does best, inhabits the moment of his labor, transcends the local and particular, and achieves a kind of self-contentment that his normal waking mind otherwise won't allow him.

With all this in mind, we can turn now to one of Henry's crucial characteristics: his lack of interest in literature. His inability to appreciate literature is correlated to the determination of his character by his vocation, as well as to his command of the other arts. Henry appreciates art and music, and I later discuss the palpable ironies of his particular preferences. It is only literature that eludes him. Henry tells himself that he fails to engage much with literature because he does not want to be "a spectator of imaginary lives." He maintains that he does not want the world to be invented, "he wants it explained," and the ease of separating these two functions is obvious to him (65). His preference for explanation leads him to reduce the texts he has read to the historical information he can glean from them. At his daughter's prompting he attempts to read *Anna Karenina* and *Madame Bovary*, only to ask, "What did he grasp, after all? That adultery is understandable but wrong, that nineteenth-century women had a hard time of it, that Moscow and the Russian countryside and provincial France were once just so" (66).

His opposition to magic realism is unsurprisingly particularly stark, and he singles out a novel that we know to be McEwan's own, *A Child in Time*, as particularly worthy of scorn, as its "visionary" narrator sees through a pub window "his parents as they had been some weeks after his conception, discussing the possibility of aborting him" (66). Some readers have seen this statement as one of the clearest signs in the novel of the ironic distance between author and character. Yet we cannot conclude definitively that McEwan would not agree with Henry's assessment. He has himself moved away from magic realism in recent years and may have entertained doubts about it even while exploring it. Indeed, I would suggest that Henry's attitude toward literature is not something that we are meant to receive with simple scorn, flattered by it because we are better than it. The gesture of self-congratulation would be very much against the spirit of the book, which is to reveal quite relentlessly Henry's own questionable means of achieving self-satisfaction. Instead, the intimate links between author, character, and reader may be precisely the point of the mode of narration. McEwan's proximity to some of Henry's defining gestures, a self-critical analysis of the kinds of comforts and complicities with which he engages, is one of his key purposes. The identity of author and narrator does not signal a lack of irony. Rather, it signals the extension of ironic distance to the author's own voice and the encouragement of the reader's own consciousness of insufficient separation from Henry's ways of being and seeing.

The novel presents Henry's indifference to literature as an extension of his overarching desire to continue on his habitual path and justify that path to himself. We can find an able guide to the ideas about literature signaled by Henry's lack of interest in it—a guide to what it is exactly that Henry lacks because he lacks literary awareness—in John Carey's 2005 book, *What Good Are the Arts?* Here Carey critiques mainstream arts policy for encouraging passive worship of "power-house" high art instead of the active involvement of all people in creative activity. Carey's polemical tone belies the fact that much New Labour policy was crafted in evident sympathy with precisely such arguments.

Carey, emeritus professor of English literature at Oxford, positions himself as a relativist and anti-elitist. He argues that research has established that art is a matter of personal taste and that our preferences for some arts over others have no objective status but rather express only what we feel. No person's feelings are more valid or dignified than anyone else's, and no person's real feelings are even accessible to any other person, so we have no firm basis on which to judge anyone's cultural experiences or tastes: "It is self-deception to imagine that our feelings, when we are in contact with what we consider 'true' art, are more valuable than the feelings others derive from 'low' or 'false' art, or from pursuits we should not consider art at all."[13] Furthermore, in Carey's view, in the case of the elite visual arts and classical music those feelings are fundamentally attached to class privilege, and the funding of those arts is a matter of one class of people attempting at once to impose their own tastes on others and to distinguish themselves from their inferiors based on their relative cultural capital.

Literature is the notable exception to all Carey's rules. Because literature has to do with language and meaning and ideas, he argues, it has to do with rational discourse, including debate about the efficacy of literature itself. Literature is the supreme art because it can "criticize itself," and it is the only art that can criticize anything at all, because "it is the only art capable of reasoning." The other arts are "locked in inarticulacy"; they can convey criticism but not make a rational case.[14] Literature thus allows for discussion of ethics and politics, for meaning and significance.

At the same time, though, Carey maintains that because literature is "indistinct," it is the form of art that allows free play to the imagination—that quality that McEwan famously said the 9/11 terrorists had to have lacked in order to have done what they did.[15] Carey argues that it is literature that requires the most active imaginative investment and participation, as the attentive reader must use imagination to "come to some kind of accommodation with the indistinctness."[16] Justin O'Connor points out the peculiarity of this argument:

In most aesthetic theory it was the other arts—especially music—that were seen as indeterminate, that could not precisely denote but only imprecisely evoke a specific content or meaning. But for Carey it is literature that is indistinct, indeterminate. Music and painting simply are—this is the picture, that is the tune—but in literature the words give free rein to the imagination. You have to fill in the gaps yourself.[17]

For Carey literature is thus an idealized realm uniting reason and imagination, rational discourse and imaginative possibility. This is very much the view of literature that McEwan seems to support in his construction of Henry's consciousness. In lacking literature, Henry lacks the premier art for instigation of critical thought and the premier source of imaginative exploration of other worlds and imaginative identification with other lives.

Consider for a moment Henry's brief moment of aesthetic transcendence, listening to his son's jazz band:

This is when [musicians] give us a glimpse of what we might be, of our best selves, and of an impossible world in which you give everything you have to others, but lose nothing of yourself. Out in the real world there exist detailed plans, visionary projects for peaceable realms, all conflicts resolved, happiness for everyone, for ever—mirages for which people are prepared to die and kill. Christ's kingdom on earth, the workers' paradise, the ideal Islamic state. But only in music, and only on rare occasions, does the curtain actually lift on this dream of community, and it's tantalisingly conjured, before fading away with the last notes. (176)

Music is for Henry a means of accessing our "best selves," but it works for him precisely because of its lack of any discursive content. It might evoke the possibility of some kind of common condition, but only very fleetingly and vaguely and without any particular injunction to act. It "fad[es] away with the last notes," and that promise of release from the vision is perhaps what gives it its appeal. It induces in him a consciousness not unlike what he achieves at work: the erasure of the "real world" external to his self, with its plans and conflicts and ideals that people argue for and die over. The lyrics of the song he is hearing at this moment of transcendence befit the effect perfectly:

> Baby, you can choose despair,
> Or you can be happy if you dare.
> So let me take you there,
> My city square, city square. (175)

These lyrics reflexively signal the novel's own focus on one man's bit of the city, his property and the threats to it, and articulate what amounts to Henry's creed: despair is a choice; you can choose instead to be happy, you can use your rational mind to talk yourself out of whatever might upset you, and that is what life is about. Don't dwell; move on; find happiness. Being lifted outside himself and into his son's music is something he can do because it is a form of the value he ascribes to his life: find comfort in transcendence of pressing realities; separate yourself from whatever dim consciousness you might have that the world might be demanding from you another kind of engagement. We see in Henry's experience of music the influence of thinking like Carey's. Carey cites Pierre Bourdieu in support of his argument that music orchestrates a "radical and absolute negation of the ordinary world's neediness and practicality, a negation that 'high' aesthetics demands of all forms of art." Music is an art that can be appreciated "freely," which means that it can be enjoyed as a form of rejection of any call from the "herd" to assert any "common moral response."[18]

The visual arts serve Henry in similar ways, as we glean from his visit to the Tate Modern for its gala opening in 1998. Built in a disused power station away from the center of London, the Tate Modern reflected and encouraged New Labour's commitment to culture-led urban renewal, based on faith in the circulation of cultural capital as a means of improving conditions in an underdeveloped area and on the idea that access to good art should be spread and dispersed throughout the city. All the Perownes attend the gala, though not due to any parental effort to inculcate in Theo and Daisy an appreciation for high culture. That appreciation appears to be simply assumed, a natural part of their elite upbringing. Upon arrival the younger Perownes disappear into the crowd to follow their own interests and design. Later, wandering the galleries with his wife, Henry particularly notes what is identified as Cornelia Parker's

Exploding Shed, in reference to *Cold Dark Matter: An Exploded View*. This work is an assemblage of pieces of a shed that the British military blew up on the artist's behalf, and it appeals to Henry as "a humourous construction, like a brilliant idea exploding out of a mind" (144). Henry's take on Parker's piece suggests that while he appreciates contemporary art, he also consumes it quite passively and superficially—he may enjoy the visual arts precisely because they allow him this sort of passive experience. Compare again John Carey's insistence on the superior political purchase of *Uncle Tom's Cabin* over a work of conceptual art that aims to critique slavery: "Reading is comparatively arduous, whereas wandering round a cotton maze is just the kind of slipshod, superficial substitute for knowledge and understanding that conceptual art's advocates imagine themselves struggling against."[19] In looking at Parker's work, a strolling Henry neglects any contextual information provided for gallery goers—any language conveying concepts, to use Carey's terms—in favor of a surface reading that he is allowed to prefer. He simply notes the work's humor and enjoys the way it evokes for him something he respects and appreciates: a brilliant mind at work.

The artist's declared purposes, clearly unknown by Henry, were far richer. Parker has said that she was interested in reflecting upon the heightened fear of explosions after 9/11; her intent would thus relate back to Henry's own thoughts throughout the day, if he could only recognize that intent. Furthermore, as commentary on the piece on the Tate Modern's website remarks,

The garden shed is a sort of halfway house, an overspill for things which, for whatever reason, aren't as wanted or needed as they once were. . . . A terribly British institution, the shed functions as a place of refuge, a safe place, a place for secrets and fantasy. By blowing up the shed Parker is taking away such a place, throwing doubt on all it represents. Its contents are revealed, damaged in the process and yet somehow more eloquent. We get an "exploded view" which creates a vast new space for our own mental activity.[20]

The irony here is quite apparent: the fact that Henry sees none of this in the piece is proof that his own ways of being are precisely what Parker is targeting. Henry routinely attempts to avoid any full consciousness of "overspill" as a way of finding his "safe place." Neglecting to engage with the art on display in the gallery is a version of this activity, and this neglect appears in the novel to be permitted by the visual arts, which invite consumers to treat them as a series of slightly amusing objects that decorate a space.

Literature in the novel appears to demand something more, and Henry's limited apprehension of its possibilities is thrown into sharp relief by his easier accommodation of the other arts. His limitation is highlighted as well by the way the narration is infused with the same literary tradition that he does not know or at best misunderstands. Sebastian Groes has exhaustively detailed the list of the writers that the novel references. It includes Sophocles, Thomas Wyatt, Shakespeare, Milton, Blake, Mary Shelley, Jane Austen, Charlotte Brontë, Dickens, Darwin, George Eliot, Browning, Arnold, Tolstoy, Flaubert, Conrad, Kafka, Joyce, Woolf, Henry James, Saul Bellow, Larkin, James Fenton, Ted Hughes, Craig Raine, and Andrew Motion.[21] Critics have noted running parallels to *Mrs. Dalloway* and *Ulysses* in particular, but Groes's persuasive reading of the novel's opening scene as an homage to Franz Kakfa's *Metamorphosis* is particularly relevant here. Both works begin with the sensation of waking and with their protagonists moving to the window. Whereas Gregor finds his arms and legs unwieldy because he has overnight become an insect, Henry feels limber and freer than usual, euphoric for reasons he attributes to his brain's chemistry. As the stories advance, Gregor is eventually ousted from his family, and his "mechanical, bureaucratic" perception of his experience symbolizes his descent into animality;[22] in *Saturday*, the person ousted from the family is the outsider Baxter, and Henry's bourgeois consciousness, no less mechanistic than Gregor's, is signaled instead by the work he does to convince himself of his own wholeness and lack of alienation.

Having read the story on his daughter's recommendation, Henry does not perceive any relation between himself and Kafka's protagonist. He identifies instead with another of the story's characters: "He liked the unthinking cruelty of the sister on the final page, riding the tram with her parents to the last stop, stretching her young limbs, ready to begin a sensual life. A transformation he could believe in" (133). Henry's reading of Kafka's work thus thoroughly infuses it with his own consciousness. He identifies with Gregor's sister because she achieves a fulfillment of his own desire to be free to live a "sensual life" without regard for its implications.

Her achieving transcendence of any concern about her brother, ridding herself of any empathy for him, vicariously fulfills Henry's own wish to be rid of niggling thoughts of any care that he might owe Baxter or to others beyond his carefully delimited borders.

Turning at last to the scene of Baxter's transformation via "Dover Beach," it should be noted that Henry does achieve a different kind of reading practice as he tries to imagine how Baxter might be understanding the poem they are both hearing. His attempt to channel Baxter's thoughts starts with his arrival as an intruder:

Henry tries to see the room through [Baxter's] eyes, as if that might help predict the degree of trouble ahead: the two bottles of champagne, the gin and the bowls of lemon and ice, the belittling high ceiling and its mouldings, the Bridget Riley prints flanking the Hodgkin, the muted lamps, the cherry wood floor beneath the Persian rugs, the careless piles of serious books, the decades of polish in the thakat table. The scale of retribution could be large. (243)

Here Henry reads his own lifestyle as a provocation to retribution. Baxter's physical presence elicits what Ross calls "a frantic class defensiveness, the troubled awareness of one whose elevated status rests on chic possessions" and—in the guise of those "careless piles of serious books"— on a "nonchalant mastery of print." Ross argues that as the scene works toward its conclusion, print culture in fact "becomes a modus operandi ensuring that the uncouth listener will not for long penetrate the hallowed boundaries of the haut-bourgeois community." Though Henry does not recognize Arnold's poem, his command of medical authority, signaled by his "ruse of reading aloud from a medical offprint," is based in another kind of print mastery, so from start to denouement the superiority of the "hyperlettered and hyperskilled remains triumphantly intact."[23]

It is evident that the Perownes' particular cultural possessions and their superior class position are intimately connected. Yet their superiority does not go unchecked, in part because Henry's ownership of "print resources" is offset by his distance from any real literary sensibility. That Bridget Riley and Howard Hodgkin are the artists they prefer for their home decor is a telling detail. In a gesture that again evokes John Carey's arguments, McEwan likely chose these particular artists as figures whose visual language would be lost on outsiders to the art world. They thus stand in marked contrast to "Dover Beach," which the scene will soon present as the kind of rational speech by which someone with no cultural education could be moved. These paintings, in their exclusiveness of address, are a better symbol of Henry's superiority than his overflowing bookshelves.

When Henry first hears "Dover Beach," he is not familiar with it and so believes—as Baxter believes—that Daisy is the author:

The lines surprise him—... They are unusually meditative, mellifluous, and willfully archaic. She's thrown herself back into another century. ... He sees Daisy on a terrace overlooking a beach in summer moonlight; ... She calls to her lover, surely the man who will one day father her child, to come and look, or rather, listen to the scene. ... Together they listen to the surf roaring on the pebbles, and hear in the sound a deep sorrow which stretches right back to ancient times. She thinks there was another time, even further back, when the earth was new and the sea consoling, and nothing came between man and God. But this evening the lovers hear only sadness and loss in the sound of the waves breaking and retreating from the shore. She turns to him, and before they kiss she tells him that they must love each other and be faithful, especially now they're having a child, and when there's no peace or certainty, and when desert armies stand ready to fight. (228–29)

Baxter's reaction is immediate: "His grip on the knife looks slacker, and his posture, the peculiar yielding angle of his spine, suggests a possible ebbing of intent" (229). From this new, yielding position, Baxter asks to hear the poem again, so Henry's second hearing of the poem makes him rethink his first interpretation:

Henry missed the first time the mention of the cliffs of England "glimmering and vast out on the tranquil bay." Now it appears there's no terrace, but an open window; there's no young man, father of the child. Instead he sees Baxter, standing alone, elbows propped against the sill, listening to the waves "bring the eternal note of sadness in." ... Even in his state, Henry balks at the mention of a "sea of faith" and the glittering paradise of wholeness lost in the distant past. Then once again, it's through Baxter's ears that he hears the sea's "melancholy, long withdrawing roar, retreating, to the breath of the night wind, down the vast edges drear and naked shingles of the world." It rings like a musical curse. The plea to be true to one another sounds hopeless in the absence of joy or love or light or peace or "help for pain." Even in a world "where ignorant armies clash by night," Henry discovers on second hearing no mention of a desert. The poem's melodiousness, he decides, is at odds with its pessimism. (230)

The poem's rereading allows us to witness a glimmer of a moment of genuine identification with Baxter. On first hearing, Henry interprets the
piece as another of Daisy's confessions, and since he now knows she is
pregnant with her Italian boyfriend's child, he imagines that boyfriend
as the scene's addressee. In Winterhalter's terms, "He is only able to draw
upon those resources that are proximal to the conditions of his life; he sees
only those he loves who are trapped in the disorder around him."[24] In the
second hearing, though, he puts himself in Baxter's position and tries to
imagine what he is hearing instead, and this identification with Baxter
makes him change fundamentally his interpretation of the work. When
he connects it only to how he imagines Daisy's life, the poem appears to
him to offer a consoling message about the possibility that personal love
will provide protection against life's uncertainties. When he sees it as he
thinks Baxter might, though, the poem strikes a pessimistic note; it "rings
like a musical curse" and leaves the haunting image of those "drear and
naked shingles of the world" foremost in one's mind.

Henry's encounter with this particular poem appears to be
unique to his experience. He is not reading it for insight into history
or social mores, as he did Flaubert and Tolstoy, or using it as a prop to
his own ego, as he did Kafka's story. Nor is he ultimately mistakenly
hearing only echoes of Daisy's biography, as he does at first. Instead, in
considering how the poem might be heard by someone else, someone
whose identity and experience have dimly concerned him throughout
the day, he is for the first time interpreting a text in terms of the
imagined significance it might have for another person. He is thinking
about how another individual might appreciate a cultural experience,
how that experience might reverberate in another life. He is identifying with Baxter imaginatively.

Of course, there is no easy way to assess Henry's mutating motivations. We might ourselves be imagining that part of what matters to
Henry is whether the poem will set Baxter on another course, and in this
light his identification with Baxter is prompted by his need to assess the
poem's potential impact on the volatile situation in his living room. Yet
he does genuinely attempt to imagine Baxter's consciousness and to see
how a literary work might make a listener reflect upon himself and his
intentions. The identification that he feels with Baxter even foments a

significant portion of empathy, when later, after conspiring with his son
to throw him down the stairs,

> he sees in the wide brown eyes a sorrowful accusation of betrayal. He, Henry
> Perowne, possesses too much—the work, money, status, the home, above all, the
> family—the handsome healthy son with the strong guitarist's hands come to res-
> cue him, the beautiful poet for a daughter, unobtainable even in her nakedness,
> the famous father-in-law, the gifted, loving wife; and he has done nothing, given
> nothing to Baxter who has so little that is not wrecked by his defective gene, and
> who is soon to have even less. (236)

Meanwhile, we know very little about how Baxter himself interprets the
poem. Having heard it read a second time, he appears "elated" and says,
"It's beautiful. You know that, don't you. It's beautiful. And you wrote it"
(231). His subsequent remark that it "reminds him of where he grew up"—
the only bit of interpretive detail we are given—could mean anything:
that he grew up by the sea, that he grew up in a place where he could
find solace from the world, or that his childhood was the uncertain, fear-
ful ground of clashing armies from which one would welcome love's protection. We can only guess what it is about the experience of hearing the
poem that Baxter finds so moving. He is perhaps affected by his mistaken
idea that the beautiful, young, pregnant reader of the poem is the author
("You wrote that. You *wrote* that"), by the beauty of the language, and
by its identification of some feature of his own experience. We can easily imagine that someone inflicted with his illness would long for comfort
against the melancholy roar of certainties inexorably withdrawn.

What we do know for certain is that he has now, at least temporarily,
been softened against his criminal intent. He tells his accomplice that he
has "changed [his] mind" and then attempts to engage Daisy in "eager"
conversation. Henry notices his striking naïveté and claims he's gone
from "lord of terror to amazed admirer. Or excited child" (231–32). Baxter
appears curious about Daisy's method: "How could you have thought of
that? I mean, you just wrote it," and the fact that we are told that he
several times repeats this statement—"You wrote it!"—perhaps indicates
that he is quite overwhelmed by the sheer fact of the poem's existence:
How could such a thing come to be? How could a human being produce
something so different from other sorts of things? The displacement of
his criminal intent by his awakened literary interest is finally confirmed

by his desire to take the book with him for further review: "I'm having this," he cries. "You said I could take anything I want. So I'm taking this. OK?" (232). His desire to keep the poem as a personal possession, close at hand, is affecting. He evidently identifies the poem with the physical book in which he believes it appears. He can hardly go from the Perownes' living room to library or bookstore to seek it out, so instead of robbing the Perownes, he will leave only with literature.

If Carey's *What Good Are the Arts?* provides an able guide to Henry's limitations, we can look to Tessa Jowell's thoughts about the arts' value, penned while she was minister of culture, for help in interpreting Baxter's pacification. Jowell's conviction is that culture is at the heart of any "healthy society," and she laments that we lack "convincing language" explaining how that is true. She notes how often politicians have been made to discuss culture only in terms of "its instrumental benefits to other agendas," thereby avoiding "investigating, questioning and celebrating what culture actually does in and of itself."[25] In response Jowell proposes to articulate the purpose of culture "in and of itself" in order to uncover legitimate noninstrumental reasons to value culture.

Jowell cites William Beveridge's famous insistence that the British nation commit itself to slaying the "five giants of physical poverty—want, disease, ignorance, squalor and idleness." She claims that it is now time to slay a sixth giant, "the poverty of aspiration," because it is this poverty "which compromises all our attempts to lift people out of physical poverty." For her, engagement with culture can alleviate this poverty of aspiration, so government should set its sights on bridging the gap between those who aspire and those who do not. Not just any culture will do. What is required is a "complex" and "engaged" culture: she is reluctant to call it "higher" but comfortable juxtaposing it to "entertainment." Providing people with more opportunities to access complex culture, providing more Baxters with chances to come to know "Dover Beach," will make them more inclined to aspire and thus more likely to succeed in improving themselves. Culture is for her linked fundamentally to the worth of people's lives. Those who do not have access to complex culture lack the tools to develop fully as human beings. Culture's ability to contribute to self-development and self-fulfillment is its most important source of noninstrumental value. Hence she affirms the government's "desire that all, not just a minority, should have access to the thrill of engagement with great art" and states that in engaging with art, we will have expert guidance in our attempts to understand "the internal world we all inhabit—the world of individual birth, life and death, of love or pain, joy or misery, fear and relief, success and disappointment." She states that those who do not attempt to engage with this culture, those who are reluctant "to attempt that challenge," are wasting their human potential, "with a concomitant loss of human realization." It is "complex cultural activity" that is "at the heart of what it means to be a fully developed human being," and a government worried about the fact that so few people are driven by pursuit of their full potential should use culture as a means to set them on a new course.[26]

Jowell claims that it was in the 1980s, under Thatcher's influence, that arts ministers began to lose any sense of the arts' inherent value: "The arts were regarded as lazy teenagers who needed to stand on their own two feet, to earn what public money they were given [so] the costs of admission to expensive art forms became more and more unaffordable for most people."[27] This led to a spiral of decline in which elite arts and accessible culture diverged more and more. For her there is a clear relationship between the elite arts and personal wealth, but this relationship is a problem. Much like the Perownes, with their "comically formidable panoply of professional skill, literary and artistic distinction, and affluence,"[28] wealthy people are disproportionately exposed to the arts and thus disproportionately exposed to the resources allowing for full human development. Everyone should be allowed the chance to benefit from the "private reserves and the lifelong enrichment" that "complex culture" provides.[29] Government funding should not go just to supporting the Royal Opera House directly, for instance, but should aim to create the kind of citizen who will want to visit it, through programs to expose schoolchildren to classical music and opera and thus give them "the equipment, the possibility, of choosing" among cultural options.[30]

She points out that she has been "lucky enough, and millions of others have been, to make sure their children grow up loving music, going to the theatre, enjoying art and reading books. We don't do that because it will get our children better jobs. We do it because we have loved doing it and we think they will too."[31] Her vision of arts funding is thus fundamentally about exposing those less fortunate than herself to the complex culture they would not otherwise have the chance to access and understand. She claims that even if people are provided with equal opportunities to achieve personal wealth and "material fulfillment," they will lack something if they fail to experience complex culture and what it provides—"an understanding of, an engagement with and the satisfying of the deepest of human needs."[32]

The scene of Baxter's transformation might appear to be a parable of Jowell's conception of the aesthetic: the arts will humanize people and contribute to their self-fulfillment; as the wealthy already know, "complex cultural activity" will make your life better and make you a better person. Aspiration to better *conditions* of life may result from encounters with culture, but that aspiration is less important than the intrinsic and noninstrumental value in the opportunity to be "elated" by encountering the work of great artists who are able guides to the human condition. I suggest though that what we find in *Saturday* is hardly a simple affirmation of such a vision of art's ameliorative capacities. What the novel intimates instead is the possibility that art will at best reconcile someone like Baxter to his life's insufficiency. Art has, in Henry's own words, "cast a spell" (288) over Baxter; it has provided a moment of magic. In this light, the novel opens the idea of art's ameliorative capacities up for critique by suggesting the poem pacifies Baxter to the point that he can be overcome again by the same professional class that misled him earlier. The change in Baxter's consciousness promises no parallel change to his social location, while Henry is insulated culturally, socially, and professionally from any proper recognition of the fact that he may need to change as much as, if not more than, Baxter does.

Henry's moment of self-critical sympathy for Baxter as he falls down the stairs—"he has done nothing, given nothing to Baxter who has so little"—is soon retracted. He faults his father-in-law for admitting to having felt sorry for Baxter, he treats Baxter as a medical case easily dispatched, and then just before the story ends, having returned from saving Baxter's life through surgery, he again firmly inhabits his habitual point of view. In a reprise of his morning, we find him looking out over his city square before sleep and telling himself that "fate" is inevitable, that biology and bad luck constrain the life of "the sort of person who can't earn a living, or resist another drink, or remember today what he resolved to do yesterday." He goes on:

No amount of social justice will cure or disperse this enfeebled army haunting the public places of every town. So what then? Henry draws his dressing gown more closely around him. You have to recognize bad luck when you see it, you have to look out for these people. Some you can prise from their addictions, others—all you can do is make them comfortable somehow, minimise their miseries. (282)

This conclusion suggests that what matters about Baxter's transformation is, ultimately, the overcoming of him that it sets in motion. Because of his exposure to "Dover Beach," Baxter can be further pacified by Henry's continuing to lie about the possibility of help for his disease, then violently injured, then placed beneath Henry's surgeon's hands on an operating table; and after the surgery Henry retreats to his comfortable home to tell himself he is perfectly right to treat misery as an inevitability whose effects one can only "minimise." Baxter's overcoming is inseparable from Henry's aversive turn away from a budding identification with Baxter— an identification made possible by, and enacted through, his own hearing of "Dover Beach"—in favor of further entrenchment in professional privilege that he wears as justification for his blinkered perspective. Just as Baxter's presence in the house is a result of Henry's own earlier actions, Baxter's literary experience fails to be meaningful because it is unaccompanied by any shift in Henry's consciousness.

The scene is in these terms very much an exposition of Herbert Marcuse's theory of "affirmative culture," a culture that rests upon "assertion of a universally obligatory, eternally better and more valuable worth that must be unconditionally affirmed: a world essentially different from the factual world of the daily struggle for existence, yet realizable by every individual for himself 'from within,' without any transformation of the state of fact." In affirmative culture, what is overthrown is not "the material order of life" but "the soul," and humanity is not the means, ends, or rationale for a just social order but simply "an inner state" easily achieved.[33]

Of course, it is also through study of Henry's bourgeois consciousness that the novel intimates another sort of perspective on art's value, asking us to decide what it is that Henry lacks because he lacks literary awareness. I have discussed how the novel singles out the literary as having a uniquely important social function that sets it apart from the culture that Henry is able to appreciate. The novel presents the arts, especially here music and the visual arts, as all too easily made into signs of one's elite status and props to one's conventional modes of self-affirmation. It in turn presents literature as uniquely able to act as what political philosopher Russell Keat has called a "meta-good," meaning a good that may cause us to reflect upon the relative value of other kinds of goods to human well-being—indeed, that may prompt critical reflection on the nature of well-being itself, as a means not of satisfying existing preferences but perhaps of transforming them into "more considered" ones.[34] Henry's lack of interest in literature manifests and signals his inability to assess properly the value of the other sorts of goods—items like his house and his car, but also his professional expertise—by which he measures his life's value. Yet if the characterization of Henry highlights literature's capacity to serve as a "meta-good," it also signals the difficulty of achieving authentic self-scrutiny and evaluation of the other goods with which one surrounds oneself and suggests, through the story of Henry's encounter with Baxter's exposure to "Dover Beach," that introspective assessment of the relative value of goods will need to lead to broad social change before someone like Baxter will benefit.

It is thus unwise to decide from McEwan's use of "Dover Beach" that he is simply interested in affirming the liberal creeds of enlightened personal love and self-fulfillment through cultural consumption. The novel by all means *explores* a conception of literature as improving for both an avaricious propertied class and for the social inferiors who threaten them. But Henry's inability to appreciate literature is correlated to his insistent rationalism and to the determination of his character by his vocation and suggests a lack of ability to engage adequately in informed debate about his own perspectives and to identify imaginatively with other people. The underclass criminal, who is thought by Henry to be condemned by "luck" to an inferior life, is softened by his encounter with a canonical poem, thus paving the way for the Perownes' final triumph over him. Yet the novel is hardly a fantasy of successful cultural governance, akin to work like Jowell's, wherein the aesthetic will contribute to self-fulfillment and to a sense of well-being and will correct any failure to aspire to the better things in life. The novel is too concerned about its own anchoring consciousness, too focused on what Henry cannot accomplish, to support such a reading.

It is not insignificant that the novel strives to be what it recommends: cultural goods that, in Keat's terms, "extend one's own range of experience" and "provide one with some understanding of the possibilities, dangers and attractions of lives one has not (yet) led, and some means of reflection on that which one already has."[35] It attempts something like Parker's *Exploded Shed*: "By blowing up the shed Parker is . . . throwing doubt on all it represents. Its contents are revealed, damaged in the process and yet somehow more eloquent. We get an 'exploded view' which creates a vast new space for our own mental activity." *Saturday* partakes of the same logic as the visual art its protagonist does not understand: it attempts to "explode" our habitual modes of apprehension, our oversights and complicities, our ways of talking to ourselves about our ways of being in the world. This suggests that while McEwan clearly has a strong sense of the value of the social practice to which he devotes so much time, he is aware of the many means through which literary experience can become a prop to mindful interiority with no social or political purchase. In other words, another form of McEwan's investment in the value of his own work—in addition, that is, to presenting literature as a privileged site of rational debate and imaginative identification, and to mining literary history throughout the narration—is the novel's way of turning back upon itself, revealing its contents as "damaged but eloquent," eloquent because they are damaged. It checks its own aspirations by avoiding any complacent sense of art's obvious social value.

Conclusion

Kazuo Ishiguro's *Never Let Me Go* shares *Saturday*'s interest in the delimitation of art's radical possibility. It imagines a late twentieth-century England in which medical science has advanced to the point that human beings now prolong their lives by mining the organs of clones. Kathy, the novel's clone narrator, has been told from an early age that after she leaves school, she will "donate" one after another organ until she "completes," or dies. She understands and accepts this process as her life's purpose and is frustratingly reticent about blaming anyone or expressing any outrage or opposition.

Making art is a major part of the curriculum at Hailsham, the school where the clones board and where most of Kathy's fondest memories originate. The students do not understand their art's real purpose, however. They do not know that the people who run the school are engaged in a campaign to prove that clones have souls, which they hope will result in their being treated humanely before they donate and die. The students' art making is crucial to the Hailsham cause because art is taken to be a portable expression of an inner life. For the noncloned humans involved, the ability to make art is an instantly recognizable sign of one's humanity. In a world in which people otherwise recoil from clones in disgust, the clones' appreciation for and creation of art are supposed to counteract prejudice. The Hailsham project's logic is thus quite contradictory: while clones should continue to exist to supply medical science, they are also human beings who possess authentic interiority and should thus have good lives. They are at once only bodies and not only bodies. That their lives will be ended artificially and at the whim of the same shadowy powers that brought them to life is not an issue the Hailsham charity sets out to address. Instead, through display of Hailsham students' creative work, they simply enjoin people to "Look at this art! How dare you claim these children are anything less than fully human?"[1] The humanitarian project is expressly designed to stop at raising awareness of the clones' humanity, having ensured that people know that the organs they rely upon do not appear "from nowhere" or grow "in a vacuum" (257). Hailsham's claims are thus managerial rather than political: it will perfect the running of the existing order rather than attempt to transform it.

The form of *Never Let Me Go* is then an expression of Ishiguro's attempt to avoid creating the kind of decorative or ameliorative work that the clones themselves are limited to. Ishiguro leads the reader to long for expressions of outrage, but mainly by refusing to articulate them. He condemns cruelty—who would object?—but refuses to horrify us with details about precise harms. He emphasizes the clones' pursuit of the truth about their lives but also undermines the value of what they might find, since whatever information they gather cannot alter the reality of their limited options. It is important to Kathy's narrative perspective that she does not emphasize her own or others' suffering and cannot name in any precise way the specifics of the system that determines their lives. The novel thereby avoids looking squarely at the vast social inequities that are nevertheless its structuring concern, preferring to consider its characters' reasons for looking away from them. This form of narration perfectly complements the novel's depiction of a world in which several traditional modes of imagining art's critical capacities—art as a form of dissent, art as a means of self-exploration, art as giving voice to the voiceless—have been invalidated, either because of the barriers to them or because these modes have themselves been turned to instrumental ends. Through these formal means the novel attempts to foster the reader's desire for the kind of outraged political utterance and critical negation that are impossible in Kathy's world. It moves us to wish for an outrage it never expresses and suggests that the best that art can hope to do is meditate upon its own insufficiency in a way that leaves readers discomfited and disconsolate.

Kathy's lover, Tommy, is the character who comes closest to producing critical art. He refuses to make anything pleasing to Hailsham. His drawings—of fragile, pitiable creatures that are at once animal and machine—are not intended for display there. Kathy's description of Tommy's art evidently struggles with its meaning: "The first impression was like one you'd get if you took the back off a radio set: tiny canals, weaving tendons, miniature screws and wheels were all drawn with obsessive precision, and only when you held the page away could you see it was some kind of armadillo, say, or a bird" (184–85). She mentions too that "for all their busy, metallic features, there was something sweet, even vulnerable about each of them," and Tommy reports "that he worried, even as he created them, how they'd protect themselves or be able to reach and fetch things" (186). We thus witness Kathy seeing and not seeing. Though she perceives some resemblance to "a radio set" and sees "miniature screws and wheels," she does not see Tommy's mechanical animals as in any way meditating on the clones' own existence as a complex blend of organic and inorganic matter, animal and machine. Nor does she see in their evident vulnerability a sign of his own worry about how he and his friends will face what is before them. It seems that, though Kathy is adept at analyzing conversations and gestures for hidden meanings, she does not see art as warranting that kind of scrutiny. In her experience it is decorative and pretty and has no meaning beyond its surface appearance.

The novel's final paragraph finds Kathy closer than she had come before to indicating that she shares in some of the intensity that Tommy's art quietly suggests. Tommy has just died, and Kathy has taken what she characteristically deems an "indulgent" trip to Norfolk, a place she and her friends used to imagine as the location of all their lost objects. Here, as Kathy reflects upon her own inescapable nostalgic remembrances, she remarks: "Once I'm able to have a quieter life, in whichever centre they send me to, I'll have Hailsham with me, safely in my head, and that'll be something no one can take away" (281). Needless to say, knowing that they will soon "take away" her vital organs, as they have done the lives of the people dearest to her, her memories of a place that did nothing to halt that process seem like poor compensation. Yet in another light her fond memories are all the more precious because the future is so bleak. Kathy is nostalgic for a time in which she was blindly innocent of any knowledge of her serious fate. Her memories are an ameliorating compensation for a reality with no fundamental comforts, in which there are only donors' "ghastly battles" (232), in which Ruth and Tommy are dead and she will soon be, too, and there is no point in getting angry or trying to object to what is happening to her because there is no evident network of resistance, no hidden army into which she might be conscripted. Kathy is utterly alone. She will die soon and in a feeble state. She exists for the use of noncloned humans. She extends the lives of those who accept her consignment to subhumanity because it secures their own well-being. Her very existence in the world is the product of the desire of those in power to put their own persistence as biological beings first in any calculation. Retreating into one's memories is, in this context, entirely understandable. That Kathy admits at all to the truth of her life, recounting Tommy's rage, recounting her gradual coming to consciousness, may be what is remarkable.

After meekly comforting herself with the thought that she can dwell in her memories, Kathy describes one last wish:

I was thinking about the rubbish, the flapping plastic in the branches, the shoreline of odd stuff caught along the fencing, and I half-closed my eyes and imagined this was the spot where everything I'd ever lost since my childhood had washed up, and I was now standing here in front of it, and if I waited long enough, a tiny figure would appear on the horizon across the field, and gradually get larger until I'd see it was Tommy, and he'd wave, maybe even call. The fantasy never got beyond that—I didn't let it— though the tears rolled down my face I wasn't sobbing out of control. I just waited a bit, then turned back to the car, to drive off to wherever it was I was supposed to be. (282)

We glimpse in this passage the kind of emotion that she routinely avoids. Kathy's desire briefly transforms trash into cherished objects, and her fantasy of Tommy's return, alongside "everything I'd ever lost since my childhood," is the closest she comes to acknowledging that his death means something to her. We are relieved here, in a sense, by the evidence that Kathy is more human than machine. To be sure, she still speaks of her loss only as something without any agency behind it. No one has taken anything from her in her account; it is simply gone. Though she longs for its return in the form of a figure on the horizon, a figure that acknowledges her own existence with a wave or a call, that longing isn't inconsolable. It isn't "out of control." Nothing ever is for Kathy, because there is somewhere she is "supposed to be," and she will just focus her energy on that requirement, recover herself, and move on. But the tears are there, and by now they are what we want. Our wish for Kathy to scream and cry, to express indignation, is our wish for an art outraged by human suffering. It is a wish for the kind of motivated political commitment that Kathy cannot make for herself or find in her world. The novel's teasing of the reader with the possibility of this sort of release simply draws attention to its refusal to indulge it in any grand way.

**

Never Let Me Go is very much a New Labour novel. In Bruce Robbins's reading, it reflects upon "the ideology of the welfare state, which gives a grateful semblance of meaning and legitimacy to the stopgap efforts of every day." He reads Kathy as that state's ideal subject, her narration emotionally empty, "bureaucratic, cravenly accepting of monstrously limited expectations, dedicated to suppressing all 'agitation' at the deep injustice that underlies the system as a whole."[2] I have suggested previously that the novel makes it possible for us to empathize with Kathy's failure to articulate her outrage. As Robbins suggests, she lives in a world in which her voice is effectively silenced. I would note, however, contra Robbins, that the British Left tends to conceive the welfare state as an attempt to bring egalitarian and equalitarian aspirations to bear on governance. For most mainstream British Left intellectuals and writers, including Ishiguro, welfare is the institutional form given to the social agreement that equalitarian distribution of wealth and privileges is a moral necessity. In these terms, the novel's unseen government is more akin to the neoliberal state that has eroded the relationship between the governance and public welfare. It is the particular realities of neoliberal governance that structure the novel's attempt to think about how and why we look away from power, how our freedoms are premised upon others' limited prospects, and how particular ideologies of individuation and creativity either directly serve or inadequately mitigate the harms that exist.

Critics have recently argued that, despite its emphasis on "subjective well-being," neoliberal capitalism has been grounds for a surge of serious mental anguish and despair and for a generalized disaffection and depression. They suggest that this disaffection should be turned into the basis of capitalism's reform, because in emphasizing despair, we acknowledge the desires that neoliberalism produces and exploits but cannot satisfy.[3] In William Davies's terms, authentic unhappiness, the kind that cannot be easily gotten over and transformed into fodder for self-improvement, is "the critical negative externality of contemporary capitalism."[4] In my reading *Never Let Me Go* provides a literary counterpoint to these claims. The novel is worried about a world in which art can only be either an instrument of those in power or silenced by them, a world in which much of human experience, especially the economic and political rationalities that arrange it, is hidden from view. It presents Tommy's art, the most nearly politicized form in the novel, as falling on deaf ears. It presents artworks conscripted into the service of humanitarian causes as ineffective and temporary fads designed to ameliorate rather than change. It presents the kind of self-knowledge that we might conventionally consider a valuable result of engagement with art as of precious little use in addressing systemic social problems. The novel is, in short, thoroughly aware of all the ways in which the social and political values conventionally ascribed to art's critical capacities have been and can be challenged and undermined.

It is in this way a signal example of the tendencies in literature that I have considered throughout this book—tendencies that emerge in relation and response to a neoliberal unification of culture, governance, and capital under New Labour. In the process of describing this unification, I have presented the ideal of artistic autonomy as fundamentally contradictory and as an ongoing focus of interest and struggle precisely because of the tensions that define it. Investment in autonomy, both affective and practical, is at once an integral feature of capitalist cultural production and an expression of the desire to be free from its constraints. The ideal of autonomy is built into attempts to imagine new working arrangements as the fruit of postmaterialist values and into the assumption that high-level cultural producers are able to transcend the marketplace upon which they rely. Conditioned by a sense of the importance of autonomy, cultural workers confront with unease their lack of substantive independence and their incorporation into creative-economy projects and vocabularies. In Mark Banks's persuasive terms, "Workers routinely fail to demonstrate . . . a clear commitment to capitalist norms such as profit maximization, disinterested exchange or wealth accumulation."[5] All the same, when this failure serves as inspiration to their ongoing cultural production and is a means by which their work is sold as the product of their authentic inner selves, it is at once an opportunity and a problem. Hence, as Banks claims, the autonomy that cultural workers experience should be read as something "socially embedded, compromised or 'negotiated,'" as they engage the "quotidian 'struggle within' to try to mediate, manage or reconcile the varied opportunities and constraints of the art-commerce relation."[6] For this reason the wavering that I highlight in this book's introduction—between holding on to the idea of artistic autonomy because of what it can afford and pointing out where those very affordances become encumbrances—seems to me the appropriate critical relation to our contemporary moment.

It has been decades since Terry Eagleton argued that the art-commerce relation is a thoroughly dialectical one. He pointed out the many ways in which autonomous art may be perceived. It may appear, for example, as a bare reflection of the commodity form, existing for "nothing and nobody in particular," independent because "swallowed up by commodity production."[7] It can serve as a "prototype" for the autonomous middle-class subject who wishes to operate as though she is "entirely self-regulating and self-determining." It can be a refuge or release from the "values of competitiveness, exploitation and material possessiveness." Finally, and Eagleton thought most hopefully, it can function as an ongoing and deeply affective "vision of human energies as radical ends in themselves."[8] Echoing Eagleton, Stewart Martin concludes that art's autonomy is "both produced *and* destroyed by capitalist culture, both its ideology *and* its critique." Moreover, "if art's autonomy is a produced, and reproduced, contradiction of developed capitalist culture then it remains a vital form through which this culture can be resisted and criticized."[9]

Today recognition of the ideal of aesthetic autonomy as an ongoing locus of struggle seems especially necessary, since the notion of the aesthetic with which Eagleton then had the most sympathy, as the realm in which human energies are envisioned as "radical ends in themselves," has itself been turned so definitively to expedient application. Faith in a cultural realm liberated from the constraints of the capitalist market has

gelled with the new vocabulary of creativity and its political and economic uses. Artists' vaunted ability to contest bureaucratic management
and other forms of regimentation is no longer at all unique. They may be
"disaffected and morally unhappy . . . sell[ing] their minds to people they
don't like for purposes they don't feel at home with,"[10] but in this they are
now more like than unlike other kinds of workers. Many nonartists now
embrace an aesthetic conception of themselves, as works in progress that
exist for their own sakes. Their search for meaning can be akin to the
production of culture: at once an imperative internal quest and a means
to tap into and augment one's inherent potential in the service of career
development. For many nonartists, too, ceaseless self-scrutiny has become
a management protocol, a marker of one's commitment to one's work, as
a spirit of opposition to assigned roles and an openness to change have
become crucial facets of the ability to labor successfully. Moreover, both
artists and nonartists routinely face contradictory imperatives: critical of
the institutions that employ them but devoted to the work they do within
them; enjoined to make work an expression of who they really are but
in circumstances that leave them little time for thought about what that
might mean and that ask us to package that expression into a readily trad-
able form.

My hope is that my approach to these imperatives might encourage
other scholars of the humanities to contribute to the formation and dissemination of the new common sense Ross advocates. I take for granted
that the arts inform the narratives available to us as we attempt to perceive the world and make sense of it and that their study can serve as a
means of reflection upon what Brian Holmes describes as the "imaginary figures" that give our world meaning and structure our self-under-
standings.[11] More pressing for me is the way in which the arts reflect
upon the possibilities of their own autonomous status. Art becomes
thereby a space where the struggle between autonomy and the market
takes place—a space in which the possibility of establishing some sort of
autonomous relation to capital is imagined and negotiated and in which
the limits of the market are made plain.

When I first started to think about how the making and meaning of literature were affected by vocabularies and phenomena tied to the
creative-economy turn, I assumed that I would find a series of defensive

and inevitably failed or compromised efforts to rescue art from any instrumental imperative. What actually emerged into view, though, was something much less definitive. Like many other analysts and practitioners, writers have been using their work to wonder about the value and relevance of conventional forms of faith in art's autonomy from political and economic imperatives and to articulate hesitant and questioning visions of their work's possible purposes—expedient and otherwise. There is, moreover, no straightforward way in which this literature is simply critique. Even when it is critique, its anti-instrumental imperatives are exemplary, marketable, consumable, and often articulated in a way that anticipates their suitability to what they contest. It is of course against this very backdrop of the marketable antimarket gesture, of recognition of the service art can do to what it contests, that the ideal of aesthetic autonomy becomes not a dead issue—a relic of modernism perhaps—but rather a vital concern for cultural producers all over again.[12] When people and their activities are reduced to mere utility, insisting upon the "uselessness of the aesthetic," "Kantian counterpoint to the brute utilitarian insistence of every other mode of cognition and social interaction" becomes all the more necessary.[13]

Notes

INTRODUCTION

1. UNESCO, *Creative Cities Network*, 2007, http://unesdoc.unesco.org/images/0015/001560/156026e.pdf, par. 1.

2. Justin O'Connor, "Intermediaries and Imaginaries in the Cultural and Creative Industries," *Regional Studies* 47 (2013): 11, doi:10.1080/00343404.2012.748982.

3. See Justin O'Connor, "The Cultural and Creative Industries: A Critical History," *Ekonomiaz: Revista Vasca de Economia* 78.3 (2011): 25–26.

4. The creative-economy turn is linked to neoliberalism by Jamie Peck, "Struggling with the Creative Class," *International Journal of Urban and Regional Research* 29 (2005): 740–70; Andrew Ross, *Nice Work If You Can Get It: Life and Labor in Precarious Times* (New York: New York University Press, 2009); and Eric Cazdyn and Imre Szeman, *After Globalization* (Malden, MA: Wiley-Blackwell, 2011), 77–99. My take on neoliberalism derives most from David Harvey, *A Brief History of Neoliberalism* (New York: Oxford University Press, 2007); Michel Foucault, *The Birth of Biopolitics: Lectures at the College de France, 1978–79*, ed. Michel Senellart, trans. Graham Burchell (London: Palgrave, 2008); and Jamie Peck, "Geography and Public Policy: Constructions of Neoliberalism," *Progress in Human Geography* 28.3 (2004): 392–405, who discusses state governments as "pre-eminent narrators of neoliberalization" (394).

5. For a succinct summary of this history, see Malcolm Miles, "The Culture Industries: Symbolic Economies and Critical Practices," *Social Analysis* 51.1 (2007): 14–15.

6. Anthony Giddens, *The Third Way: The Renewal of Social Democracy* (London: Polity, 1998), 24. On the language of the Third Way and its concession to economic rationality, see Norman Fairclough, *New Labour, New Language?* (London: Routledge, 2000), 15.

7. Alan Finlayson, *Making Sense of New Labour* (London: Lawrence and Wishart, 2003), 185.

8. Perri 6, "Governing by Cultures," *Demos Quarterly* 7 (1995): 11.

9. For celebratory treatments of the cultural worker as model flexible personality, see Richard Florida, *The Rise of the Creative Class: And How It's Transforming Work, Leisure, Community and Everyday Life* (Boston: Basic Books, 2002), 8–12, 67–82; and Charles Leadbeater and Kate Oakley, *The Independents: Britain's New Cultural Entrepreneurs* (London: Demos, 1999), 20–30. For critiques of the model, see Mark Banks, *The Politics of Cultural Work* (London: Palgrave, 2007), 69–93; Brian Holmes, "The Flexible Personality: For a New Cultural Critique," 2005, http://eipcp.net/transversal/1106/holmes/en; Ross, *Nice Work If You Can Get It*, 1–10; and Imre Szeman, "Neoliberals Dressed in Black; or, The Traffic in Creativity," *English Studies in Canada* 36.1 (March 2010): 15–36.

10. Work Foundation, *Staying Ahead: The Economic Performance of the UK's Creative Industries* (London: DCMS, 2007), 102.

11. For critiques of the rhetoric of the new economy, see Andrew Ross, *No-Collar: The Humane Workplace and Its Hidden Costs* (Philadelphia: Temple University Press, 2004); and Doug Henwood, *After the New Economy* (New York: New Press, 2003).

12. Holmes, "The Flexible Personality."

13. Luc Boltanski and Eve Chiapello, *The New Spirit of Capitalism*, trans. Gregory Elliott (London: Verso, 2005), 491.

14. Aravind Adiga, *The White Tiger* (New York: Free Press, 2008), 32.

15. Jeff Karem, *The Romance of Authenticity: The Cultural Politics of Regional and Ethnic Literatures* (Charlottesville: University of Virginia Press, 2004), 205.

16. Ibid., 206–7.

17. Marshall Berman, *The Politics of Authenticity: Radical Individualism and the Emergence of Modern Society*, new ed. (London: Verso, 2009), 163.

18. Russell Keat, *Cultural Goods and the Limits of the Market* (London: Palgrave, 2000), 14.

19. Scott Lash and John Urry, *Economies of Signs and Space* (London: Sage, 1994).

20. Timothy Aubry, *Reading as Therapy: What Contemporary Fiction Does for Middle-Class Americans* (Iowa City: University of Iowa Press, 2011), 17, 25.

21. Nikolas Rose, *Inventing Our Selves: Psychology, Power, and Personhood* (Cambridge: Cambridge University Press, 1996), 157.

22. See O'Connor, "Cultural and Creative Industries," 43.

23. Claire Bishop, *Artificial Hells: Participatory Art and the Politics of Spectatorship* (London: Verso, 2012), 22; see also Nicolas Bourriaud, *Relational Aesthetics* (Dijon: Presses Du Reel, 2002).

24. Bishop, *Artificial Hells*, 189.

25. See O'Connor, "Cultural and Creative Industries," 43; Brian Holmes, "Artistic Autonomy and the Communication Society," *Third Text* 18.6 (2005): 548.

26. See in particular Nicholas Brown, "The Work of Art in the Age of Its Real Subsumption under Capital," *nonsite.org*, accessed August 20, 2013, http://nonsite.org/editorial/the-work-of-art-in-the-age-of-its-real-subsumption-under-capital, par. 28; Mark Banks, "Autonomy Guaranteed? Cultural Work and the 'Art-Commerce Relation,'" *Journal for Cultural Research* 14.3 (2010): 251–70; and Stewart Martin, "The Absolute Artwork Meets the Absolute Commodity," *Radical Philosophy* 146 (November–December 2007): 15–25. I explore the politics of autonomous creative productivity in relation to the neoliberal university in Sarah Brouillette, "Academic Labor, the Aesthetics of Management, and the Promise of Autonomous Work," *nonsite.org*, no. 9, accessed August 20, 2013, http://nonsite.org/article/academic-labor-the-aesthetics-of-management-and-the-promise-of-autonomous-work.

27. Holmes, "Artistic Autonomy," 550.

28. Pierre Bourdieu, *The Rules of Art: Genesis and Structure of the Literary Field* (Stanford, CA: Stanford University Press, 1996), 56.

29. Jasper Bernes, "The Work of Art in the Age of Deindustrialization" (PhD diss., University of California, Berkeley, 2012), 11, 7.

30. On the "antagonism toward counting" that has discouraged literature scholars from engaging with sociology, see James F. English, "Everywhere and Nowhere: The Sociology of Literature after 'the Sociology of Literature,'" in "New Sociologies of Literature," special issue, *New Literary History* 41.2 (Spring 2010): v–xxiii.

31. Stephen Schryer, *Fantasies of the New Class: Ideologies of Professionalism in Post–World War II American Fiction* (New York: Columbia University Press, 2011), 200, 201.

32. Massimo De Angelis and David Harvie, "'Cognitive Capitalism' and the Rat-Race: How Capital Measures Immaterial Labour in British Universities," *Historical Materialism* 17 (2009): 15.

CHAPTER I

1. The term "thought-leader" is one Florida applies to himself; see his website, http://www.creativeclass.com/richard_florida/.

2. Florida, *Rise of the Creative Class*, 68–69.

3. Ibid., 68.

4. David Wilson and Roger Keil, "The Real Creative Class," *Social & Cultural Geography* 9.8 (2008): 846.

5. Leadbeater and Oakley, *Independents*, 15.

6. Florida, *Rise of the Creative Class*, 13.

7. Peter Drucker, *Landmarks of Tomorrow: A Report on the New "Post-modern" World* (1959; repr., Edison, NJ: Transaction, 1996), 81; Daniel Bell, *The Coming*

of Post-industrial Society: A Venture in Social Forecasting (New York: Basic Books, 1973); Erik Olin Wright, *Class Structure and Income Determination* (New York: Academic Press, 1979), and *Classes* (London: Verso, 1985); Alvin W. Gouldner, *The Future of Intellectuals and the Rise of the New Class: A Frame of Reference, Theses, Conjectures, Arguments, and an Historical Perspective on the Role of Intellectuals and Intelligentsia in the International Class Contest of the Modern Era* (New York: Seabury, 1979); Barbara Ehrenreich and John Ehrenreich, "The Professional-Managerial Class," *Radical America*, pt. 1, 11 (March–April 1977): 7–31, and pt. 2, 11 (May–June 1977): 7–22; Paul Fussell, *Class: A Guide through the American Status System* (New York: Summit Books, 1983); Robert B. Reich, *The Work of Nations: Preparing Ourselves for 21st-Century Capitalism* (New York: Knopf, 1991); Paul H. Ray and Sherry Ruth Anderson, *The Cultural Creatives: How 50 Million People Are Changing the World* (New York: Three Rivers Press, 2000); and John Howkins, *The Creative Economy: How People Make Money from Ideas* (New York: Penguin, 2002).

8. Peck, "Struggling with the Creative Class," 740.

9. See Martin Prosperity Institute, "About Us," accessed August 20, 2013, http://martinprosperity.org/about/.

10. See Creative Class Group, "Corporate Advising," http://www.creative-class.com/services/corporate_advising; and "Economic Development," http://www.creativeclass.com/services/economic_development.

11. Edward Glaeser makes this case in his review of *The Rise of the Creative Class*, available at http://creativeclass.com/rfcgdb/articles/GlaeserReview.pdf, accessed August 20, 2013, in which he concludes that the book is substantially correct, mistaken only in suggesting there is any difference between its findings and Glaeser's own work. Anne Markusen comes to similar conclusions, but is less self-serving, in "Urban Development and the Politics of a Creative Class: Evidence from a Study of Artists," *Environment and Planning* 38 (2006): 1921–40.

12. Sustained critical analysis of *The Rise of the Creative Class* is in Peck, "Struggling with the Creative Class"; Mark Banks, "Fit and Working Again? The Instrumental Leisure of the 'Creative Class,'" *Environment and Planning A* 41 (2009): 668–81; Paul Maliszewski, "Flexibility and Its Discontents," *Baffler* 16 (2004): 69–79; Alec MacGillis, "The Ruse of the Creative Class," *American Prospect*, December 18, 2009, http://prospect.org/cs/articles?article=the_ruse_of_the_creative_class; Cazdyn and Szeman, *After Globalization*, 77–100.

13. The best overviews of the history of reference to the creative industries are in Justin O'Connor, *The Cultural and Creative Industries: A Review of the Literature* (London: Creative Partnerships, Arts Council England, 2007); and Banks, *Politics of Cultural Work*. See also John Hartley, ed., *Creative Industries* (Malden, MA: Blackwell, 2005); and Richard E. Caves, *Creative Industries: Contracts between Art and Commerce* (Cambridge, MA: Harvard University Press, 2002).

George Yúdice, *The Expediency of Culture: Uses of Culture in the Global Era* (Durham, NC: Duke University Press, 2003), provides the most trenchant and sustained analysis of the configurations of government, capitalism, and culture to which creative-economy discourse points.

14. Kate Oakley, "Not So Cool Britannia: The Role of the Creative Industries in Economic Development," *International Journal of Cultural Studies* 7 (2004): 69.

15. Qtd. in Leadbeater and Oakley, *Independents,* 10–11.

16. DCMS, *International Strategy 2006* (London: DCMS, 2006), 14.

17. DCMS, *Creative Industries Economic Estimates Statistical Bulletin* (London: DCMS, 2007), n.p.

18. Work Foundation, *Staying Ahead: The Economic Performance of the UK's Creative Industries* (London: DCMS, 2007), 6.

19. Qtd. in Paul Roberts, *Nurturing Creativity in Young People: A Report to Government to Inform Future Policy* (London: DCMS, 2006), 5.

20. The phrase "competitive threat" is from Sir George Cox, *Cox Review of Creativity in Business: Building on the UK's Strengths* (Norwich, UK: Her Majesty's Stationery Office, 2005).

21. Qtd. in Charlie Tims and Shelagh Wright, *So, What Do You Do? A New Question for Policy in the Creative Age* (London: Demos 2007), 24.

22. Justin O'Connor suggests the tactical origins of reference to the creative industries in "Surrender to the Void: Life after Creative Industries," *Cultural Studies Review* 18.3 (December 2012): 390.

23. Ibid., 391.

24. Tony Blair, "Progressive Governance," *Progressive Politics* 2.1 (2003), http://www.policy-network.net/uploadedFiles/Publications/Publications/Blair(1).pdf.

25. Catherine Needham, "Citizen-Consumers: New Labour's Marketplace Democracy," Catalyst Working Paper (London: The Catalyst Forum, 2003), 17.

26. Philip Schlesinger, "Creativity and the Experts: New Labour, Think Tanks, and the Policy Process," *International Journal of Press/Politics* 14.1 (2009): 11.

27. Charles Leadbeater, *Living on Thin Air: The New Economy* (London: Penguin, 1999), 244.

28. Needham, "Citizen-Consumers," 9.

29. Stuart Hall, "New Labour's Double-Shuffle," *Soundings* 24 (July 2003): 14.

30. UK Government, *Modernising Government* (Norwich, UK: Her Majesty's Stationery Office, 1999), 5–10, 35.

31. See Banks, *Politics of Cultural Work,* 42.

32. Ross, *Nice Work If You Can Get It,* 24–28.

33. Angela McRobbie, "Re-thinking Creative Economy as Radical Social Enterprise," *Variant* 41 (Spring 2011), http://www.variant.org.uk/41texts/amcrobbie41.html, par. 1.

34. Qtd. in Alan Finlayson, "Cameron, Culture and the Creative Class: The Big Society and the Post-bureaucratic Age," *Political Quarterly* 82.s1 (2011): 41, 43.

35. David Cameron, "The Big Society" (speech), November 10, 2009, http://www.conservatives.com/News/Speeches/2009/11/David_Cameron_The_Big_Society.aspx.

36. Alan Finlayson, "The Broken Society versus the Social Recession," in *After the Crash: Reinventing the Left in Britain*, ed. Richard S. Grayson and Jonathan Rutherford (London: Lawrence Wishart, 2010), 33. My treatment of Cameron's politics is extensively indebted to this particular chapter and to Finlayson, "Cameron, Culture and the Creative Class."

37. Qtd. in Finlayson, "The Broken Society versus the Social Recession," 33.

38. Matt Stahl, *Unfree Masters: Recording Artists and the Politics of Work* (Durham, NC: Duke University Press, 2012), 11.

39. Perri 6, "Governing by Cultures," 8. See Finlayson, *Making Sense of New Labour*, 195.

CHAPTER 2

1. See Moishe Postone, *Time, Labor, and Social Domination: A Reinterpretation of Marx's Critical Theory* (Cambridge: Cambridge University Press, 1993), 33; cf. Karl Marx, *The Grundrisse* (1857–61; repr., London: Penguin, 1973), 325, 705–6.

2. Daniel Bell, *The Cultural Contradictions of Capitalism* (New York: Basic Books, 1976), 14–19.

3. Florida, *The Rise of the Creative Class*, 77–81, 193–94.

4. Bourdieu, *Rules of Art*, 56.

5. Jerrold Seigel, *Bohemian Paris: Culture, Politics, and the Boundaries of Bourgeois Life, 1830–1930* (Baltimore: Johns Hopkins University Press, 1986).

6. Bourdieu, *Rules of Art*, 60.

7. César Graña, *Modernity and Its Discontents: French Society and the French Man of Letters in the Nineteenth Century* (New York: Harper Torchbooks, 1967), 72.

8. Michel Feher, "Self-Appreciation; or, The Aspirations of Human Capital," *Public Culture* 21.1 (2009): 23, 33.

9. Maurizio Lazzarato, "Immaterial Labor," in *Radical Thought in Italy: A Potential Politics*, ed. Paolo Virno and Michael Hardt (Minneapolis: University of Minnesota Press, 1996), 133.

10. Ibid., 134–35.

11. Tiziana Terranova, "Free Labor: Producing Culture for the Digital Economy," *Social Text* 63 (2000): 51.

12. Lazzarato, "Immaterial Labor," 136.

13. Paolo Virno, "Notes on the 'General Intellect,'" in *Marxism beyond Marxism*, ed. Saree Makdisi, Cesare Casarino, and Rebecca E. Karl (New York: Routledge, 1996), 265; see also Terranova, "Free Labor," 51.

14. Paolo Virno, "General Intellect," trans. Arianna Bove, accessed August 20, 2013, http://www.generation-online.org/p/fpvirno10.htm, par. 5.

15. Lazzarato, "Immaterial Labor," 141.

16. Paolo Virno, "The Ambivalence of Disenchantment," in Virno and Hardt, *Radical Thought in Italy*, 21; Cf. Marx, *Grundrisse*, 692–93.

17. Virno, "General Intellect," par. 6.

18. Ibid., par. 7.

19. Ibid.

20. Paolo Virno, *A Grammar of the Multitude*, trans. Isabella Bertoletti, James Cascaito, and Andrea Casson (Los Angeles: Semiotext[e], 2004), 98.

21. Virno, "General Intellect," par. 8.

22. Virno, *Grammar*, 52.

23. Lazzarato, "Immaterial Labor," 144–46.

24. Antonio Negri, "Art and Culture in the Age of Empire and the Time of the Multitudes," *Substance* 36.1 (2007): 55.

25. Ibid.

26. Sylvère Lotringer, "Foreword: We, the Multitude," in Virno, *Grammar*, 15–16; See also Michael Hardt and Antonio Negri, *Empire* (Cambridge, MA: Harvard University Press, 2001), 359–64.

27. Lotringer, "Foreword," 16.

28. The phrase is from Timothy Brennan, "The Empire's New Clothes," *Critical Inquiry* 29 (2003): 347, where he also faults the autonomists for their focus on "noninvolvement and insubordination rather than on alliances or agendas," making resistance to capitalism not an action but "a mode of being."

29. Richard Florida, *The Flight of the Creative Class* (New York: HarperCollins, 2005), 188.

30. See Angela McRobbie, "From Holloway to Hollywood: Happiness at Work in the New Cultural Economy?," in *Cultural Economy*, ed. Paul du Gay and Michael Pryke (London: Sage, 2002), 97–114, and "Clubs to Companies," in *Creative Industries*, ed. John Hartley (Malden, MA: Blackwell, 2005), 375–90; Ross, *No-Collar*; Tiziana Terranova, *Network Culture: Politics in the Information Age* (London: Pluto, 2004); Ross, *Nice Work If You Can Get It*.

31. "Self-work" is from Paul Heelas, "Work Ethics, Soft Capitalism and the 'Turn to Life,'" in du Gay and Pryke, *Cultural Economy*, 78–96.

32. Feher, "Self-Appreciation."

33. See Axel Honneth, "Organized Self-Realization: Some Paradoxes of Individualization," *European Journal of Social Theory* 7.4 (2004): 463–78; Alain

Ehrenberg, *La fatigue d'être soi: Dépression et société* (Paris: Odile Jacob, 1998), and "Le sujet cérébral," *Esprit* 209 (2004): 130–55.

34. See Brennan, "Empire's New Clothes," 344.

35. See Peck, "Struggling with the Creative Class."

36. Florida, *Rise of the Creative Class*, 72.

37. See Silvia Federici, "Precarious Labor: A Feminist Viewpoint," *In the Middle of a Whirlwind* (blog), accessed August 20, 2013, http://inthemiddleofthewhirlwind.wordpress.com/precarious-labor-a-feminist-viewpoint.

38. Jason Read, *The Micro-politics of Capital: Marx and the Prehistory of the Present* (New York: State University of New York Press, 2003), 8, 6.

39. See Brennan, "Empire's new Clothes"; David Graeber, "The Sadness of Post-workerism, or, 'Art and Immaterial Labor' Conference, a Sort of Review," *Commoner*, January 19, 2008, http://www.commoner.org.uk/wp-content/uploads/2008/04/graeber_sadness.pdf.

40. Mario Tronti, "The Strategy of Refusal," in *Autonomia: Post-political Politics*, ed. Sylvère Lotringer and Christian Marazzi (Cambridge, MA: MIT Press, 2007), 32, 28.

41. Harry Cleaver, *Reading Capital Politically* (Austin: University of Texas Press, 1979), 74. See also Michael Ryan, *Politics and Culture: Working Hypotheses for a Post-revolutionary Society* (Baltimore: Johns Hopkins University Press, 1989), 55–56; Nick Dyer-Witheford, *Cyber-Marx: Cycles and Circuits of Struggle in High-Technology Capitalism* (Chicago: University of Illinois Press, 1999), 64–66.

42. Cleaver, *Reading Capital Politically*, 67, 70.

43. Accounts of this history are in ibid., 51–66; Ryan, *Politics and Culture*, 46–61; and, most comprehensively, Steve Wright, *Storming Heaven: Class Composition and Struggle in Italian Autonomi* (London: Pluto Press, 2002).

44. Lotringer, "Foreword," 11–12. See also Boltanski and Chiapello, *New Spirit of Capitalism*, 97; Martin Hartmann and Axel Honneth, "Paradoxes of Capitalism," *Constellations* 13.1 (2006): 47.

45. See Graeber, "Sadness of Post-workerism," 13.

46. Hardt and Negri, *Empire*, 294.

47. Virno, *Grammar*, 110; Ryan, *Politics and Culture*, 57.

48. Ryan, *Politics and Culture*, 46, 57.

49. Foucault, *Birth of Biopolitics*, 272.

50. The two classic studies are Mark Rose, *Authors and Owners: The Invention of Copyright* (Cambridge, MA: Harvard University Press, 1993); and Martha Woodmansee, *The Author, Art, and the Market: Reading the History of Aesthetics* (New York: Columbia University Press, 1996).

51. Bill Ryan, *Making Capital from Culture: The Corporate Form of Capitalist Cultural Production* (Berlin: Walter de Gruyter, 1992), 41–45.

52. Ibid., 44–45, 34. See also Banks, *The Politics of Cultural Work*, 185; Pierre Bourdieu, *The Field of Cultural Production*, ed. Randal Johnson (Cambridge: Polity Press, 1993).

53. Ryan, *Making Capital from Culture*, 49. See also Banks, *Politics of Cultural Work*, 6–7.

54. Ryan, *Making Capital from Culture*, 117.

55. Boltanski and Chiapello, *New Spirit of Capitalism*, 450, 449.

56. Graña, *Modernity and Its Discontents*, 63, 66.

57. Ibid., 68.

58. Berman, *The Politics of Authenticity*, 312 (italics in the original).

59. Graña, *Modernity and Its Discontents*, 168.

60. Qtd. in Bourdieu, *Rules of Art*, 60.

61. Graña, *Modernity and Its Discontents*, 41.

62. Honneth, "Organized Self-Realization," 470.

63. Ibid.

64. See Hartmann and Honneth, "Paradoxes of Capitalism," 43.

65. Foucault, *Birth of Biopolitics*, 225.

66. Charles Taylor, *The Ethics of Authenticity* (Cambridge, MA: Harvard University Press, 1991), 62.

67. Maurizio Lazzarato, "From Capital-Labour to Capital-Life," *ephemera* 4.3 (2004): 204.

68. Brennan, "Empire's New Clothes," 367.

CHAPTER 3

1. J. P. Guilford, "Creativity," *American Psychologist* 5 (1950): 446, 448.

2. Robert Weisberg, *Creativity: Beyond the Myth of Genius* (New York: W. H. Freeman, 1993), 242–43.

3. Frank Barron, "Putting Creativity to Work," in *The Nature of Creativity: Contemporary Psychological Perspectives*, ed. Robert J. Sternberg (Cambridge: Cambridge University Press, 1988), 81.

4. Donald W. MacKinnon, "The Nature and Nurture of Creative Talent," given first as The Walter Van Dyke Bingham Lecture at Yale University on April 11, 1962; published in *American Psychologist* 17.7 (July 1962): 485, 494.

5. Writers were not always willing subjects. When Amy Lowell was asked to visit IPAR, she wrote a poem titled "To the Impudent Psychologist," or "To a Gentleman Who Wanted to See the First Drafts of My Poems in the Interest of Psychological Research into the Workings of the Creative Mind" (MacKinnon, "Nature and Nurture," 491); poet Kenneth Rexroth reacted similarly, publishing an attack on the IPAR's attempted "Vivisection of the Poet" in the *Nation* in 1959.

6. Frank Barron, "Complexity-Simplicity as a Personality Dimension," *Journal of Abnormal and Social Psychology* 48.2 (1953): 164.

7. Ibid., 194–95.

8. Frank Barron, *Creativity and Personal Freedom* (New York: D. Van Nostrand, 1968), 238.

9. Barron, "Putting Creativity to Work," 84.

10. Cecil Day-Lewis, *The Poetic Image* (London: Jonathan Cape, 1946), 89.

11. Barron, "Putting Creativity to Work," 88.

12. Ibid., 92.

13. Barron, *Creativity and Personal Freedom*, 244–47.

14. Barron, "Putting Creativity to Work," 89.

15. Barron, *Creativity and Personal Freedom*, 223–44.

16. Mike Arons, "Frank Barron and the Creativity Revolution," in *Unusual Associates: A Festschrift for Frank Barron*, ed. Alfonso Montuori (Cresskill, NJ: Hampton Press, 1996), 63–64.

17. Ibid., 65.

18. Ibid., 66.

19. Barron was, however, the chief psychological consultant for a museum exhibit called *Creativity: The Human Resource*, sponsored by Chevron. One-third of the exhibit featured profiles of eighteen Americans who had had notably "creative careers." It also included some of the tests Barron had devised on an interactive terminal where people could test themselves ("Putting Creativity to Work," 78). It was accompanied by a film and a resource book that were distributed to local schools where the exhibit was mounted and was seen by more than five million people in twenty-one cities before becoming a permanent feature at the Pacific Science Center in Seattle.

20. Frank Barron, "Barron's Ordinary Wars," in Montuori, *Unusual Associates*, 441.

21. Abraham Maslow, *The Farther Reaches of Human Nature* (New York: Viking Press, 1971), 81, 93.

22. Abraham Maslow, *Toward a Psychology of Being* (Princeton: D. Van Nostrand, 1962), 137.

23. Maslow, *Farther Reaches of Human Nature*, 57.

24. Rose, *Inventing Our Selves*, 161.

25. Frank G. Goble, *The Third Force: The Psychology of Abraham Maslow* (New York: Grossman Publishers, 1970), 93–94.

26. Qtd. in ibid., 172.

27. Abraham Maslow, *Eupsychian Management: A Journal* (Homewood, IL: Richard D. Irwin and the Dorsey Press, 1965), xi, 192.

28. Ibid., 1, 7, 88, 103.

29. Maslow, *Toward a Psychology*, 131.

30. Richard J. Lowry, *A. H. Maslow: An Intellectual Portrait* (Belmont, CA: Wadsworth Publishing, 1972), 55.

31. Maslow, *Farther Reaches of Human Nature*, 59–70.

32. Ibid., 135.

33. Maslow, *Farther Reaches of Human Nature*, 305–7.

34. Maslow, *Eupsychian Management*, 188.

35. Ibid., 192–93.

36. Maslow, *Farther Reaches of Human Nature*, 58.

37. Ibid., 59.

38. Ibid., 96–99.

39. Maslow, *Eupsychian Management*, 264.

40. Abraham Maslow, "See No Evil, Hear No Evil: When Liberalism Fails," in *Future Visions: The Unpublished Papers of Abraham Maslow*, ed. Edward Hoffman (London: Sage, 1996), 165.

41. Teresa Amabile, *Creativity in Context: Update to "The Social Psychology of Creativity"* (Boulder, CO: Westview Press, 1996), 90.

42. Teresa Amabile, *The Social Psychology of Creativity* (New York: Springer-Verlag, 1983), 5.

43. Ibid., 14.

44. Ibid., 8–14.

45. Ibid., 15.

46. Amabile, *Creativity in Context*, 90, 109, 115.

47. Stephen Overell, *Inwardness: The Rise of Meaningful Work* (London: The Work Foundation, 2008), 24.

48. Ronald Inglehart, *Modernization and Postmodernization: Cultural, Economic, and Political Change in 43 Societies* (Princeton, NJ: Princeton University Press, 1997), 70.

49. Ibid., 67–80 (my emphasis).

50. Ibid., 44.

51. Overell, *Inwardness*, 25.

52. Tom Peters, *Thriving on Chaos: Handbook for a Management Revolution* (New York: Knopf, 1987), xi–xii.

53. Tom Peters, *Liberation Management: Necessary Disorganization for the Nanosecond Nineties* (New York: Knopf, 1992), 173.

54. Ibid., 468–79, 741.

55. Ibid., 496, 473, 489.

56. Ibid., 609.

57. Tom Peters, "The Work Matters," address delivered in Boston, March 1, 1999, http://www.providersedge.com/docs/leadership_articles/The_Work_Matters_Movement.pdf, 19.

58. Ibid., 20.

59. Tom Peters, *The Brand You 50: Fifty Ways to Transform Yourself from an "Employee" into a Brand That Shouts Distinction, Commitment, and Passion!* (New York: Knopf, 1999), 24 (ellipses and boldface in the original). Many other self-help books informing people how and why to brand themselves have appeared in recent years, and they differ little from Peters's. These include Jay Levinson and Seth Godin, *Get What You Deserve!* (New York: William Morrow, 1997), and nearly every title in Pearson's momentum series (published in Harlow, UK), such as Carmel McConnell, *Soultrader: Find Purpose, Find Success* (2002); Thomas Gad and Anette Rosencreutz, *Managing Brand Me: How to Build Your Personal Brand* (2002); and Carmel McConnell and Mick Cope, *Float You: How to Capitalize on Your Talent* (2001). The entrepreneur's biography is another popular genre, blending advice to readers with revelations of the author's journey of self-discovery; see, for example, Randy Komisar, *The Monk and the Riddle: The Art of Creating Life While Making a Living* (Cambridge, MA: Harvard Business Press, 2000), who states: "Like painting and sculpting, business can be a venue for personal expression and artistry, at its heart more like a canvas than like a spreadsheet. Why? Because business is about change. Nothing stands still. Markets change, products evolve. . . . Business is one of the last remaining social institutions to help us manage and cope with change" (55).

60. Peters, *The Brand You 50*, 26, 18.

61. Ibid., 125–29, 154.

62. Ibid., 72, 86.

63. Ibid., 86, 177, 181.

64. Ibid., 99, 149.

65. Richard Reeves, *Happy Mondays: Putting the Pleasure Back into Work* (Cambridge: Perseus, 2001). Titles similar to *Happy Mondays* in emphasis and outlook are legion and include Leadbeater, *Living on Thin Air* (1999); Kimberly Seltzer and Tom Bently, *The Creative Age: Knowledge and Skills for the New Economy* (London: Demos, 1999), produced for Demos; Linda Holbeche and Nigel Springett, *In Search of Meaning in the Workplace* (West Sussex, UK: Roffey Park Institute, 2004), produced for the Roffey Park Institute, a UK-based trust whose focus is "management development"; and Overell, *Inwardness* (2008), produced for The Work Foundation.

66. Reeves, *Happy Mondays*, 133, 145, 4.

67. Ibid., 70, 18, 2.

68. Ibid., 24, 7, 37, 177.

69. Ibid., 22, 128, 66.

70. Ibid., 28–29, 43, 50.

71. Barron, *Creativity and Personal Freedom*, 226.

72. Reeves, *Happy Mondays*, 53.

73. Maslow, "See No Evil, Hear No Evil," 165.

74. Reeves, *Happy Mondays*, 102.

75. Ibid., 154.

76. In a discussion paper released just a few years after *Happy Mondays*, Reeves admits that "the 'free' market may now be making us less free" and that "late capitalism" fails to give us "companionship, time for reflection, spirituality, security, intellectual development and joy in our children" (*The Politics of Happiness* [London: The New Economics Foundation, 2003], 4–5). The problem is again, however, our "barometers of success." Reeves suggests that the "market ethos" tyrannizes us because we let it; if we are exposed to a less materialist mind-set by, for instance, a course on "the good life" required until age sixteen, we will find more compelling work and happiness.

77. Richard Sennett, *The Culture of the New Capitalism* (New Haven, CT: Yale University Press, 2006); Heelas, "Work Ethics, Soft Capitalism."

CHAPTER 4

1. Eva Illouz, *Oprah Winfrey and the Glamour of Misery* (New York: Columbia University Press, 2003), 128.

2. Aubry, *Reading as Therapy*, 199, 201–2.

3. Joseph Slaughter, *Human Rights Inc.: The World Novel, Narrative Form, and International Law* (New York: Fordham University Press, 2007), 267.

4. Adiga, *The White Tiger*, 101. Subsequent page references appear in the main text.

5. Sanjay Subrahmanyam, "Diary," *London Review of Books* 30.21 (November 6, 2008): 43.

6. Ibid., 42.

7. Amitava Kumar, "Bad News: Authenticity and the South Asian Political Novel," *Boston Review* 33.6 (2008), http://bostonreview.net/kumar-bad-news.

8. See, for example, Salil Tripathi, "Unconvincing Dehumanization," *Philadelphia Inquirer*, November 16, 2008, http://www.philly.com/philly/entertainment/literature/34457084.html (site discontinued).

9. Man Booker Prize, "Man Booker Prize 2008 Winner Announced," accessed August 20, 2013, http://www.themanbookerprize.com/press-releases/man-booker-prize-2008-winner-announced.

10. Aravind Adiga, "Taking Heart from the Darkness," *Tehelka* 5.38 (September 27, 2008), http://www.tehelka.com/story_main40.asp?filename=hub270908Takingheart.asp; Stuart Jeffries, "Roars of Anger," *Guardian*, October 15, 2008, http://www.guardian.co.uk/books/2008/oct/16/booker-prize.

11. Man Booker Prize, "Aravind Adiga: 'Life Goes On As Before,'" http://www.themanbookerprize.com/perspective/articles/1125 (site discontinued).

12. Illouz, *Oprah Winfrey*, 118.

13. Tripathi, "Unconvincing Dehumanization."

14. Illouz, *Oprah Winfrey*, 118.

15. Claire Squires, *Marketing Literature: The Making of Contemporary Writing in Britain* (London: Palgrave, 2007), 119–46.

16. See, for example, Aravind Adiga, "The Delights of Delhi," *Time* (Asia ed.), February 20, 2006, Arts & Entertainment, 8; and "India's Growth Paradox," *Time* (Asia ed.), November 27, 2006, Arts & Entertainment, 49.

17. Jason Overdorf, "The Alleged Booker Prize," *Outlook India*, October 27, 2008, http://www.outlookindia.com/full.asp?fodname=20081027&fname=Arvind+Adiga+%28F%29&sid=3.

18. Qtd. in Sanjukta Sharma, "Aravind Adiga Wins Booker for Debut Novel," *Livemint*, October 16, 2008, http://www.livemint.com/2008/10/16003924/Aravind-Adiga-Wins-Booker-for.html?h=B.

19. Man Booker Prize, "Man Booker Prize 2008 Winner Announced."

20. Sharma "Aravind Adiga Wins Booker for Debut Novel."

21. Kumar, "Bad News."

22. W. H. Jensen, "Incredible Journey through a Changing India," customer review of *The White Tiger*, by Aravind Adiga, September 5, 2008, http://www.amazon.com/review/R3QJUMF85S80ZS.

23. Shiloh True "Rabid Reader," "All He Longed For Was a BIG BELLY, How Bad Could That Be," customer review of *The White Tiger*, by Aravind Adiga, October 28, 2008, http://www.amazon.com/review/R2C93PAZDZ3M1B/ref=cm_cr_pr_perm?ie=UTF8&ASIN=1416562605&nodeID=&tag=&linkCode=.

24. Talha F. Basit, "Great Insight into Indian Culture! Highly Recommended," customer review of *The White Tiger*, by Aravind Adiga, March 16, 2009, http://www.amazon.com/review/RIN6CHHWT5NKK/ref=cm_cr_pr_perm?ie=UTF8&ASIN=1416562605&nodeID=&tag=&linkCode=.

25. Beinggerrie "Kizzie," "White Tiger: Audiobook," customer review of *The White Tiger*, by Aravind Adiga, January 6, 2009, http://www.amazon.com/review/R3IToI1FBLTU11/ref=cm_cr_pr_perm?ie=UTF8&ASIN=1400106656&nodeID=&tag=&linkCode=.

26. Mr. Dip, "Balram Would Approve," customer review of *The White Tiger*, by Aravind Adiga, October 26, 2008, http://www.amazon.com/review/R2VUMPSN1ZPWJ5/ref=cm_cr_pr_perm?ie=UTF8&ASIN=1416562605&nodeID=&tag=&linkCode=.

27. Parth H. Mehta, "If I Could Give Less Than One, I Would Liberally Give It. Completely Artificial," customer review of *The White Tiger*, by Aravind Adiga, November 11, 2008, http://www.amazon.com/review/RP73U7OB-HIW4R/ref=cm_cr_pr_perm?ie=UTF8&ASIN=1416562605&nodeID=&tag=&linkCode=.

28. Ashish Kumar, "Brilliant, a Book That Was Needed—but Shallow," customer review of *The White Tiger*, by Aravind Adiga, December 20, 2008, http://www.amazon.com/review/RSQ344YXUURZ7/ref=cm_cr_pr_perm?ie=UTF8&ASIN=1416562605&nodeID=&tag=&linkCode=.

29. AD "AD," "Pandering to the West," customer review of *The White Tiger*, by Aravind Adiga, November 8, 2008, http://www.amazon.com/review/R3VKEN9ERX5PV6/ref=cm_cr_pr_perm?ie=UTF8&ASIN=1416562605&nodeID=&tag=&linkCode=.

30. See Jeffries, "Roars of Anger"; and Nick DiMartino, "Nick Interviews Aravind Adiga," *The Shelf Life* (blog), October 6, 2008, http://universitybook-store.blogspot.com/2008/10/nick-interviews-aravind-adiga.html.

31. Monica Ali, *In the Kitchen* (London: Transworld, 2009), 243. Subsequent page references appear in the main text.

32. John Marx's work, drawing attention to the "collaboration between fiction and scholarship" in Ali's work, is exceptional in this respect. See John Marx, "The Feminization of Globalization," *Cultural Critique* 63 (Spring 2006): 23.

33. I discuss the *Brick Lane* controversy in detail elsewhere. See Sarah Brouillette, "Literature and Gentrification on Brick Lane," *Criticism* 51.3 (Summer 2009): 425–49.

34. Alan Liu, *The Laws of Cool: Knowledge Work and the Culture of Information* (Chicago: University of Chicago Press, 2004), 8, 9.

CHAPTER 5

1. Richard Lloyd, *Neo-Bohemia: Art and Commerce in the Postindustrial City* (London: Routledge, 2006), 78.

2. Arts Council England, "About Us: Decibel," http://www.artscouncil.org.uk/aboutus/project_detail.php?sid=8&id=79&page=2 (site discontinued).

3. Problems with the program are outlined in Arts Council England, "Decibel Evaluation: Key Findings," April 2005, http://www.artscouncil.org.uk/publications/publication_detail.php?sid=8&id=465 (site discontinued).

4. Nick Tanner, "Literary Prize Bows to Pressure over Racial Discrimination," *Guardian*, January 18, 2007, http://books.guardian.co.uk/news/articles/0,,1992476,00.html.

5. Ibid.

6. Evans's sentiment echoes Anish Kapoor's reaction to having been invited to participate in *The Other Story*, a key 1989 exhibition of visual art by black British artists: "Being an artist is more than being an Indian artist. I feel supportive to that kind of endeavour. . . . It needs to happen once; I hope it is never necessary again" (qtd. in Sonja Dyer, *Boxed In: How Cultural Diversity Policies Constrict Black Artists* [London: Manifesto Club, 2007], 7).

7. "In Full Colour: Cultural Diversity in Book Publishing Today," ed. Danuta Kean, *The Bookseller*, March 12, 2004, supplement.

8. Sara Selwood, "The Politics of Data Collection: Gathering, Analysing and Using Data about the Subsidised Cultural Sector in England," *Cultural Trends* 12.47 (2002): 29–31.

9. Richard Appignanesi, "Introduction: 'Whose Culture?' Exposing the Myth of Cultural Diversity," in *Beyond Cultural Diversity: The Case for Creativity*, comp. and ed. Richard Appignanesi (London: Third Text Publications, 2010), 6.

10. Richard Hylton suggests that *decibel* has "compounded the problems of tokenism and racial separation within the visual arts sector" (*The Nature of the Beast: Cultural Diversity and the Visual Arts Sector* [Bath, UK: Institute of Contemporary Interdisciplinary Arts, 2007], 19). Jean Fisher writes: "It has been symptomatic of cultural diversity policies in general that a 'culturally different' artist is presumed to be 'representative' of that community" ("Cultural Diversity and Institutional Policy," in Appignanesi, *Beyond Cultural Diversity*, 63). Dyer notes, too, that black artists and curators are expected to "produce projects that are geared towards attracting a black and minority ethnic audience," and that can be mainly interpreted in relation to their racial backgrounds (*Boxed In*, 11). All of these commentators are concerned with the visual arts. Comparable research on the implications of recent diversity initiatives for the publishing sector has not yet been done.

11. Leon Wainwright, "Art (School) Education and Art History," in Appignanesi, *Beyond Cultural Diversity*, 101.

12. Jeff Karem, *The Romance of Authenticity: The Cultural Politics of Regional and Ethnic Literatures* (Charlottesville: University of Virginia Press, 2004), 205, 206–7.

13. Berman, *Politics of Authenticity*, 163.

14. Daljit Nagra, "Look We Have Coming to Dover!," in *Look We Have Coming to Dover!* (London: Faber and Faber, 2007), 32.

15. Rachel Cooke, "Hilda Ogden Is My Muse," *Observer*, February 4, 2007, Books sec.

16. Patrick Barkham, "The Bard of Dollis Hill," *Guardian*, January 18, 2007, Arts sec.

17. Ibid.

18. For further instances, see AE, "A Gourd Time," *Guardian*, February 9, 2007, http://books.guardian.co.uk/review/story/0,,2009444,00.html; and Sean O'Brien, "Poet of a Streetwise School of Eloquence," review of *Look We Have Coming to Dover!*, by Daljit Nagra, *Independent*, October 12, 2007, Books sec.

19. Nagra, "In a White Town," in *Look We Have Coming to Dover!*, 18.

20. Dave Gunning, "Daljit Nagra, Faber Poet: Burdens of Representation and Anxieties of Influence," *Journal of Commonwealth Literature* 43 (2008): 100.

21. YouTube, "Daljit Nagra Poetry Reading for Oxfam," August 8, 2007, http://youtube.com/watch?v=QzlabElZx2c.

22. WritersServices, "Oxfam Poetry," accessed August 20, 2013, http://www.writersservices.com/mag/07/Oxfam%20Life_Lines_2.htm.

23. Meet the Author, Daljit Nagra, "Look We Have Coming to Dover!," video, http://www.meettheauthor.co.uk/bookbites/1577.html.

24. David Harvey, *Spaces of Capital* (Edinburgh: Edinburgh University Press, 2001), 409, 397, 399.

25. Gautam Malkani, *Londonstani* (London: Penguin, 2006), 40. Subsequent page references appear in the main text.

26. Gautam Malkani, "About Londonstani," accessed August 20, 2013, http://www.gautammalkani.com/about_londonstani.htm; see also Gautam Malkani, "Sounds of Assimilation," *New York Times*, August 19, 2006, http://www.nytimes.com/2006/08/19/opinion/19malkani.html, and "Mixing and Matching: What's ~~Wrong~~ Right with Asian Boys?," *Financial Times*, April 22, 2007, 16.

27. See Gary Younge, "Londonistan Calling," review of *Londonstani*, by Gautam Malkani, *Nation*, September 25, 2006, http://www.thenation.com/article/londonistan-calling.

28. Anita Sethi, "The Curse of Being Labelled the 'New Zadie,'" *Guardian*, November 13, 2005, http://www.guardian.co.uk/media/2005/nov/14/pressandpublishing.bookscomment.

29. Qtd. in ibid; see also Sarfraz Manzoor, "Why Do Asian Writers Have to Be 'Authentic' to Succeed?" *Guardian*, April 29, 2006, http://observer.guardian.co.uk/review/story/0,,1764420,00.html.

30. Diana Evans, "Very Rudeboy," review of *Londonstani*, by Gautam Malkani, *Financial Times*, April 29, 2006, 32.

31. Trevor Lewis, "Way Out West," review of *Londonstani*, by Gautam Malkani, *Sunday Times*, April 20, 2006, 47.

32. Tim Martin, "U Hear Wot the Critix Chattin?," review of *Londonstani*, by Gautam Malkani, *Independent on Sunday*, May 7, 2006, 21.

33. Zoë Paxton, "He Speaks Their Language," review of *Londonstani*, by Gautam Malkani, *Times*, April 15, 2006, 7.

34. Malkani, "About Londonstani."

35. Ibid.

36. Jill Lawless, "Novelist Grew Up in Hounslow Himself," *Montreal Gazette*, July 8, 2006, 16.

37. Gautam Malkani, "Mixing and Matching," 16.

38. Ibid.

39. Malkani, "About Londonstani."

40. Malkani, "Mixing and Matching."

41. Malkani, "About Londonstani."

42. Sianne Ngai, *Ugly Feelings* (Cambridge, MA: Harvard University Press, 2005).

43. Malkani, "Mixing and Matching."

44. Malkani, "About Londonstani."

45. Paxton, "He Speaks Their Language."

46. Terry Eagleton, *The Idea of Culture* (Oxford: Blackwell, 2000), 34.

47. Michael Denning, *Culture in the Age of Three Worlds* (London: Verso, 2004), 79, 92, 96.

48. Harvey, *Spaces of Capital*, 394–411.

49. Denning, *Culture in the Age of Three Worlds*, 94.

50. De Angelis and Harvie, "'Cognitive Capitalism' and the Rat-Race," 15.

51. Other works of interest include Zadie Smith, *Autograph Man* (London: Hamish Hamilton, 2002); Tony White, *Foxy-T* (London: Faber and Faber, 2003); Nirpal Singh Dhaliwal, *Tourism* (London: Vintage, 2006); and Adiga, *The White Tiger*, which won the 2008 Man Booker Prize.

CHAPTER 6

1. David Harvey, *Rebel Cities: From the Right to the City to the Urban Revolution* (London: Verso, 2012), 27–66.

2. "Schools, Communities and Young Writers," *Spread the Word*, accessed June 23, 2012, http://www.spreadtheword.org.uk/index.php?id=education (site discontinued).

3. "Encompass," *Spread the Word*, accessed August 20, 2013, http://www.our-words.co.uk/index.php?id=projects&text=2683.

4. Sarah Butler, "Public Displays . . . ," *Mslexia* 42 (July–August–September 2009): 16.

5. "A Place for Words: A Sense of Place," *UrbanWords*, 2008, http:/www.urbanwords.org.uk/aplaceforwords/sense-of-place.php.

6. Ibid.

7. Sarah Butler, "Narrating the City," seminar presentation, Leeds Metropolitan University, Leeds, UK, October 3, 2008, http://www.urbanwords.org.uk/aplaceforwords/narratingTheCity.pdf, 4, 5.

8. Sarah Butler, with Inua Ellams, Subhadassi, Melanie Abrahams, Sophie Hope, David Ogunmuyiwa, and Paul Shepheard, "Writing the City: What Role Can Writers Play in the Process of Regeneration?," October 24, 2008, http://www.urbanwords.org.uk/aplaceforwords/TINAG.pdf, 4.

9. "A Place for Words: Communication and Articulation," *UrbanWords*, 2008, http://www.urbanwords.org.uk/aplaceforwords/communication-and-articulation.php.

10. "A Place for Words: Creative Consultation," *UrbanWords*, 2008, http://www.urbanwords.org.uk/aplaceforwords/creative-consultation.php.

11. "A Place for Words: Communication and Articulation."

12. Ibid.

13. Sarah Butler, "A Place for Words," *Writing in Education* 45 (September 2008): 42.

14. Butler, "Narrating the City," 10.

15. Sarah Butler, "Can Writing Shape Place?," conference presentation, University of Surrey, Guildford, UK, February 23, 2010, http://www.urbanwords.org.uk/aplaceforwords/can%20writers%20shape%20place.pdf, 5.

16. Ibid., 6.

17. Qtd. in Butler, "Public Displays . . . ," 17.

18. Bishop, *Artificial Hells*, 22.

19. Linda France, "Words in the World," unpublished Microsoft Word file, National Association of Writers in Education, 2010, http://www.nawe.co.uk/Private/17610/Live/Web-Resource-1.doc, 1.

20. Chris Meade, "A Place That Makes You Go 'Aaaaaaaaaahhhhhh,'" *UrbanWords*, 2009, http://www.urbanwords.org.uk/aplaceforwords/A%20Place%20That%20Makes%20You%20Go%20Ahh.pdf, 2.

21. Ibid., 4.

22. Ibid.

23. Rosa Ainley, "(Re)generating Change: Writing the Public Realm," *UrbanWords*, May 2010, http://www.urbanwords.org.uk/aplaceforwords/regenerating%20change.pdf, 1.

24. Ibid., 2.

25. Gerry Hassan, Melissa Mean, and Charlie Tims, *The Dreaming City: Glasgow 2020 and the Power of Mass Imagination* (London: Demos, 2007), http://www.demos.co.uk/files/Dreaming%20city.pdf, 10, 66–68.

26. Ibid., 208.

27. Ibid., 22.

28. Ibid., 22–23.

29. Ibid., 23.

30. Butler, "Narrating the City," 9, 6.

31. Qtd. in Butler, "Can Writing Shape Place?," 4.

32. Butler et al., "Writing the City," 3.

33. Butler, "Narrating the City," 10.

34. Ibid., 11.

35. Adrian Riley, interview by Neelam Shah, "The Shop of Priceless Things: An Interview with Adrian Riley," September 6, 2011, *UrbanWords*, http://www.urbanwords.org.uk/2011/09/the-shop-of-priceless-things-an-interview-with-adrian-riley/.

36. Ibid.

CHAPTER 7

1. For the clearest versions of the former tendency, see John Banville, "A Day in the Life," *New York Review of Books* (May 26, 2005), 8–9; and Elizabeth Kowaleski Wallace, "Postcolonial Melancholia in Ian McEwan's *Saturday*," *Studies in the Novel* 39.4 (Winter 2007): 465–80. For the latter, see Molly Clark Hillard, "'When Desert Armies Stand Ready to Fight': Re-reading McEwan's *Saturday* and Arnold's 'Dover Beach,'" *Partial Answers: Journal of Literature and the History of Ideas* 6.1 (January 2008): 181–206; and Teresa Winterhalter, "'Plastic Fork in Hand': Reading as a Tool of Ethical Repair in Ian McEwan's *Saturday*," *JNT: Journal of Narrative Theory* 40.3 (Fall 2010): 338–63.

2. Selwood, "Politics of Data Collection," 34.

3. Policy Action Team 10, *Arts & Sport. A Report to the Social Exclusion Unit* (London: Department for Culture, Media and Sport, 1999), 2; see also Selwood, "Politics of Data Collection," 36.

4. Bishop, *Artificial Hells*, 14.

5. Finlayson, *Making Sense of New Labour*, 154.

6. Winterhalter, "'Plastic Fork in Hand,'" 342.

7. Ian McEwan, *Saturday* (New York: Anchor, 2006), 3. Subsequent page references appear in the main text.

8. Ellis, "The Politics of Ian McEwan's 'Saturday,'" *Barbaric Words* (blog), February 4, 2005, http://barbaricwords.blogspot.ca/2005/02/politics-of-ian-mce-wans-saturday.html.

9. Hillard, "'When Desert Armies Stand Ready to Fight,'" 188.

10. Michael L. Ross, "On a Darkling Planet: Ian McEwan's *Saturday* and the Condition of England," *Twentieth-Century Literature* 54.1 (Spring 2008): 89.

11. Winterhalter, "'Plastic Fork in Hand,'" 343.

12. Ross, "On a Darkling Planet," 89.

13. John Carey, *What Good Are the Arts?* (London: Faber and Faber, 2005), 171.

14. Ibid., 174, 177.

15. "Among their crimes was a failure of the imagination," McEwan writes. See Ian McEwan, "Only Love and Then Oblivion," *Guardian* (September 15, 2001), http://www.guardian.co.uk/world/2001/sep/15/september11.politicsphilosophyandsociety2.

16. Carey, *What Good Are the Arts?*, 214.

17. Justin O'Connor. "Art, Popular Culture and Cultural Policy: Variations on a Theme of John Carey," *Critical Quarterly* 48.4 (2006): 50.

18. Carey, *What Good Are the Arts?*, 119.

19. Ibid., 258.

20. Jonathan Watkins, "On Cold Dark Matter," *Tate Modern*, accessed August 20, 2013, http://www2.tate.org.uk/colddarkmatter/texts4.htm.

21. Sebastian Groes, "Ian McEwan and the Modernist Consciousness of the City," in *Contemporary Critical Perspectives: Ian McEwan*, ed. S. Groes (London: Continuum, 2009), 102.

22. Ibid., 103.

23. Ross, "On a Darkling Planet," 89, 87.

24. Winterhalter, "'Plastic Fork in Hand,'" 359.

25. Tessa Jowell, "Government and the Value of Culture," May 2004, http://www.shiftyparadigms.org/images/Cultural_Policy/Tessa_Jowell.pdf, 8.

26. Ibid., 3–7.

27. Ibid., 12.

28. Ross, "On a Darkling Planet," 77.

29. Jowell, "Government and the Value of Culture," 14.

30. Tessa Jowell, "Why Should Government Support the Arts?," *engage review* 17 (Summer 2005): 3.

31. Ibid.

32. Jowell, "Government and the Value of Culture," 15.

33. Herbert Marcuse, "The Affirmative Character of Culture," in *Negations: Essays in Critical Theory* (Boston: Beacon Press, 1968), 95, 103.

34. Keat, *Cultural Goods and the Limits of the Market*, 157.

35. Ibid., 156.

CONCLUSION

1. Kazuo Ishiguro, *Never Let Me Go* (London: Faber and Faber, 2005), 256. Subsequent page references appear in the main text.

2. Bruce Robbins, "Cruelty Is Bad: Banality and Proximity in *Never Let Me Go*," *Novel* 40.3 (2007): 294, 296.

3. Mark Fisher, *Capitalist Realism: Is There No Alternative?* (Winchester, UK: O Books, 2009), 79.

4. William Davies, "The Political Economy of Unhappiness," *New Left Review* 71 (September–October 2011): 68.

5. Banks, *Politics of Cultural Work*, 184.

6. Banks, "Autonomy Guaranteed?," 252, 262.

7. I am citing Terry Eagleton, *The Idea of Culture* (Oxford: Blackwell, 2000), 9, 368, which presents a summation of his earlier work *The Ideology of the Aesthetic* (Oxford: Blackwell, 1990).

8. Eagleton, *The Idea of Culture*, 9.

9. Martin, "The Absolute Artwork Meets the Absolute Commodity," 17.

10. This was C. Wright Mills's take on intellectuals' agonized and antagonistic relationship to the white-collar workplace. Qtd. in Kevin Mattson,

Intellectuals in Action: The Origins of the New Left and Radical Liberalism, 1945–1970 (University Park: Pennsylvania State University Press, 2002), 55.

11. Holmes, "Artistic Autonomy," 549.

12. Brown, "Work of Art in the Age of Its Real Subsumption under Capital," par. 28.

13. Imre Szeman, "Manhattanism and Future Cities: Some Provocations on Art and New Urban Forms," in *Transnationalism, Activism, Art*, ed. Kit Dobson and Aine McGlynn (Toronto: University of Toronto Press, 2012), 25.

Index

Adam, Robert, 178
Adiga, Aravind, 8–9, 84–100, 114
aesthetics, 7–12, 15–19, 32–36, 42–
54, 112, 175–200. *See also* artists;
creativity; culture; the self
affective attachments, 2, 16, 31, 39–40,
84, 99–115, 120, 144, 205
affirmative culture, 197
Ainley, Rosa, 156, 165
Ali, Monica, 9, 85, 99–115, 129, 135,
223n32
"Almost an Island" (project), 171
Amabile, Teresa, 69–70
American Psychological Association, 58
Amis, Martin, 134
Anand, Mulk Raj, 96
Anderson, Sherry Ruth, 22
Armitage, Simon, 165
Arnold, Matthew, 12, 125, 149–50
artists: authenticity discourses and,
94–115, 132–48, 172, 205; capitalist
production and, 34–35, 40–42,
50, 86–94, 154–56, 172–74, 205–8;
creative self discourses and, 5, 8,
16–18, 31–32, 34–35, 55–56, 86–94,
220n59; flexibility and instability
of, 45, 58, 62, 66–70, 73–82, 89–90,
99–115; markets and marketing and,
6, 49–50, 53, 207; nonconformity
and, 57–63, 66–73; psychological
studies of, 55–56, 63–77;
regeneration projects and, 11, 154–74;
social resposniveness and, 15, 43–45,
66–67, 70, 90–91, 94–99, 175–205;

state relations to, 2–4, 12, 20–26,
33, 116–19, 131, 155–58, 175–76, 185,
194–96; workers as, 1, 4–5, 7–8,
34–43, 45, 49, 63–84, 86–99. *See also*
capitalism; creativity; labor
Arts Council England, 131, 157
Aubry, Timothy, 13, 84
authenticity: community
representations and, 116–17, 120–32,
136–48, 152–53, 157–58, 224n20;
diversity discourses and, 9–11,
94–99, 105–9, 120–32, 134, 223n6;
literary critiques of, 120–32, 137–
48; marketability of, 45, 51, 94–99,
101–2, 112–13, 134, 148–53; neoliberal
discourses and, 7, 13–14, 51–54, 109,
119–20, 133–48; self-expression and,
26, 36–39, 42–43, 54, 69, 148–53,
172, 205–8. *See also* artists; creativity;
literature; the self
authors and authorship: authenticity
discourses and, 94–99, 138–48; as
immaterial labor, 50–52, 148–53,
205; self as commodity and, 116–32,
135–37, 145, 151, 207, 224n10; social
science research and, 20–26, 139–45,
211n30, 223n32; writer-consultants
and, 154–65. *See also specific works
and writers*
autonomia movement, 34–36, 39–49,
51–54, 215n28
autonomy (aesthetic), 5–9, 15–19, 29–35,
69–70, 99–115, 158, 205, 208. *See also*
aesthetics; artists; creativity

CPSIA information can be obtained
at www.ICGtesting.com
Printed in the USA
LVOW11s2242280317
528827LV00001B/1/P